LA VIOLENCIA AND THE HEBREW BIBLE

SEMEIA STUDIES

Number 82

SBL PRESS

LA VIOLENCIA AND THE HEBREW BIBLE

The Politics and Histories of Biblical Hermeneutics

on the American Continent

Edited by

Susanne Scholz and Pablo R. Andiñach

SBL PRESS

SBL PRESS

Atlanta

Copyright © 2016 by SBL Press

Library of Congress Cataloging-in-Publication Data

Names: Scholz, Susanne, 1963– editor.
Title: La violencia and the Hebrew Bible : the politics and histories of biblical hermeneutics on the American continent / edited by Susanne Scholz and Pablo R. Andiñach.
Description: Atlanta : SBL Press, 2016. | Series: Semeia studies ; Number 82 | Includes bibliographical references and index.
Identifiers: LCCN 2016005377 (print) | LCCN 2016014135 (ebook) | ISBN 9781628371307 (pbk. : alk. paper) | ISBN 9780884141327 (hardcover : alk. paper) | ISBN 9780884141310 (e-book)
Subjects: LCSH: Violence in the Bible. | Bible. Old Testament—Criticism, interpretation, etc.—United States. | Violence—Religious aspects—Christianity.
Classification: LCC BS1199.V56 V57 2016 (print) | LCC BS1199.V56 (ebook) |
DDC 221.6097—dc23
LC record available at http://lccn.loc.gov/2016005377

Printed on acid-free paper.

CONTENTS

CONTENTS

Part 3: Responses

ACKNOWLEDGMENTS

This book is the result of a three-day research seminar organized by the editors of this volume at Perkins School of Theology in October 2012. We express our sincere gratitude to the Center for the Study of Latino/a Christianity and Religions at Perkins School of Theology at Southern Methodist University in Dallas, Texas, for awarding our project with a grant in support of the seminar. We especially thank the director of the center, Hugo Magallanes, for his multiyear support and enthusiasm for our project as it progressed from the research seminar to this book. The grant enabled us as the organizers of the research seminar and later as the editors of this volume to extend invitations to the contributors, with the certainty that we would be able to take care of their creature comfort during their visit in Dallas.

We also thank the faculty assistant at Perkins School of Theology, Carolyn Douglas, for her invaluable help in making travel arrangements, assisting with the organization of our various meals, and preparing handouts and lecture materials during the seminar. During our three-day gathering, we read our papers to each other, discussed them in collegial spirit, and enjoyed time with previously known and new colleagues, while we were away from our normal teaching and administrative responsibilities.

We thank the librarians of Bridwell Library at Perkins School of Theology, especially the reference librarians Jane Lenz Elder and David Schmersal, as well the Interlibrary Loan and Reserves assistant Sally Hoover, who helped reliably, patiently, and knowledgably with any book-related issue. We thank David Schones, a Graduate Program in Religious Studies doctoral student of Old Testament at Southern Methodist University, for his help in proofreading the manuscript and for the creation of this volume's indices.

Most of all, a hearty thank you to our contributors who participated in this multifaceted project which included their carefully preparation of their papers into publishable essays. We are also most grateful to our respondents who agreed to read the manuscript in its final form and to offer their insights and comments about reading the Hebrew Bible on the American continent. Surely, their responses enhance, deepen, and bring together our broad-ranging perspectives on *La Violencia and the Hebrew Bible*.

We also thank Robert Hunt, Director of Global Theological Education at Perkins School of Theology, whose organizational passion brought five Perkins faculty members, including Susanne Scholz, to the Instituto Superior Evangélico de Estudios Teológicos (ISEDET) in Buenos Aires in March 2010. During this trip, which was made possible by a Henry Luce Foundation Grant given to the Center for the Study of Latino/a Christianity and Religions at Perkins School of Theology, we—Pablo and Susanne—met for the first time, and then and there we came up with the idea to collaborate across geographical and linguistic boundaries on a project related to the contextual study of the Hebrew Bible. In short, without the Luce Grant to the Center and the faculty trip, this book would not have come into existence.

We are also grateful to the members of the Semeia Studies board for including this volume among its scholarly works. We thank the general editor of Semeia Studies, Gerald West, for his support in helping us get this book into the series. Last but not least, we thank Nicole L. Tilford, production manager at SBL Press, without whose professional assistance and patience the preparation of this manuscript could not have been accomplished. A big thank you to all of you.

Susanne Scholz and Pablo R. Andiñach
July 26, 2015

Abbreviations

AB	Anchor Bible
AOTC	Abingdon Old Testament Commentaries
ApOTC	Apollos Old Testament Commentary
BASOR	*Bulletin of the American Schools of Oriental Research*
BTB	*Biblical Theology Bulletin*
BZAW	Beihefte zur Zeitschrift für die alttestmentliche Wissenschaft
ErFor	Erträge der Forschung
EuroJTh	*European Journal of Theology*
FOTL	Forms of the Old Testament Literature
FRLANT	Forsshungen zur Religion und Literatur des Alten und Neuen Testaments
HDR	Harvard Dissertations in Religion
HSM	Harvard Semitic Monographs
IBC	Interpretation: A Bible Commentary for Teaching and Preaching
IEJ	*Israel Exploration Journal*
Int	*Interpretation*
ITC	International Theological Commentary
JAAR	*Journal of the American Academy of Religion*
JBL	*Journal of Biblical Literature*
JFSR	*Journal of Feminist Studies in Religion*
JPS	Jewish Publication Society
JSOT	*Journal for the Study of the Old Testament*
LXX	Septuagint
MÉTIS	*MÉTIS*: História e cultura
MT	Masoretic Text
NAC	New American Commentary
NICOT	New International Commentary on the Old Testament
NRSV	New Revised Standard Version

NSKAT	Neuer Stuttgarter Kommentar, Altes Tesament
OBT	Overtures to Biblical Theology
OTL	Old Testament Library
OTM	Old Testament Message
PUF	Presses Universitaires de France
RevExp	*Review and Expositor*
SB	Sources bibliques
SBAB	Stuttgarter biblische Aufsatzbände
SBS	Stuggarter Bibelstudien
SemeiaSt	Semeia Studies
SJOT	*Scandinavian Journal of the Old Testament*
SHBC	Smyth & Helwys Bible Commentary
SSN	Studia Semitica Neerlandica
StBibLit	Studies in Biblical Literature (Lang)
SWBA	Social World of Biblical Antiquity
SymS	Symposium Series
TOTC	Tyndale Old Testament Commentaries
USQR	*Union Seminary Quarterly Review*
VF	*Verkündigung und Forschung*
VT	*Vetus Testamentum*
WAW	Writings from the Ancient World
WBC	World Biblical Commentary
WMANT	Wissenschaftliche Monographien zum Alten und Neuen Testament
ZBK	Zürcher Bibelkommentare

INTRODUCTION

Susanne Scholz and Pablo R. Andiñach

La violencia is a technical term that Central and South Americans of every background know. It refers to the brutal, repressive, and murderous policies of state-sponsored violence, practiced in various Central and South American countries during the twentieth century. Sometimes these decades of internal war, supported and fostered by external powers such as the United States, are called "civil war." Colombia's population lived through *la violencia* from 1948 to 1958 (Palacios 2006). The people of Argentina experienced *la violencia*, usually called "the Dirty War" (Guerra Sucia), from 1974 to 1983, during which military and security forces tortured and killed left-wing guerrillas and political dissidents (Feitlowitz 1998). In Chile, the twentieth-century period of *la violencia* began in 1973 when a military coup overthrew President Salvador Allende, and General Augusto Pinochet began to rule the country with fear and terror (Collier and Sater 2004). In Central American countries such as Nicaragua, El Salvador, Guatemala, and Honduras, the period of their respective civil wars began in the 1960s, increased in the 1970s, and culminated in the 1980s. For instance, Nicaragua was continuously in the international headlines when the Sandinista National Liberation Front (FSLN) campaigned to violently oust the Somoza dictatorship in the late 1970s, governed from 1979 to 1990, and fought the "Contra War" while the Contras received financial assistance from the United States from 1981 to 1990 (Webb 2014). Thus, the term *la violencia* goes far beyond the literal translation of "violence." It captures one of the most brutal and repressive periods on the American continent that involved political, economic, social, and religious institutions on every level. Complicity, corruption, and fear permeated all areas of life and society. Yet biblical scholarship does not usually engage in reading the Bible in the context of *la violencia*. This book suggests that such engagement is long overdue, because the correlation provides interpreters with critical insights about the politics and histories of biblical hermeneutics on the American continent.

Interestingly, books on violence in the Hebrew Bible have appeared in abundance during the past decade. Many of their authors ground their investigations in historical methods, detaching discussions on violence in ancient Israel and the ancient Near East from contemporary considerations (Kelle and Ames 2008), although their forewords, prefaces, or introductions often refer to global experiences of violence and war in the aftermath of 9/11. Accordingly, some scholars disclose that they examine violence in the Old Testament because of contemporary events such as 9/11 (Bekkenkamp and Sherwood 2003; Zehnder and Hagelia 2013). Others acknowledge that they are particularly concerned over the Old Testament God legitimizing genocide and blood shed (Collins 2004; Seibert 2012; Schnocks 2014). Still others place their Hebrew Bible interpretations within the context of the church hoping to find redemption from Old Testament violence there (Creach 2013; Schlimm 2015), or they read the Old Testament within the church to identify scholarly responsible ways of dealing with issues of biblical violence (e.g., Fischer 2013). Occasionally, interpreters classify the Bible as an inherently violent text, claiming that violence is at the very center of "God's being" (Emilsen and Squires 2008, xiii). Several writers focus on violence in the Bible and the Qur'an, trying to nurture Christian, Jewish, and Muslim dialog and fend against views that identify violence in the Qur'an without accounting for biblical violence (e.g., Jacobs 2009; Jenkins 2011, Nelson-Pallmeyer 2003; Stanley, 2008).

Although the past two decades are surely not unique in the pervasiveness of violence among nations and peoples, the invasion of Iraq by United States American military followed by so-called "shock and awe" bombing, the relentless warring in Afghanistan, United States drone strikes, the rhetoric and execution of "targeted bombing" with so-called "collateral damage," and the billions of dollars spent on the United States military operations instead of taking care of the millions upon millions of people living on one dollar a day have certainly taken violence to a significant height in the world. When so much recent violence is experienced in the lives of so many people, does it matter if the Hebrew Bible, God, or interpreters endorse or reject violence?

The contributors in this volume assert that violence is indeed a worthy topic in biblical studies, because it permeates the American continent. Accordingly, all essays locate themselves within selective settings on this continent, and in contrast to the plethora of recent publications on violence and the Hebrew Bible, this book contributes to the scholarly discussion from a decidedly contextualized hermeneutic. It locates itself on the American continent with its manifold, diverse, and long-standing experiences of violence, military dictatorships, the disappearances of thousands upon thousands of people in Latin American countries during the twentieth century, the murder of indigenous peoples, the collaboration with the powerful North, the existence of secret prisons, as well as the resistance to political-military domination, not only since 9/11 but also decades prior to that event. Perhaps even the Spanish colonization was not the beginning point to *la violencia* as the Incan and Mayan histories indicate. The book's key Spanish phrase, *la violencia*, locates the discussions of this book in the context of the political, social, and military forms of oppression and brutalization characteristic in Latin and Central American countries during the twentieth century. Accordingly, the various contributions remain focused on violence on the American continent in the encounter with the Hebrew Bible. As such, this book explores the topic of violence beyond the empiricist-scientific epistemological paradigm. It examines how past and present experiences of violence have shaped biblical meanings within various past and present American contexts, enhancing and deepening exegetical scholarship on the Hebrew Bible. As a whole, the volume analyzes the collision of Hebrew Bible interpretations within the political, cultural, and religious dynamics present on the American continent.

The book consists of nine essays and three responses that consider various biblical texts, interpretation histories, and American contexts. The contributors come from the Caribbean, North, Central, and South America. The studies demonstrate that the histories, cultures, and politics of the American continent provide rich and important resources for the interpretation of the Hebrew Bible. Each contribution encourages readers to think contextually about biblical interpretation in a place and at a time when massive quantities of violence appear on every continent of the Earth. It should be obvious that this book does not provide a comprehensive treatment of violence and biblical interpretation on the American continent, really an impossible task. Rather, it aims to inspire further scholarship to locate biblical readings geopolitically wherever the Bible is read today and tomorrow. As such, this anthology addresses fellow Bible scholars, students, and lay people wanting to learn more about biblical interpretations located explicitly on the American continent and examined as part of the enormous violence in American people's lives.

About the Contributions

The nine essays and three responses discuss, examine, and evaluate the topic of *la violencia* in selected historical, geographical, and theoretical frameworks that the vastness of the topic allows. The book is divided into three parts. The first part, entitled "Reading the Hebrew Bible on the American Continent," begins with a study of the oracles against the nations by Steed Vernyl Davidson. In the essay entitled "Violence in National Security Arrangements: The Case of the United States, the Caribbean, and the Nations in the Oracles against the Nations," he examines the biblical oracles, as they appear in the prophetic literature, in conversation with United States foreign policy documents related to the Caribbean. Davidson argues that in each set of texts, the rhetoric of violence is masked in similar ways despite the vastly different settings. Davidson discusses texts such as the Monroe Doctrine, the Roosevelt Corollary, drug enforcement, and deportation policies to illustrate the hegemonic nature of the relationship among imperial and subordinate nations. As such, his analysis reflects upon the potency of violent language in geopolitical relationships tinged with imperialist overtones.

Entitled "Contesting State Violence: The Bible, the Public Good, and Divinely Sanctioned Violence in the Texas Borderlands," the contribution by Gregory Lee Cuéllar examines the connections between the United States biblical Protestant tradition and the Anglo-imagined persona of the Texas Rangers as men of "good character" in the Texas-Mexico border region during the early twentieth century. Cuéllar reminds readers of the violent encounters at the Texas-Mexico Border between 1910 and 1920 when the area was a site of racial violence in which an estimated five thousand men of Mexican ethnicity died largely at the hands of the state's primary paramilitary police force, the Texas Rangers (i.e., *Los Rinches*). The chapter gives particular attention to the theobiblical underpinnings of the Texas state representative of Brownsville, José T. Canales. It becomes clear that United States citizenship on the frontier and the biblical Protestant tradition were heavily invested in biblical texts, legitimating the Texas Rangers's physical violence against the Mexican "Other." In the effort to provide a nonviolent horizon in this bloody encounter, Cuéllar also refers to J. T. Canales who fought against racial violence. His counter testimony, serving as a borderland theology of liberation, sides with the suffering and survival of ethnic Mexicans in the Texas-Mexico borderlands region.

Next is a reading of the book of Habakkuk by Renata Furst who connects her reading to the long-lasting violence in Central America. Entitled "'How Long, Oh God? I Cry for Help': Habakkuk, Violence, and the Quest for a Just God in Honduras," the essay explores "random" social violence and survival through the theological lens of Habakkuk, a book written during a time (605–597 BCE) when social violence peaked in the kingdom of Judah. Similarly, so Furst, random violence of gangs and socioeconomic abandonment has characterized her native country of Honduras during the past several decades. It becomes clear that both in Honduras and Habakkuk, violence is experienced as "random," because victims perceive it as senseless and meaningless. Lack of meaning threatens the personal and social perception of victims and the belief that a just world is possible. For the victims of such random violence, the central question is whether God is a passive observer or an active agent who guarantees that a just world will ultimately prevail. In this sense, then, Furst's reading finds hope in Habakkuk that soon *la violencia* will end not only in ancient Israel but also in Honduras.

In "The Culture of Fear: About Internalized Violence in Ancient Near Eastern and Biblical Literatures," José Enrique Ramírez-Kidd analyzes violence as a cultural and literary expression as found in ancient Near Eastern and biblical texts. He emphasizes that fear must be understood as an extreme form of violence that often has more lasting and destructive effects than concrete forms of violence. Ramírez-Kidd observes that imperial politics of domination does not always resort to military action. It demonstrates its military power only when subjugated peoples do not accept their subjugation. The chapter details internalized forms of violence with carefully selected references to various biblical and ancient Near Eastern texts to argue that the internalization of violence has obvious similarities to the political situations in contemporary Latin America. Examples from Nicaragua's and Haiti's political history as well as literary writings from Columbia and Uruguay further clarify the impact of cultures of violence. They give people psychological "skins" to adapt to feelings of impotency, lack of faith in one's own abilities, and passivity into one's fate so that people do not even imagine anymore that peace and justice would also be available to them. Thus, so Ramirez-Kidd, violence is not perceived to be unusual anymore for people living in the ancient Near East or in Latin America today.

A second part gathers explorations into "Reading Biblical Texts in American Contexts." It begins with Pablo R. Andiñach's essay on

"Denouncing Imperialism: An Argentine Rereading of the Tower of Babel (Gen 11:1–9)." Relying on a literary approach, Andiñach finds in the biblical narrative a strong testimony against any form of imperial violence. This finding is significant, because, as Andiñach argues, today's imperial violence is not limited to countries from the hemispheric South and poor countries but also extends to poor and lower-class people in Europe, the United States, and Latin America. Genesis 11 must be understood with this dynamic in mind.

Cheryl B. Anderson focuses on the inherent violence in interpretations of Gen 19 and Judg 19. Entitled "Biblical Interpretation as Violence: Genesis 19 and Judges 19 in the Context of HIV and AIDS," the essay employs Johan Galtung's concept of cultural violence to expose the inherent violence prominently argued for in traditional interpretations of the biblical narratives. Anderson criticizes ecclesial and exegetical stances as inflicting cultural violence on people who do not fit the "mythical norm." She urges Bible scholars to recognize their culturally harmful reading practices and to identify ways of offering alternative readings that eliminate the underlying harmful cultural and structural patterns of violence.

Susanne Scholz posits that the internal United States violence, experienced by so many people, is aided and abetted by the biblical hermeneutics dominantly practiced in the United States. Her essay, "How To Read the Bible in the Belly of the Beast: About the Politics of Biblical Hermeneutics within the United States of America," shows that mainstream Bible scholarship does not make connections to internal US-American violence. It is mostly silent about it, sometimes even endorsing it. Far too many interpretations are grounded in exegetical methods and reading strategies that distance biblical meanings from the various forms of violence plaguing the country, be it poverty, the death penalty, police brutality, or sexual violence. Scholz discusses the historical-cultural background of the reliance of mainstream US-American exegesis on hermeneutical principles that are complicit with violence in its own society. Illustrating the exegetical complicity within selected contemporary US-American interpretations of Judg 21, she elaborates on three of their dominantly used reading strategies. She proposes a sociology of biblical hermeneutics as a way to read the Bible in resistance to violence in the United States and to the complicity apparent in the commentary literature on Judg 21.

In an essay entitled "'They Will Be Yours for Corvée and Serve You': Forced Labor in the Hebrew Bible, Modern America, and Twentieth-Century Communist States," Serge Frolov tends to biblical passages, such as Deut 20 and 1 Kgs 9, that seem to condone and even encourage the practice of corvée. Frolov shares that he had had first-hand experience of certain aspects of *la violencia*. Although he knows that he has been fortunate enough never to be directly touched by war, as a Soviet citizen he was subjected not only to political oppression (which was especially harsh due to his Jewish origin), but also to the most immediate and naked form of economic exploitation: forced labor. His essay raises questions about one person's liberation becoming another person's oppression, about utopian dreams becoming dystopian nightmares, and, of course, about the role of the monotheistic deity in these disturbing dynamics. He begins by introducing the central passage for his topic, Deut 20:10–14, against its historical background. He reviews selected scholarly and popular interpretations of the last few decades and explains why these interpretations are unacceptable to many readers in the Americas, including to Frolov. He also offers an alternative reading that makes Deut 20:10–14 meaningful without accepting its problematic content.

In "Trauma All Around: Pedagogical Reflections on Victimization and Privilege in Theological Responses to Biblical Violence," Julia M. O'Brien explores how the cultural particularities of interpreters' lived experiences of trauma shape their theological responses to the violence portrayed in the Bible. Her essay draws on examples from a course on Violence and the Bible that O'Brien taught twice at Lancaster Theological Seminary in Lancaster, Pennsylvania. She explains how class status, national privilege, and gender constructions, including constructions of domestic violence, foster interpretations of biblical violence that differ significantly from those who read the Hebrew Bible in light of trauma studies. O'Brien asserts that contextual factors limit the effectiveness of scholarly "fixes" to the "problem" of biblical violence. In a future iteration of this course, she hopes that she and her students will meet each other as biblical interpreters and as human beings while processing their life experiences inside and outside the classroom. After all, as O'Brien reminds us, violence is real in people's lives and reading the Bible must take account of this recognition.

Three responses from Nancy Bedford, Todd Penner, and Ivoni Richter Reimer further deepen, expand, and interrogate the positions taken and envisioned by the nine contributors. The conversation about *la violencia* and the politics and histories of reading the Hebrew Bible in America is just beginning, but it demonstrates that violence in its wide range of horrifying expressions is real in people's lives, and biblical interpreters ought to take violence in the world seriously to arrive at exegetically noteworthy and culturally-theologically relevant ideas about the place of the Bible in the world.

Works Cited

Bekkenkamp, Jonneke, and Yvonne Sherwood. 2003. *Sanctified Aggression: Legacies of Biblical and Post Biblical Vocabularies of Violence*. New York: T&T Clark.

Collier, Simon, and William F. Sater. 2004. *A History of Chile, 1808–2002*. Cambridge: Cambridge University Press.

Collins, John J. 2004. *Does the Bible Justify Violence?* Minneapolis: Fortress.

Creach, Jerome F. D. 2013. *Violence in Scripture*. Louisville: Westminster John Knox.

Emilsen, William W., and John T. Squires, ed. 2008. *Validating Violence—Violating Faith? Religion, Scripture and Violence*. Adelaide: ATF Press.

Feitlowitz, Marguerite. 1998. *Lexicon of Terror: Argentina and the Legacies of Torture*. New York: Oxford University Press.

Fischer, Irmtraud, ed. 2013. *Macht—Gewalt—Krieg im Alten Testament: Gesellschaftliche Problematik und das Problem ihrer Repräsentation*. Freiburg im Breisgau: Herder.

Jacobs, Steven Leonard. 2009. *Confronting Genocide: Judaism, Christianity, Islam*. Lanham, MD: Lexington Books.

Jenkins, Philip. 2011. *Laying Down the Sword: Why We Can't Ignore the Bible's Violent Verses*. New York: HarperOne.

Kelle, Brad E., and Frank Ritchel Ames, eds. 2008. *Writing and Reading War: Rhetoric, Gender, and Ethics in Biblical and Modern Contexts*. SymS 42. Atlanta: Society of Biblical Literature.

Nelson-Pallmeyer, Jack. 2003. *Is Religion Killing Us? Violence in the Bible and the Quran*. Harrisburg, PA: Trinity Press International.

Palacios, Marco. 2006. *Between Legitimacy and Violence: A History of Colombia, 1875–2002*. Durham: Duke University Press.

Schlimm, Matthew Richard. 2015. *This Strange and Sacred Scripture: Wrestling with the Old Testament and Its Oddities*. Grand Rapids: Baker Academic.

Schnocks, Johannes. 2014. *Das Alte Testament und die Gewalt: Studien zu göttlicher und menschlicher Gewalt in alttestamentlichen Texten und ihren Rezeptionen*. WMANT. Neukirchen-Vlyn: Neukirchener Verlagsgesellschaft.

Seibert, Eric A. 2012. *The Violence of Scripture: Overcoming the Old Testament's Troubling Legacy*. Minneapolis: Fortress.

Stanley, Christopher D. 2008. "Words of Life: Scriptures and Non-Violence in Judaism, Christianity and Islam." Pages 39–56 in *Validating Violence—Violating Faith? Religion, Scripture and Violence*. Edited by William W. Emilsen and John T. Squires. Adelaide: ATF Press.

Webb, Gary. 2014. *Dark Alliance: The CIA, the Contras, and the Crack Cocaine Explosion*. New York: Seven Stories Press.

Zehnder, Markus, and Hallvard Hagelia. 2013. *Encountering Violence in the Bible*. Sheffield: Sheffield Phoenix.

PART 1
READING THE HEBREW BIBLE
ON THE AMERICAN CONTINENT

Violence in National Security Arrangements: The Case of the United States, the Caribbean, and the Nations in the Oracles against the Nations

Steed Vernyl Davidson

Resumen: El presente ensayo examina la violencia expresada en la política exterior de los Estados Unidos hacia las naciones del Caribe y analiza los "oráculos contra las naciones" que pueblan los libros proféticos. En la recorrida de estos textos bíblicos se busca demostrar que tienen como función ofrecer el sustento teológico e ideológico para una teoría de la seguridad nacional que proteja los intereses del imperio. Se describe un paralelo entre la doctrina de la seguridad nacional como soporte ideológico de la dominación del imperio sobre el Caribe, mientras que en los textos de los oráculos se muestra que expresan los intereses del Imperio persa, en este caso representados por la élite gobernante en Judá cuyos intereses coinciden con los del país dominante. Del mismo modo que los persas procuraban encontrar naciones amigas que ayudaran a consolidar su poder en las zonas aledañas de su imperio donde se generaban ciertas rebeldías, se muestra que los Estados Unidos ha ejercido su dominio sobre el Caribe, una zona antes dominada por otras naciones europeas. Yehud, la pequeña colonia judía dominada por los persas, utiliza sus oráculos contra las naciones como soporte ideológico y teológico del imperio. La noción de "providencia divina" aplicada a los Estados Unidos produjo que ésta asuma que la libertad y la democracia como valores propios y exclusivos, y que su misión era expandirlos geográficamente, lo que justifica su acción imperial y dominadora.

This essay examines the rhetorical similarities between the biblical oracles against the nations, found in the prophetic books, and foreign policy statements from the United States regarding the Caribbean to expose the biblical oracles as literary-colonial devices that support empire ideology within the Persian-colonized Yehud of the sixth century BCE. The oracles against the nations are found in Amos 1–2, Isa 13–23, Jer 46–51, Ezek 25–32, Nahum, and Obadiah (Clements 1975, 58). Sometimes the oracles in Joel 3:1–21, Zeph 2:4–15, and Zech 9:1–8 are also included in this list, and so this study refers to all of them. My central claim is that the oracles against the nations represent theological statements by the elite of Yehud that support the security arrangements of the Persian Empire. I use the US-American foreign policy statements as a contemporary cultural reference for the interpretation of the biblical oracles, because the US-American documents also address the ordering of a territorial neighborhood, in this case the Caribbean. The geopolitical differences between sixth-century Persian imperial arrangements and a system of client-states that the United States has pursued in the Caribbean since the nineteenth century are obvious (Coatsworth 1994, 4), but the correlation allows me to assess how both sets of texts assume and legitimate violence. It will become clear that both the biblical oracles and the US-American policy statements enact symbolic violence that signals the desired political and military security arrangements. Importantly, both the oracles and the US-American foreign policy statements deploy rhetorical forms that communicate the centrality of security but minimize the violence perpetuated upon the respective target populations.

A general comment about the placement of the biblical oracles against the nations needs to be made. The oracles present vivid images of gruesome destruction resulting from vengeful wrath. Rather than historical accounts of actual events, they are probably fantasies of revenge. Still, scholars have debated the origins of the oracles. For instance, early scholarship observed that the oracles did not fit well into the prophetic books,[1] as they lacked the social engagement of the presumed historical prophets. The oracles were thus attributed to later editors who may have added them into the prophetic books (Peels 2007, 84; Christensen 1975, 1; Carroll 2006, 753; Barton 2003, 78). Another hypothesis suggests that the oracles were leftover invocations of liturgical forms normally associated with war (Christensen 1972, 592; Hayes 1968, 83). These and other scholarly hypotheses, focusing on the historical origins of the oracles, provided a sense of their

---

1. Sigmund Mowinckel (2002, 55) contributed to this scholarly notion in his study of Jeremiah. He assumed that Jer 45:1–5 marks the limits of the book of Jeremiah and designated the remaining chapters (except Jer 46–52) as "originally a collection, a tradition complex of its own … considerably later than Jeremiah."

performativity. Yet these hypotheses seem inadequate, because they do not explain why the oracles abandon so completely the high ethical standards of the vast majority of the prophetic texts. The oracles fall even below "an eye for an eye."[2] In the final form of the biblical canon, the oracles constitute significant sections of the prophetic books. My analysis accepts the placement of the oracles within their literary context and interprets them in their present forms and literary settings as integral to prophetic books.

The oracles as initial oral performances now present in texts require comment. Whether they were originally performed orally as unauthorized actions within the public square or as communal laments within the cult, in the early stage the oracles reached only a limited audience (Hayes 1968, 87–90, Clements 1975, 61). Yet once they were placed within the prophetic books, their audiences grew considerably. It is also important to remember that the oracles were not heard by the referenced nations (Hayes 1968, 81), which strengthens their literary significance.[3] The oracles should thus be primarily regarded as literature that features prominently within the prophetic books, even though they cannot be traced back to the biblical prophets themselves (Ben Zvi 2009, 73; Brueggemann 1998, 113; Carroll 2006, 753).

Historically, I locate the oracles in the Persian period, as suggested by studies showing that the oracles were compiled during the sixth century BCE. I also concur that they were only read by a small, learned number of readers (Ben Zvi 2009, 83; Carr 2011, 221). I also assume that this literate elite was concerned about security, since they lived after the Babylonian devastation of Jerusalem. The Persian-era Yehud was an obscure and isolated colony located in relative vicinity to major political and cultural centers like Egypt. It is likely that the geopolitical location of Yehud raised security concerns for the Persian Empire (Berquist 1995, 10).[4] The Persian

---

2. John Barton (2003, 78) raises similar questions regarding the oracles in Amos. Barton explores the inclusion of foreign nations in a list, based upon an unmentioned ethical standard, and wants to understand the inclusion of the foreign nations as central for the understanding of the entire book of Amos.

3. Clements (1975, 62) insists that prophets intended the oracles to be heard by audiences in ancient Israel. I agree with him that the final versions of the written prophetic texts were intended for a select readership in Yehud.

4. Scholars disagree on the strategic importance of Yehud to the Persians. Jon Berquist (1995, 63) thinks that Yehud was a way station for Persian forces on route to Egypt. Oded Lipschits (2006, 30) regards Yehud's agricultural worth as valuable only as a base of taxation to the Achaemenids.

defeat of the Babylonian Empire had neutralized the main geopolitical threat for both Persians and Yehudites. Despite anxieties caused by their relationship with neighboring Samaria (Neh 4, 6), the elite residents of Yehud probably knew that Tyre and Sidon had achieved substantial autonomy from the Persian Empire. Tyre and Sidon supported and controlled maritime trade in the eastern Mediterranean as a buffer zone against Greek imperial interests (Lipschits 2006, 27). Presumably, Persian security interests consisted in enlisting neighboring states against distant imperial threats. The oracles indicate that Yehud's elite, seeking to buy favor from the Persian Empire, was probably willing to support the security arrangements of the Persian Empire.

The situation in Persian-controlled Yehud compares to the geopolitical relationship between the United States and the territories located in the ring of the Caribbean Sea. From its founding as a nation, the United States recognized that was located in the midst of powerful European colonial interests. With the accumulation of sufficient military and economic strength to engage potential rivals, the United States adopted policies that created security arrangements and guaranteed supremacy. The security arrangements resulted in US-American military involvement in so-called "unthreatening territories" (Crandall 2006, 11–15). In my view, the oracles against the nations as a body of texts expose a possible scenario in the relationship between Yehud and the Persian Empire during the early Persian period. Persian-controlled Yehud consisted of a geopolitical dynamic similar to the one constructed by the United States with its neighbors. Pressure tactics were put upon militarily unthreatening territories in order to intimidate mighty competitors. The domination of the unthreatening territories provided an imaginary security zone that perhaps aided both broader Persian policies and Yehud's security. As a result, the Persian Empire probably gained a compliant and cooperative colony that helped in preserving "peace" in the region while the Yehudite population agreed to being protected against real and imagined threats.

The following analysis proceeds in three steps. First, it narrates the history of US-American foreign policy statements in the Caribbean. Second, it examines the function of the oracles as foreign policy statements in the Yehud. Third, it explains how literary systems of power, defining both the oracles and the United States self-identity, establish symbolic and actual violence in a new world order. A conclusion reflects on the importance of geography as a means of drawing out the implications of living near a national-security seeking country.

About the History of United States Foreign Policy Statements in the Caribbean

The notion of the United States as a national security state originates in the National Security Act of 1947 that shifted the military posture of the United States from defense to aggression (Stuart 2008, 8). After the victories of World War II, the United States recognized that it was not a wise strategy to stand on the sidelines hoping that geopolitical threats would be diffused by friendly states and not become a US-American concern (Hogan 1998, 2). Changes in nuclear technology also meant that oceans were insufficient buffers to contain threats to the United States. Thus the National Security Act of 1947 represents years of planning to ensure that another Pearl Harbor would not occur again. Consequently, large sections of the US-American government became militarized, and intense resources went into the creation of institutions, such as the "National Military Establishment" (Stuart 2008, 8), later renamed the Department of Defense in 1949, the National Security Council, and Central Intelligence Agency (Hogan 1998, 2–3). Of course, the practice of what can be called the national security state existed before 1947, but this terminology should be used sparingly for the United States, as it tends to be associated with centralized and militarized states that lack several of the institutions characteristic of a functioning democracy. Yet as historians explain, the National Security Act created such a state in the midst of a functioning democracy; it effectively produced "a constitutional dictatorship" (Michaels 2002, 27). The Caribbean, as a space created by the impulse and accident of European colonization,[5] has experienced various and severe forms of violence at the hands of larger nation-states throughout its history. Yet the policy positions of the United States as a neighbor within the Caribbean region, albeit a bigger, stronger, and richer neighbor than any individual country or all of them, presented a vision for the ordering of the Caribbean in favor of US-American security concerns.

While the turn to technical versions of the term "national security state" was a mid-twentieth-century phenomenon, the Caribbean experienced the heavy handed relationship from the beginning of the United States as a nation-state and major player in the region (Coatsworth 1994,

---

5. By *Caribbean*, I refer primarily to all the territories—islands and coastlands—touched by the Caribbean Sea. Certain United States policy is invoked in this essay that does not include Caribbean basin territories, such as Guatemala and El Salvador.

3). Marcus Raskin and Robert Spero (2007, 254) assert a pattern in US-American military intervention in "third world countries" dating back to the nineteenth century. The articulation of security concerns through the prism of its neighbor's independence has served as the platform through which the United States realized its goal of becoming a global power. For instance, Gordon Connell-Smith (1984, 432) observes that the recognition of the weakness of its neighbors was foundational to US-American security concerns. In fact, the neighbors, posing no direct dangers to the United States, generated the need for protection against possible threats from the outside through these neighbors.

The Monroe Doctrine of 1823 stands as the single and most important foreign policy position that determined the posture of the United States in the Caribbean and the Americas as a whole. When US-American Secretary of State John Kerry announced the end of the Monroe Doctrine era to the Organization of American States in October 2013, his declaration indicated the extent to which this policy defined the United States in the region. In December 1823, President James Monroe announced a policy position that aimed at containing imperial impulses in the Americas, particularly from European powers. Described at the time by its detractors as a "big brother" function (Bingham 1914, 335), the Monroe Doctrine marked the hemisphere as a no-go area for European powers. The policy placed the United States in an aggressive posture toward European nations. It was fueled in part by fears that European powers, putting down resistance movements in Italy and Greece, might also turn their attention to newly emerging Latin American nations (Gilderhus 2006, 6). Lawrence Martin (1940, 525) suggests that John Quincy Adams, who was Secretary of State in the 1920s, was concerned about Russian ambitions related to California, Oregon, and Alaska, all non-United States territories at the time. Adams asserted in July 1823 the need to say "frankly and explicitly to the Russian government that the future peace of the world, and the interest of Russia itself, cannot be promoted by Russian settlements upon any part of the American continent" (525). By the end of that year, President Monroe laid out this foreign policy position known as the Monroe Doctrine. As Mark Gilderhus (2006, 5) notes, the Monroe Doctrine, like several other US-American policy documents, is written in a lofty style that uses "the language of idealism and high principle" and emphasizes notions such as freedom, democracy, and peace. Gilderhus also explains that the Monroe Doctrine established a rhetorical style that persisted into the Cold War period and beyond. While the text of the policy statement invokes high ideals, Gilderhus also observes that it affirms "defensive objectives" (5).

The space between the rhetoric of the Monroe Doctrine and the practice of "Monroeism" (Bingham 1914, 336) reflects the space between ideals and military objectives, as well as the space between lofty rhetoric and the lived experience of violence.[6] Historians observe that the US-American concern to protect hemispheric states from European imperialism appears overblown given the constitution of the hemisphere in 1823.[7] In fact, in the 1820s, the empire of Brazil was geographically larger than the United States, and there were less than a dozen states that would have benefited from protection, namely, Columbia, Peru, Chile, Paraguay, and Mexico (Martin 1940, 525). Despite the paternalism of the Monroe Doctrine, the United States used it as one of the bases for its involvement in the Mexican-American War. At the end of that war, in 1846, large tracts of Mexico were ceded to the United States (Bingham 1914, 341; Martin 1940, 525). In 1898, at the end of the Spanish-American War, the United States acquired territories and protectorates that permanently ended Spain's hold on any Caribbean territory. The Monroe Doctrine was a bland diplomatic statement. In practice, however, it was the foundation and authorization for military and violent engagement in the region for years to come.

At the start of the twentieth century, Theodore Roosevelt ramped up the aggressive tendencies of the Monroe Doctrine with what is called the "Roosevelt Corollary." Fueled by fears of competing military and economic interests in the region, Roosevelt made a much harsher announcement in December 1904. He pronounced:

> Chronic wrongdoing, or an impotence which results in a general loosening of the ties of civilized society, may in America as elsewhere, ultimately require intervention by some civilized nation, and in the Western Hemisphere the adherence of the United States to the Monroe Doctrine may force the United States, however, reluctantly, in flagrant cases of such wrongdoing or impotence, to the exercise of an international police power. (Ricard 2006, 18)

---

6. Elihu Root (1914, 442) distinguishes between the rhetoric and the perception of the Monroe Doctrine. He asserted that "grandiose schemes of national expansion" derived too much inspiration from the statement.

7. For instance, Root (1914, 429) noted that at the time of the declaration of the Monroe Doctrine, not a single European nation claimed the right to take possession of territory in the region.

Essentially, Roosevelt took what many regarded as the defensive self-inter-
est of the nineteenth century and made it more aggressive; he turned "an
initially defensive dictum … into an aggressive policy" (ibid.).

If the Monroe Doctrine was a way to announce the US-American presence on the American continent and to safeguard the interests of the United
States from European encroachment, Roosevelt made force explicit where
none existed previously. While the sentiments of the Monroe Doctrine did
not rule out the use of force, the practice known as Monroeism consisted of
interventionist tendencies that stood behind the Roosevelt Corollary. Serge
Ricard (2006, 18) explains that the Roosevelt Corollary was the guide for
the actions of the United States in the Caribbean region for the rest of the
twentieth century. Along with the Platt Amendment,[8] the Monroe Doctrine
effectively handed Cuba over to the United States. The Roosevelt Corollary
dealt specifically with a case in the Dominican Republic that led to the US-
American military occupation of the Dominican Republic in 1904. United
States actions forestalled European collections of debts and other matters
similar to European intervention in Venezuela from 1902 to 1903. A total
of seventeen different US-American military interventions occurred from
1900 to 1933 in four separate countries of Central America (Coatsworth
1993, 34–35). Gilderhus (2006, 10) explains that Roosevelt's actions were
an extension of the Monroe Doctrine along with the Platt Amendment, and
they directed United States military actions in Panama, Nicaragua, Haiti on
several occasions, and the Dominican Republic on several occasions. Gilderhus also includes notable US-American foreign policy incursions in the
Caribbean, such as in the Cuban Bay of Pigs affair in 1961and the Cuban
Missile crisis in 1962. Under the guise of containing Soviet style communism, the United States intervened in the case of the Dominican Republic
in 1965 to prevent "another Cuba." Interestingly, during and after the Cold
War few military interventions took place, the notable exceptions where
those in Grenada and Panama (Crandall, 2006, 3).

The list of military interventions demonstrates a link between United
States foreign policy statements and violence. While the statements
espouse the ideals of "neighborliness" and security guarantees, they also
legitimize military action. Raskin and Spero's (2007, 231) observation

---

8. The Platt Amendment is an amendment to a 1901 appropriations bill under the
name of Senator Orville H. Platt, espousing the control of Cuba to its inhabitants but
at the same time preserving the United States in the role of a guardian, thereby ensur-
ing permanent military interventions (Keach 2008, 140).

demonstrates that idealism has accompanied bellicosity as the posture of most US-American Presidents and words intending to ensure security eventually manifested into violent outcomes. The articulation of its own security in relation to its weaker neighbors while calculating the reactions of other major world powers has made the Caribbean into a zone severely impacted by the US-American security state. United States foreign policy statements about the Caribbean established regional stability as the over-arching goal. These statements appealed to both the United States popula-tion and regional nations to support this vision of stability and the mecha-nisms necessary to ensure its achievement. Charles H. Sherrill (1914, 321), a US-American diplomat to Argentina from 1909 to 1911, laid out the benefit of the Monroe Doctrine; it prevented the hemisphere from turning into Tripoli, Algeria, or Morocco. By showing hemispheric states that the US-American policy ensures regional stability, several South American countries appeared to offer support for the Monroe Doctrine. In an assess-ment of the Monroe Doctrine, Charles Chandler (1914, 518) suggested that the inducements of independence from European colonial powers to countries like Columbia eased the welcome of the Monroe Doctrine. Chandler even claimed that "the South Americans asked *for* the Monroe Doctrine" (ibid). Securing the consent of regional states to the exercise of military power as envisaged through these foreign policy statements, the United States in effect rendered these states as protectorates and cre-ated "an empire without colonies in the Caribbean" (Gilderhus 2006, 10). The adoption and conferral of the "Big Brother" role enabled the United States as neighbor-*cum*-imperial power to deploy violence in pursuit of the undisputed and generally desired goal of regional stability.

US-American military interventions based on the Monroe Doctrine, the Roosevelt Corollary, and the Platt Amendment populated the Carib-bean landscape during the twentieth century. As a result, various Carib-bean nations suffered considerable violence due to the US-American pre-occupation with its own security. The names of countries and dates seem like a bland recitation in the ledger, but they translate into military occu-pations and actions that led to much death and destruction. Most of all, they induced fear of the consequences of a lethal military force. Whether the violence was military intervention, the funding of insurgent groups, silent support of autocrats, the destabilization of economies, or the with-drawal of international relations, the impact upon Caribbean populations was the same: violence coming from an aggressive power that sought to define its interests under the rhetorical cover of peace and stability.

The Function of the Oracles against the Nations
as Foreign Policy Statements in Yehud

The invocation of US-American military involvement in the Caribbean helps me to foreground a reading of the biblical oracles against the nations as foreign policy statements (Daschke 2010, 174). As a collection in the prophetic literature of Persian-period Yehud, the oracles function as a vision for a new world order facilitated by the Persian Empire. Accordingly, the oracles reflect the perspective of elite residents of Yehud, a small colonized territory lacking any kind of military capability. The oracles implicitly appeal to elite members of Yehud, asking them to regard the Persian Empire as the divine instrument for establishing a different world order.

Across the prophetic corpus, the oracles stand as a motley collection that sustains no clear pattern. Yet despite their diversity, the oracles are a distinct genre, as all of them are preoccupied with subjecting foreign nations to divine violence. The term "oracles against the nations" proves elusive because the word oracle, מַשָּׂא, occurs inconsistently in the prophetic texts. In Isaiah, the term מַשָּׂא, appears only with the dominant introductory formula, which consists of מַשָּׂא plus the nation named.[9] The oracles in Nahum also follow this pattern. In Jeremiah, the term does not appear, and so a preposition performs the same task.[10] Ezekiel employs a unique set of patterns that range from opening indictments (e.g., Ezek 25:8) to the formulaic "set your face against x and prophesy against x" (e.g., Ezek 25:2). Despite the diverse structures and glimmers of hope for restoration, the characterization of the oracles as oracles "concerning the nations" (Childs 2001, 114; Fretheim 2002, 575) or as "oracles about the nations" (Geyer 2004, 3) overlooks the poetry's antagonistic position against foreign nations.

Notwithstanding the variability of styles, literary locations, the order of the nations mentioned, and the elements in the various collections, every oracle features geopolitical concerns. The oracles thus fit within the political contours of the prophetic literature (Gottwald 1964, 45) and make

---

9. Exceptions to this formula appear in Isa 14:28, where a historical reference occurs, and 18:1, which begins without an introduction.

10. Jeremiah uses the prepositions לְ (e.g., Jer 46:2) and אֶל (e.g., Jer 47:1). The preposition עַל introduces the general collection (Jer 46:1). Obadiah attaches the preposition לְ to Edom (Obad 1:1).

their international political dimensions clearer due to the focus on foreign nations. With the exception of the collection in Amos 1–2, the geographic maps of the oracles direct the reader's attention exclusively outside of Yehud.[11] As the earliest form of this genre (Barton 2003, 78), Amos hardly provides the template found in other prophetic books. Yet Amos 1–2 and several oracles in Ezek 25 reflect the general ethos of the oracles. They contain clear indictments against nations that go beyond generic accusations of pride. Rhetorically, only the Amos collection draws an orbit around Judah and Israel, climaxing with Israel's impending judgment. In addition, only the Amos collection includes oracles against Israel and Judah.

The placement of the oracles in the prophetic books supports their geopolitical outlook. For instance, Amos premises the judgment of Israel upon the divine punishment of other nations that breaches unstated and perhaps unknown international codes (Hayes 1995, 166; Barton 2003, 118). Undermining claims of election as a buffer against divine punishment (Amos 9:7), Amos deploys the international reach of Israel's deity to the discomfort of the domestic audience. Breaking with Amos's "exclusively national" (Gottwald 1964, 94) interests, other prophetic books situate the oracles in literary contexts that deal with international issues. Isaiah's collection follows the nationalist narratives of Isa 11 and prefigures the apocalyptic section of Isa 24–27 that begins with global destruction (Isa 24:1). As Brevard Childs (2001, 116) states, the concern with the nations in Isaiah hints at the hope for a decisive divine victory over Babylon and the global control of the nations. The two editions of Jeremiah deploy the oracles for geopolitical purposes. The LXX places them after 25:14 to loosely follow the nations listed in 25:19–26, leaving the decisive destruction of Babylon to the Baruch narrative of Jer 46. Yet the MT sets the collection at the end of the book, a rearrangement of the earlier order of the list that thereby ends the book of Jeremiah with an oracle against Babylon (Jer 50–51; Holt 2003, 188), the last global superpower at the time (Peels 2007, 82). In Ezekiel, the oracles lie between the judgment on Jerusalem and the future vision of a restored Jerusalem (Clements 1996, 114). Louis Stulman and Hyun Chul Paul Kim (2010, 203) diagram the

---

11. The case of Isa 22, the oracle on the "valley of vision," is perhaps an exception. The reference to breaches in the city of David and the destruction of houses in Jerusalem in 22:9 could possibly make this text an oracle about Judah. However, much of the oracle, like most of the oracles against the nations, consists of nondescript statements that could apply to almost any situation.

arrangement of the Book of the Twelve that shows the oracles from Amos to Zechariah forming a ring around the oracles in Obadiah to Zephaniah. This diagram centers on the crimes of the foreign nations as a means of asserting divine justice and of addressing the question of theodicy raised by the destruction of Israel and Judah. While Stulman and Kim limit their diagram to a theological concern, their study demonstrates that on the macrolevel the prophetic texts include the oracles to articulate their vision about international relationships with other nations.

As a whole, then, the oracles make geopolitical concerns evident for the Yehudite audience, even though the nations listed in the various collections include nations that neither harbor nor possess the capacity to threaten Jerusalem. By raising the image of threat, albeit imagined threats, the oracles make security an issue for the stability of the envisioned future. Prophetic texts create "a transtemporal bridge" (Ben Zvi 2009, 77) between the past and the future, enabling ancient readers to inscribe the concerns of the past onto their own time. The oracles thus hand ancient readers a past that is ideologically framed by YHWH controlling empires and nations.[12] They co-opt the original audience into an anti-imperial ideology (Ben Zvi 2009, 75) that stands against named empires while simultaneously embracing the structure of empire as the basis of resistance. The oracles explain that along Judah's path from judgment to salvation stand foreign nations needing to be controlled so that Judah will be secure in the future. Prophetic texts not only theologize military engagements, they also indicate earthly powers as crucial divine instruments. Importantly, the oracles leave unnamed the earthly powers that could achieve the systematic containment of the foreign powers. No doubt, the elite educated readership of these oracles in early Persian period Yehud, "a retainer (or retainer-religious) 'class'" (Ben Zvi 2009, 75), likely envisaged the Persian Empire as the divine instrument.

The systematic destruction and containment of foreign nations listed in the oracles implies salvation for Israel and Judah (Hayes 1968, 81; Clements 1975, 59). In my reading of the oracles, salvation takes the form of security guarantees for Persian-era Yehud. The oracles conscript support

---

12. The oracles represent divine power exercised through earthly agents: Isaiah depicts the mustered army against Babylon (13:4–6); Jeremiah shows the Ethiopians confronting Egypt (46:9), the Babylonians punishing Egypt (46:25–27), and an unnamed fierce army destroying Babylon (50:8–10, 29, 41–43). In Ezekiel, Moab is handed over to the people of the East (25:10) and Nebuchadnezzar attacks Tyre (26:7).

for Persia as the divinely chosen superpower and guarantor of peace from among Yehud's elite while at the same time convincing those elites that Persian rule bodes well both for Yehud's security and its vested territorial interests. Folding Yehud's security needs within the Persian imperial project helps explain the relentless violence that pervades the oracles. Despite their negativity toward certain empires, the oracles embrace the structures of empire to achieve security and therefore inexorably pursue the path of violence.

Violence and the New World Order

Both US-American foreign policy statements toward the Caribbean and the oracles envision an ordering of the world that would ensure peace and stability. Further, both texts proceed from the perspective of the dominant power for whom security concerns supersede other considerations. Given the inevitability of violence in the pursuit of security goals, the victims of that violence are easily made invisible. Ignoring the victims of violence, the oracles illustrate how the original writers embraced empire. They constructed territorial relationships among nations that were not only sustained by violence but also depended on violence. Living in a weak nation, they aimed to leverage their place within the empire. The oracles thus assert the effectiveness of imperial power, and they place this power at the disposal of divine power. Yehud becomes the beneficiary of lethal power that orders the world to its advantage. The combined force of earthly and heavenly empires possesses the capability to produce horrific violence.

A description of the structures of violence, as they appear in the oracles and the US-American foreign policy statements, requires a differentiated view of violence. The equation of violence with force results in simplistic assessments of violent situations (Bufacchi 2005, 194; Arendt 1970, 45). Force draws attention to the effects of violence, in the case of the oracles instances of death, destruction, deportation, or despair. Salvoj Žižek (2008, 1) describes images of violence as "subjective violence" in which the agent of violence is clearly visible. In contrast, objective violence is violence required to keep things at the normal state, at a level of so-called "peace." Since objective violence remains invisible, it can be ignored. Yet it is necessary to keep its invisibility in mind to avoid making irrational assessments about the captivating visibility of subjective violence (2). As literature, the oracles produce symbolic violence that is distinct from the actual effects of violence. The images in the oracles represent the standard images of war in the ancient Near East. The relentless descriptions may shock modern readers who are unacquainted with forms of symbolic and subjective violence, as, for instance, typical during the time of the Neo-Assyrian Empire and codified in Assyrian palace reliefs. Consequently, when modern readers recoil in horror from the oracles, the violence represents the objective violence in the ancient Near East, the type of violence necessary to maintain empires, given that "war was a recognized instrument of foreign policy in the ancient Near East" (Gottwald 1964, 31). By deploying such violence, the oracles participate in the imperial logic that imagines a divine imperium taking form throughout the Persian Empire.

If the oracles present a normative view of imperial power, their appeal lies not in frightening readers into compliance but in conscripting their assent to the legitimacy of this vision. By separating out violence as a concept dependent upon factors such as power and legitimacy, Hannah Arendt (1970, 50) shows that regimes of power do not exist simply based upon violence; they require networks of support and communal organization that grant acceptability to the use of violence. They make violence "a characteristic of relationality" (Castelli 2004, 3). Violence serves as the instrument that power uses to achieve its purposes. Since power remains a communal rather than simply an individual entity (Arendt 1970, 52; Carlson 2011, 18), power constantly needs renewal from the community to maintain its legitimacy. Inevitably, the extraction of violence as a definable concept from power and force proves difficult since violence often protects power and is seen in technologies that amplify force (Arendt 1970, 4). Nonetheless, in order to avoid rendering the term violence meaningless by subsuming all actions of force and destruction under the category of violence (Arendt 1970, 52; Bufacchi 2005, 197), the integration of technologies in the discourse on violence proves useful. The oracles thus invite readers to approve the imagined global arrangements that are set up to promote the well-being of Yehud. As such, the oracles grant legitimacy to the use of divine power in direct actions of violence and through its imperial proxy to advance the aims of the divine imperium or "countergovernance" (Brueggemann 1998, 113).

High ideals serve as another feature that legitimizes violence. Rather than an end in itself, violence functions as the means to achieve lofty goals. Both the biblical oracles and the US-American foreign policy statements appeal to high ideals for which violence serves only as a necessary tool. Thus, the legitimization of violence in the oracles does not rely upon a legal process but appeals to the internal logic of the covenant relationship between

Yehud and its deity. Apart from the indictments in the Amos oracles and those of Ezekiel 25, hubris emerges as the only clearly identifiable charge against other nations (Isa 16:6; Jer 48:29; Ezek 28:17; Zeph 2:10; Zech 9:6). In all other instances, the oracles offer no reason for the judgment against the nations; they create a seemingly irrational and legally untenable situation and fit closer to the curse form than to legal forms. They do not make a case for crime and punishment (Geyer 2004, 179). Rather than establishing a fair process that could pass legal scrutiny, the oracles are preoccupied with fidelity to the covenant relationship. In this regard, the oracles are not so much xenophobic as they are nationalistic in the most idealistic form of nationalism. Precisely because they appeal to the lofty ends of nationalism to legitimize violence, the oracles require careful attention and analysis. In the oracles, idealistic nationalism remains blind to its own faults, magnifying its needs (the pursuit of a moral crusade to punish wrongs[13]) and hurts (vengeance for the destruction of Jerusalem[14]).

The use of violence as the means to enable a national vision unites the oracles and the US-American foreign policy statements. In both cases, violence appears as a preferred option, but it is not a character trait that motivates either context. An idealized world constructed in the national image motivates the US-American statements and the oracles. In the case of the United States, a strong belief in the purpose as a redeemed people saved from the excesses and decadence of "old" Europe to build the "city of God" (Carlson and Ebel 2012, 11; Webb 2012, 97) animates actions in the world. A sense of providence produces a civic religion that is characterized by national certainty and the narrow binaries of good and evil. The contours of this civic religion, based in Puritan theologies of providence, views violence through an evaluative lens of acceptable national performance. Consequently, the interpretation of instances of violence and catastrophe as divine punishment for failure, as well as the sanctioning of violence as a suitable means to achieve those national ideals is commonplace in US-American political history and practice (Murphy and Hanson 2012, 30; Webb 2012, 99).

---

13. While specific wrongs are hard to identify, the oracles operate on the idea that these nations deserve punishment. See, e.g., Isa 13:11; 14:3–7; Jer 46:25; Ezek 28:1–10; Amos 1–2; Nah 3: 4–7; Zech 9:3–4.

14. The issue of vengeance for the temple comes up in almost all of the collections. See, e.g., Jer 46:10–12; Ezek 25:2–7, 12–14; Obad 12–14; Nah 2:2; Zeph 2:8–11.

Biblical texts serve as one source for the US-American political ethos of violence[15] that results in the idealism of a nation that understands violence as redemptive. In most instances, however, the United States hardly experiences violence but perpetrates violence upon other nations in pursuit of high ideals. Both the US-American foreign policy statements and the biblical oracles thus represent national aspirations to fulfill collective identities forged in the context of violence and catastrophe.[16] Yehud emerges from the Babylonian devastations shaped by a theology of trauma that regards the violence of that trauma as redemptive (Carr 2011, 213). Various experiences from the Puritan interpretation of the sufferings in the former life and the new lease granted in the "new world" to Abraham Lincoln's influential assessment of the Civil War have fed a national narrative in which violence is a just instrument of divine punishment and redemption (Hauerwas 2012, 224; Daschke 2010, 168). The obvious ethnocentricities of these two contexts blur the larger concerns of the civic and theological discourses committed to violence as a means of ushering in an ideal world. In both discourses, the moral claims of the one wielding the sword masks troubling concerns about concentrations of power.

The US-American relationship with Cuba represents one of the starkest cases in the pursuit of an ideal through violence. Since the end of the Spanish-American war when Cuba entered the United States orbit, the relationship has been imperialistic. The Platt Amendment that granted United States power over Cuba's sovereignty (Hernández-López 2010, 121) features prominently in this relationship (Keach 2008, 140; Hernández-López 2010, 126). Undoubtedly, the relationship of the United States with Cuba has been defined in large measure by these policy documents that seek to limit the presence of external powers in the hemisphere. In the case of Cuba, this would be the former Soviet Union and the ideology of communism. Failed attempts at military aggression to change Cuba's path left the United States with a series of laws that have functioned largely as siege warfare to starve

---

15. Dereck Daschke (2010, 165) observes the intersection of "politics, religion, and warfare" in the presidency of George W. Bush that was marked by rhetoric derived from prophetic texts and the notion of prophetic authority.

16. Interestingly, Thomas Jefferson considered the Monroe Doctrine as "the most momentous [text] which has ever been offered to my contemplation since that of independence. That made the U.S. a nation; this sets our compass and points the course which are to steer through the ocean of time opening on U.S." (Root 1914, 429).

the nation of resources.[17] Amnesty International reports on the deleterious social and economic impact of the United States embargo against Cuba. For instance, Amnesty International (2009, 18) reports that in 2007 the restrictions of medicines increased levels of iron deficiency anemia to 37.5 percent for children under three years old. The lack of access to nutritional products or the ability to import medical equipment from research facilities in the United States significantly impairs the delivery of health care. The Amnesty International report highlights the objective violence done to Cuba partly in the name of US-American security. However, the obvious violence that has taken place at the Guantanamo Base, Camp Delta, in pursuit of US-American security and high ideals fit within the context of this current discussion. Despite the abrogation of the Platt Amendment in 1934 during the Batista era and its replacement with a Treaty of Relations, the aims of the Platt Amendment have remained in effect when the United States was granted perpetual rights over the naval station at Guantánamo Bay. In this anomalous space where Cuba has "ultimate sovereignty" over the land, the United States maintains "jurisdiction and complete control" (Hernández-López 2010, 126). My point here lies not so much in the inherent ambiguity of the Guantánamo agreement, which the US-American government continues to exploit for its own purposes. Rather I draw attention to the violence that accompanies these foreign policy statements. Since Guantánamo serves as a symbol for some of the worst excesses of the so-called "war on terror," connecting known and unknown violence in that space to the idealism of the policy statements explains how objective violence underlies the interests of peace and stability.

Technologies authorize and sanction the use of violence in pursuit of stated ends. Apart from requiring legitimacy, "violence is by nature instrumental" (Arendt 1970, 51). Thus superior technology, making violence more effective, achieves greater support, because sophisticated instruments ensure accomplishment of the desired end. The biblical oracles envision a combination of divine force and imperial strength to create the new global arrangements. These forces include well-armed warriors[18] and outfitted

---

17. The United States passed the first law restricting trade with Cuba in 1960 after the nationalization of sugar estates. Other laws passed in 1961 and 1963 would follow. The sanctions regime got even tighter with the Torricelli Act of 1992, Helms-Burton Act of 1996, and the Trade Sanctions Reform and Enhancement Act of 2000.

18. See Isa 13:4, 17–18; 18:1–2; Jer 46:3, 9; 50:9, 11, 29; 51:11; Ezek 28:7–8; Nah 2:3–5.

war horses (Jer 45:4; 50:40–41; Ezek 26:7–14). YHWH wields the most impressive and effective instruments of violence in the form of "divine terror" (Holt 2003, 192). Instruments consist of direct divine combat with and without weapons,[19] the use of unseen forces,[20] and marshaling the forces of nature and the cosmos (e.g., Isa 13:13; 14:9; 19:5–6; Ezek 27:34; 31:15–18; Nah 1:2–8). The instruments revolve around the divine warrior and *Chaoskampf* motifs.[21] In deploying the divine warrior motif, the oracles reveal the mythological connections in the oracles (Geyer 2004, 21) and their links to war oracles.[22] The divine warrior motif also helps communicate rhetorically the rightness of the instruments of violence, as the direct involvement of YHWH in the fictive battle guarantees success. In addition, the use of *Chaoskampf* relies upon the notion of cosmic perfection. This rhetorical strategy hands over to the power, believed to be the arranger of creation, the right to make the necessary arrangements to fix the distortions present in the creative order (Kitts 2013, 354; Crouch 2011, 490). The transcendent nature of the agent of violence in the oracles lends it legitimacy because violence enacted by the divine fits with "the domain of sovereignty" (Žižek 2008, 198) and the "divine king" (Crouch 2011, 485).

Updated technological instruments and the superior military technology grants the United States the ability to wield a "big stick" in the Caribbean. That the use of violence achieves its desired outcomes in a largely asymmetrical landscape renders violence a fairly easy tool of United States foreign policy in the Caribbean (Crandall 2006, 13). The US-American invasion of Grenada in 1983 illustrates how technologies enable violence and the sanctioning of violence. The disproportionate use of force in Grenada reflects the structure of violence that requires effectiveness as a chief outcome. In Grenada, the United States deployed 8,000 soldiers with a symbolic compliment of 353 soldiers from Caribbean nations (Crandall

---

19. Almost every collection of the oracles invokes the divine warrior motif in some fashion. See, for instance, Isa 14:22–23, 25; Jer 46:25–27; Ezek 25:4–5, 7–11, 13–14, 16–17; Obad 2–4, 8–9; Nah 2:13; 3:5–7; Zeph 2:5, 11–15; Zech 9:4, 7–10.

20. See Isa 13:15–16; Jer 46:28; 48:18, 35, 41; 49:8, 28–32; 50:2–3, 21–24; Ezek 27:28–33; Nah 2:2; Zeph 2:4.

21. C. L. Crouch (2011, 485) observes the theme of *Chaoskampf* in the destruction of Egypt in Ezek 32 where Egypt is depicted as the chaos monster.

22. Barton (2003, 83) remains skeptical of these connections with regards to the Amos oracles since he believes that a state of war would be needed for these oracles to hold such a setting.

2006, 144) to meet a challenge of no more than 800 Grenadian forces (Raines 2010, 168) and perhaps 250 Cuban soldiers (Raines 2010, 92). As far as military operations go, it took three days to subdue the insurgents, nineteen US-American soldiers were lost (Raines, 2010, 532), and 8,635 medals were awarded, but the Grenada invasion proved successful. Yet this success does not take account of 300 Grenadian and Cubans killed (Crandall 2006 148) or the indiscriminate bombing of sites like a mental hospital due to inaccurate maps and military intelligence. Behind the expenditure of $134.4 million (Crandall 2006, 162) and the loss of life and property in Grenada lie various actions openly and tacitly pursued by the United States that contributed to the instability leading up to the invasion that supposedly restored peace to Grenada. In effect, the military and other actions subjected Grenada to forms of violence that ensured its future participation in the security plan as established by the United States.

Violence is visibly present in the texts of the biblical oracles against the nations, but it is not visible in the US-American foreign policy statements, except in later military actions authorized by these statements. Preoccupation with visible violence distracts attention from the objective forms of violence that rely upon constant renewal for its legitimacy. In other words, attention to the objective violence present in concentrations of power, such as states, empires, and disciplinary regimes of faith, opens up the scope of the discourse on violence. The national ends in the United States and the province of Yehud legitimize violence, and both contexts articulate ways of conscripting consent for its legitimacy. The oracles against the nations describe a divine imperium that operates through an earthly proxy, most likely the Persian Empire, to produce a world ordered according to covenant visions. Even as the oracles depict the fall of empires, they replace these empires with a divine empire that leaves the structures and logics of empire intact. Of course, the US-American foreign security statements do not mention a divine power. Yet the language of objectivity, bureaucratic beneficence, and political opportunism legitimizes the violence with the terminology of peace, freedom, and democracy. The vision of the new world order appears to be benevolent and advantageous to all, even to the enemies of the worldly empires.

Conclusion

The study of the biblical oracles against the nations and the US-American foreign policy statements about the Caribbean reveals the importance of geography. Both the oracles and the foreign policy statements imagine nearby territories as compliant states as necessary to the creation of political security. The biblical and the US-American texts guarantee a world in which the respective populations enjoy their way of life. The oracles present a new world without the threats of major empires such as Assyria, Babylon, and Egypt. The oracles also envision smaller neighbors, such as Moab and Edom, as sufficiently chastened for their offenses and presumably accepting Yehud's presence and leadership. This vision assumes a geographic spread of influence equal to that of empires. Similarly, the United States charts its geographical neighborhood, particularly to its southern borders, as an "American Lake" (Coatsworth 1994, 8). The other southern countries turn into client states compliant to US-American national security interests. The lists of nations relevant to the United States resemble the lists in the oracles. In both cases, the geography of nations assumes that national ideals and influence is spread geographically and changes the world. In this bold vision, violence ensures the implementation and maintenance of the respective ideals and their influence in the region.

Attention to geography also reveals that the geographic scope of the oracles against the nations and the US-American foreign policy statements envision the transformation of the world. The lists of nations in the respective collections defy logic (Hamborg 1981, 157; Clements 1975, 63–64) or attempts to discern geographical ordering (Peels 2007, 82), similar to Egyptian execration texts (Hayes 1995, 163; Gottwald 1964, 103). Instead, the lists represent geographies of influence and control according to imperial interests. While no single collection of the biblical oracles completely maps the known territory, the cumulative impact of reading the collections in the prophetic corpus reinforces the global scope of the divine imperium. The situation is slightly different in the US-American policy statements where no single policy was pursued in every case, even though the overarching goal of territorial security directed a common set of tactics. Empires possess the capacity to imagine such geographies of influence and control. They also have the resources necessary to maintain them for as long as possible. The geographies grant such tools and, in the case of the biblical oracles, they also grant the use of those tools to the divine imperium in pursuit of the creation of the new world order. In effect, the biblical oracles deploy the weapons of empire. Given that greater resources mean more lethal instruments of violence, the nature of the violence matches the capacity of those instruments, whether the violence can be seen in grotesque images or masked by precision weaponry. In either case the vision for the world's transformation according to imperial interests is clearly articulated.

Furthermore, the US-American foreign policy statements serve the ideological purpose of creating a sphere of influence for the promotion of unique US-American values in the Caribbean. The United States self-understanding of its role in divine providence results in the belief that "democracy and freedom" are US-American values that ought to be spread geographically. When received through the prism of this theology of providence, violence becomes one of the means for carrying out the divine mandate. The self-presentation of the United States as the "city on a hill" within the Caribbean region marks the unbalanced relationship in which a regime of power becomes necessary to sustain its preeminent role. The oracles reflect the violence necessary to implement the vision of the new world. The reconstituted community that forms in the Persian province of Yehud serves as the target audience for the final collection of prophetic books. They call their readers to imagine a new world while grounding them in a version of history that links them to a fictive present and future world. The political contours of the prophetic books take on significance in the oracles that guide the reader on a geographic survey of the world. This survey demonstrates that the Yehudite elite wanted security, and the oracles depicted it as consonant with the divine will. Both the biblical oracles and the US-American security policy statements thus illustrate that on the rhetorical level worthy goals may hide the specter of violence taking place intentionally or unintentionally through the pursuit of narrowly worded policies. By making the security of the nation superior to other concerns, such as just relations among nations, both the biblical and the United States texts justify the violence rhetorically that the people endure in their respective neighborhoods during their respective eras.

Works Cited

Amnesty International. 2009. *The US Embargo against Cuba: Its Impact on Economic and Social Rights*. London: Amnesty International.

Arendt, Hannah. 1970. *On Violence*. New York: Harcourt Brace Jovanovich.

Barton, John. 2003. *Understanding Old Testament Ethics: Approaches and Explorations*. Louisville: Westminster John Knox.

Ben Zvi, Ehud. 2009. "Towards an Integrative Study of Authoritative Books." Pages 15–28 in *The Production of Prophecy: Constructing*

Prophecy and Prophets in Yehud. Edited by Diana V. Edelman and Ehud Ben Zvi. London: Equinox.

Berquist, Jon. 1995. *Judaism in Persia's Shadow: A Social and Historical Approach.* Minneapolis: Fortress.

Bingham, Hiram. 1914. "Should We Abandon the Monroe Doctrine?" *Journal of Race Development* 4:334–58.

Brueggemann, Walter. 1998. *Isaiah 1–39.* Louisville: Westminster John Knox.

Bufacchi, Vittorio. 2005. "Two Concepts of Violence." *Political Science Review* 3:193–204.

Carlson, John D. 2011. "Religion and Violence: Coming to Terms with Terms." Pages 7–22 in *The Blackwell Companion to Religion and Violence.* Edited by Andrew R. Murphy. Malden, MA: Wiley-Blackwell.

Carlson, John D., and Jonathan H. Ebel. 2012. "John Brown, Jeremiad, and Jihad: Reflections on Religion, Violence, and America." Pages 1–25 in *From Jeremiad to Jihad: Religion, Violence, and America.* Edited by John D. Carlson and Jonathan H. Ebel. Berkeley: University of California Press.

Carr, David. 2011. *The Formation of the Hebrew Bible: A New Reconstruction.* New York: Oxford University Press.

Carroll, Robert P. 2006. *Jeremiah.* Vol. 2. Sheffield: Sheffield Phoenix.

Castelli, Elizabeth A. 2004. "Feminists Responding to Violence: Theories, Vocabularies, and Strategies." Pages 1–9 in *Interventions: Activists and Academics Respond to Violence.* Edited by Elizabeth A. Castelli and Janet R. Jakobson. New York: Palgrave Macmillan.

Chandler, Charles Lyon. 1914. "The Pan American Origin of the Monroe Doctrine." *The American Journal of International Law* 8:515–19.

Childs, Brevard. 2001. *Isaiah.* Louisville: Westminster John Knox.

Christensen, Duane L. 1972. "Studies in the Oracles against the Nations: Transformations of the War Oracle in the Old Testament." *HTR* 65:592–93.

———. 1975. *Transformations of the War Oracle in the Old Testament: Studies in the Oracles against the Nations.* HDR 3. Cambridge: Harvard University Press.

Clements, R. E. 1975. *Prophecy and Tradition.* Atlanta: John Knox.

———. 1996. *Ezekiel.* Louisville: Westminster John Knox.

Coatsworth, John H. 1994. *Central America and the United States: The Client and the Colossus.* New York: Twayne.

Connell-Smith, Gordon. 1984. "The Grenada Invasion in Historical Perspective: From Monroe to Reagan." *Third World Quarterly* 6:432–45.

Crandall, Russell. 2006. *Gunboat Democracy: U.S. Interventions in the Dominican Republic, Grenada, and Panama.* Lanham, MD: Rowan & Littlefield.

Crouch, C. L. 2011. "Ezekiel's Oracles against the Nations in the Light of a Royal Ideology of Warfare." *JBL* 130:473–92.

Daschke, Dereck, 2010. "'A Destroyer Will Come against Babylon': George W. Bush's Oracles Against the Nations." Pages 157–81 in *A Cry Instead of Justice: The Bible and Cultures of Violence in Psychological Perspective.* Edited by Dereck Daschke and Andrew Kille. New York: T&T Clark.

Fretheim, Terence E. 2002. *Jeremiah.* Macon, GA: Smyth & Helwys.

Geyer, John B. 2004. *Mythology and Lament: Studies in the Oracles about the Nations.* Hants, England: Ashgate.

Gilderhus, Mark T. 2006. "The Monroe Doctrine: Meaning and Implications." *Presidential Studies Quarterly* 36:5–16.

Gottwald, Norman K. 1964. *All the Kingdoms of the Earth: Israelite Prophecy and International Relations in the Ancient Near East.* New York: Harper & Row.

Hamborg, G. R. 1981. "Reasons for Judgment in the Oracles against the Nations of the Prophet Isaiah." *VT* 31:45–59.

Hauerwas, Stanley. 2012. "Why War Is a Moral Necessity for America." Pages 220–32 in *From Jeremiad to Jihad: Religion, Violence, and America.* Edited by John D. Carlson and Jonathan H. Ebel. Berkeley: University of California Press.

Hayes, John B. 1968. "The Usage of Oracles against the Nations in Ancient Israel." *JBL* 87:81–92.

———. 1995. "Amos' Oracles against the Nations." *RevExp* 92:153.

Hernández-López, Ernesto. 2010. "Guantánamo as a Legal Black Hole: A Base for Expanding Space, Markets, and Culture." *University of San Francisco Law Review* 45:141–213.

Hogan, Michael J. 1998. *A Cross of Iron: Harry S. Truman and the Origins of the National Security State 1945–1954.* Cambridge: Harvard University Press.

Holt, Else. 2003. "The Meaning of an *Inclusio*: A Theological Interpretation of the Book of Jeremiah." *SJOT* 17:183–205.

Keach, William. 2008. "Guantanamo, Empire, and the War on Terror." *Raritan* 27:130–42.

Kitts, Margo. 2013. "Violent Death in Religious. Imagination." Pages 351–60 in *The Oxford Handbook of Religion and Violence*. Edited by Mark Juergensmeyer, Margo Kitts, and Michael Jerryson. New York: Oxford University Press.

Lipschits, Oded. 2006. "Achaemid Imperial Policy and the Status of Jerusalem." Pages 19–52 in *Judah and the Judeans in the Persian Period*. Edited by Oded Lipschits and Manfred Oeming. Winona Lakes, IN: Eisenbrauns.

Martin, Lawrence. 1940. "The Geography of the Monroe Doctrine and the Limits of the Western Hemisphere." *Geographical Review* 30:525–28.

Michaels, C. William. 2002. *No Greater Threat: America after September 11 and the Rise of a National Security State*. New York: Algora.

Mowinckel, Sigmund. 2002. *The Spirit and the Word: Prophecy and Tradition in Ancient Israel*. Edited by K. C. Hanson. Philadelphia: Fortress.

Murphy, Andrew R., and Elizabeth Hanson. 2012. "From King Philip's War to September 11: Religion, Violence, and the American Way." Pages 29–47 in *From Jeremiad to Jihad: Religion, Violence, and America*. Edited by John D. Carlson and Jonathan H. Ebel. Berkeley: University of California Press.

Peels, H. G. L. 2007. "'You Shall Certainly Drink!': The Place and Significance of the Oracles against the Nations in the Book of Jeremiah." *EuroJTh* 16:81–91.

Raines, Edgar F. 2010. *The Rucksack War: U.S. Army Operational Logistics in Grenada, 1983*. Washington, DC: Center of Military History, US Army.

Raskin, Marcus, and Robert Spero. 2007. *The Four Freedoms under Siege: The Clear and Present Danger from Our National Security State*. Westport, CT: Praeger.

Ricard, Serge. 2006. "The Roosevelt Corollary." *Presidential Studies Quarterly* 36:17–26.

Root, Elihu. 1914. "The Real Monroe Doctrine." *The American Journal of International Law* 8:427–42.

Sherrill, Charles H. 1914. "The Monroe Doctrine from a South American Viewpoint." *The Journal of Race Development* 4:319–323.

Stuart, Douglas T. 2008. *Creating the National Security State: A History of the Law that Transformed America*. Princeton: Princeton University Press.

Stulman, Louis, and Hyun Chul Paul Kim. 2010. *You Are My People: An Introduction to Prophetic Literature*. Nashville: Abingdon.

Webb, Stephen H. 2012. "American Providence, American Violence." Pages 91–108 in *From Jeremiad to Jihad: Religion, Violence, and America*. Edited by John D. Carlson and Jonathan H. Ebel. Berkeley: University of California Press.

Žižek, Slavoj. 2008. *Violence: Six Sideways Reflections*. New York: Picador.

Contesting State Violence: The Bible, the Public Good, and Divinely Sanctioned Violence in the Texas Borderlands

Gregory Lee Cuéllar

Resumen: Este ensayo investiga la ideología y teología que hay detrás del concepto de "destino manifiesto" presente en la historiografía y autoimagen de los Estados Unidos. Señala que unido a este concepto se encuentra el de la "providencia," esa fuerza impulsada por Dios que se enraíza en textos bíblicos como los relativos a la tierra prometida o a la idea de "pueblo elegido," que en este caso es comprendido como encarnada en los inmigrantes puritanos Protestantes que eran llamados por Dios a mejorar el mundo. Bajo esta concepción ideológica y teológica se interpretó la anexión de Texas como parte del plan de Dios en su afán por imponer el bien a través de la conquista de todo el continente. El ensayo presenta y discute el concepto de "bien público," la ideología por al cual se afirma que haber ganado la guerra por el territorio era la prueba de que los Estados Unidos estaban en lo correcto y de que México era el país equivocado, porque el "Dios de la ejércitos" no hubiera permitido que triunfe el error. Se analiza que también alimentó esta ideología la polémica anticatólica que identificó a México con el catolicismo y a la que se oponía la versión cristiana del Protestantismo anglosajón. Se destaca el papel de "Los rinches" (Texas rangers) que actuaba no solo como policía sino en primer lugar como fuerza que favorecía la llegada e instalación de los granjeros estadounidenses. Finalmente, el ensayo revela el papel de la Biblia en la construcción de la ideología expansionista que a través de violencia y brutalidad se aplicó a la población de estos territorios invadidos.

The imperialist impulses of Manifest Destiny were unleashed under Anglo-Protestant notions of the public good. As stated by nineteenth-century Democratic politician and journalist John Louis O'Sullivan (1845, 7), it was the "manifest design of Providence" that Anglos occupy the North American continent. Indeed, the pernicious effects ensuant to Manifest Destiny were attenuated by seizing upon the Old Testament biblical motifs such as the Promised Land, the chosen people, and the warrior God. Among the first published iterations of Manifest Destiny as an Anglo-American expansionist ideology was O'Sullivan's 1845 editorial column on the annexation of Texas for *Democratic Review*. He argues in it:

> Why, were other reasoning wanting, in favor of now elevating this ques-
> tion of the reception of Texas into the Union ... for the avowed object of
> thwarting our policy and hampering our power, limiting our greatness
> and checking the fulfillment of our manifest destiny to overspread the
> continent allotted by Providence for the free development of our yearly
> multiplying millions. (5)

Essential to Manifest Destiny's legitimacy as a genuine North American ideology was its appeal to "Providence." This belief echoed the seventeenth century Puritan view that Anglo-Saxon immigrants were a special, chosen people, destined by God to better the world (Horsman 1981, 82; Bailey 2011, 30). Enmeshed within this language, United States annexation of the republic of Texas served as the inaugural expression of God's plan for Anglo-American Protestant occupation of the continent. In O'Sullivan's (1845, 7) view, this "manifest design of Providence" was "the inevitable fulfillment of the general law which is rolling our population westward." Here Anglo-American expansion was the inevitable result of divinely ordained force of good in the world.

Although granting Texas statehood served to confirm United States providential destiny, some writers pointed to Texas's independence in 1836 as the precursor event to Anglo-Protestant expansion over Mexican territory. As Presbyterian minister A. B. Lawrence commented in his 1840 *Emigrant's Guide to the New Republic*, "To Protestant Christians the events of Texas are further deeply interesting, as an indication of Providence in relation to the propagation of divine truth in other parts of the Mexican dominions" (xviii). Early on, the master narrative of Texas's emergence often attributed Anglo military victory to God's favor over Protestants. Seizing upon this theological assumption were the political proponents of Manifest Destiny, especially as it pertained to the United States annexation of Texas. Within this metanarrative framework, Mexico constituted a natural foe of Anglo-American Protestant progress.

The United States decision to annex Texas was ratified in 1845 as a result of a resolution passing in the United States Senate during a conventions in Austin, Texas, on March 1 and on July 4. Included in the annexation agreement was the United States' claim to the disputed territory lying between the Nueces River and the Rio Grande. In 1845, war ensued with Mexico after American troops marched to claim the Rio Grande as the official United States-Mexico territorial boundary (Montejano 1987, 18–19). In just two years, the United States acquired nearly one million square miles of Mexico's northern territories, which consisted of the present-day states of California, New Mexico, northern Arizona, Nevada, Utah, Colorado, Kansas, Oklahoma, and Wyoming. With the signing of the Treaty of Guadalupe-Hidalgo in 1848, which opens with the words, "In the name of Almighty God," the United States-Mexico boundary was drawn from the Gulf of Mexico westward along the Rio Grande to a point just above El Paso del Norte, Chihuahua, and through the Sonoran Desert onto the Pacific just below San Diego, California (Caballos-Ramírez and Martínez 1997, 136–37).[1] The appeal to the biblical notion of the "chosen people" and Anglo-Protestant providential destiny provided rationale for resetting the boundaries of United States sovereignty. Under this religious worldview, the Río Grande had been divinely preordained as the official United States nation-state boundary (Diener and Hagen 2012, 41–42). Implicit here, however, was how a natural river came to represent a humanly marked divide between a litany of polarized conflicting forces—Anglo versus Mexican, Protestant versus Catholic, freedom versus despotism, and civility versus criminality.

The essay outlines the argument in several sections. It begins with a rehearsal of United States arguments about geopolitical expansion as a public good. It then outlines the prevalence of deep anti-Catholic prejudices as a significant part of Anglo-American notions of the public good as a justification for discriminating against Mexicans living in the land. It continues with a discussion of biblical references made to the biblical God as a "warrior God," military justifications for murdering Mexicans living in Texas, and Anglo-American sermons that imagined the war as a "holy war" and enabled the United States conquest as a divine mandate. The essay then explains how the newly defined public good endorsed a

---

1. According to David Weber (2003, 140), southern Arizona remained Mexican territory until 1853.

new Anglo-American conceptualization of the Texas-Mexico border that reinforced stigmatizing views about Mexican Catholic identity. This dynamic led to another facet in this war that yet another section describes. It relates to the paramilitary group of the Texas Rangers who turned into "sacred warrior heroes" justifiably coercing Mexican ranchers off their lands. A conclusion sums up the arguments that indicate that the Bible played a central role in the construction of a credible United States expansionist ideology.

United States Expansionism and the Public Good

During the United States congressional debates on the Mexican-American War, politicians gave form to a conception of the public good that was easily insinuated by Manifest Destiny's master-narrative. Elected officials supporting Anglo-American expansion often portrayed the United States war efforts against Mexico as a force of good in a land fraught with savagery and imbecility. In an 1847 speech on the merits of the Mexican-American War, Senator Lewis Cass of Michigan declared:

> We do not want the people of Mexico, either as citizens or subjects. All we want is a portion of territory, which they nominally hold, generally uninhabited, or, where inhabited at all, sparsely so, and with a population, which would soon recede, or identify itself with ours. (5–6)

Yet silenced in Cass's remarks was the longstanding history of Mexican-*mestizo* townships and ranching communities in the territories he contended were "generally uninhabited" (Weber 2003, 140). For Cass (1847, 5), absorbing the Mexicans into the United States "would be a deplorable amalgamation" and an "evil." To occupy and possess Mexico's northern territory was, in Cass's view a charitable aim, which was "extending the dominion of civilization and improvement over the domain of nature" (2). In the following year, Cass modified his segregationist stance on incorporating Mexican citizens, specifically in relation to the annexation of the entire Mexican Republic (Horsman 1981, 229–41). In a March 1848 speech, he reiterated: "If we were to swallow all Mexico, it would not kill us" (Cass 1848, 3). For him, the full meaning of "swallow" was tied to its historical use in Hos 8:8. As he explained:

> It is at least as old, in our language, as the time of the translators of the Bible. How much more aged, I do not stop to inquire; but in the lan-

guage, whence our Bible was translated, it is at least thirty centuries older. *"Israel is swallowed up,"* said one of her prophets when the throne of David was overturned, and his kingdom annexed, aye, annexed, to the empire of Assyria. *"Israel is swallowed up."* Now, sir, I may congratulate myself upon my position. (12, emphasis original)

The analogy intimated here parallels the United States annexation of Mexico with the Assyrian conquest of northern Israel. Similar to the role of the Neo-Assyrian Empire in the book of Hosea, Cass viewed United States expansion as God's retributive justice against Mexico. Cass's use of the Bible not only granted further authority to the expansionist claims espoused in Manifest Destiny, but also equated United States geopolitical ambitions in Mexico with divine will. In this instance, however, he diverged from the abiding Israel-Puritan analogy, preferring instead an Assyria-United States correspondence as a way of justifying the conquest of Mexico. In efforts to align the United States imperial mission with a divine mandate, Cass deviated from the normal script and used a biblical text in a way that recognized the United States as an empire divinely sanctioned to dispense justice.

Asserting a similar connection was Congressman Andrew Johnson of Tennessee. In August 1848, he spoke these words on the floor of Congress:

Conviction forces itself on my mind that this war was just, or it could never have been crowned with such unparalleled success. Our country must have been in the right, or the God of Battles would sometimes have been against us. Mexico must be in the wrong; she is a doomed nation. The right red arm of an angry God has been suspended over her, and the Anglo-Saxon race has been selected as the rod of her retribution. (Graf and Haskins 1967, 456)

Like Cass and Johnson, political advocates of the Mexican-American War often pointed to Mexico's military invasion of United States soil as its initial act of aggression—an argument predicated on the view that the Río Grande and not the Nueces River marked the official Texas-Mexico territorial boundary (Schroeder 1973, 11, 27). Johnson's articulation of United States expansionism by way of Old Testament formulations, such as "the God of battles," "the arm of an angry God," and "the rod of her retribution," built on Manifest Destiny's master narrative that designated Anglo-Protestant America as the primary divine instrument for developing a more just and free society. Within this justifying rationale, Mexico's attempts to defend its sovereignty were deemed nefarious or in Johnson's words: "Mexico must be in the wrong" (Graf and Haskins 1967, 456).

Implicit within this appropriation of biblical motifs like God of battles or warrior God was a notion of the public good that stood in stark contrast to the Catholic Mexican-*mestizo* social order. In an 1848 speech, Senator Thomas J. Rusk of Texas, a Mexican-American War supporter, delivered these words:

> My opinion, then, Mr. President, is, that we should prosecute this war with vigor, and that the necessary consequence of such vigorous prosecution will be, to show the Mexicans that we are resolved to bring them to reason.... It is said, Mr. President, that it would be robbery to take away their country from the Mexicans. On this point, I would ask whether the principles of our Government do not guaranty to all of our citizens the full enjoyment of life, liberty, and property? If so, would not the extension of our Government throughout Mexico give perfect security to the inhabitants, who would, in that event, be entitled to the protection of our laws? Could this be called robbery, or would the right of property be divested? (11)

Rusk's view of the public good was predicated upon the idea that Mexican-*mestizo* culture and society were innately deficient and backward. If only the Mexican people could be brought "to reason," then they would recognize United States invasion not as "robbery" but as a magnanimous effort to provide Mexico with "perfect security to the inhabitants," "the protection of our laws," and "the right of property." In this regard, United States military conquest was little more than the benevolent articulation of a better society for Mexico. In Rusk's (1848, 11–12) words, "Instead of being an injury to these people, it would be to do them the greatest service possible to take them under our protection." Yet emphasis on the public benefits of United States expansion dismissed the established identity of Mexico as a self-determined nation-state with set laws, religion, language, and territorial boundaries. After the war, the acclaimed benefits of life, liberty, and property ultimately were to be the primary sites of social struggle for colonized ethnic Mexicans in the United States Southwest.

Bound by the greater good, Rusk viewed United States seizure of Mexican territory as a gesture of "service" and not "injury" to the Mexican people. Indeed, conquest was recast as an instrument of protection rather than a vehicle for nullifying Mexican history, values, and cultural identity. For Representative T. J. Turner of Illinois, the improvement of Mexican society was "no less our right than our duty to go on extending liberty and law over the provinces now occupied by those who are unable or unwilling to govern themselves" (1848, 3). This sense of duty to the public good rendered the violent seizure of Mexican territory negligible. As Senator Cass propounded in the Senate near the end of Mexican-American War:

> I believe it the happiest fate that could befall them; and I believe that this war, injurious in many respects, as it may have been, and must have been, is destined to work a great good for the Mexican people. I believe it will meliorate their condition, civil, religious, social, and political. I believe that the contact with our citizens will bring many advantages, permanently beneficial. (1848, 12).

Cass's construction of the public good contended that advancing Mexico toward a more civilized state necessitated acts of violence, and from the standpoint of providential destiny, these acts of violence were linked to God's wrath on Mexico.

Virulent Anti-Catholic Sentiments

In mid-nineteenth century United States frontier society, an abiding anti-Catholic attitude also informed Anglo-American notions of the public good. English hostilities toward Spanish Catholics, which had found expression in the Black Legend and sixteenth-century Reformation thought, were imported to the British colonies (Limerick 1987, 223). As Charles Gibson (1971, 21) describes, the Black Legend is "the legend of an inquisitorial, ignorant, and fanatic Spain, incapable of taking its place among cultivated peoples either now or in the past, disposed always toward violent forms of repression, enemy of progress and change." For Anglo-Americans in the newly annexed state of Texas, this anti-Catholic sentiment was naturally directed at Mexican society, who even after their independence from Spain maintained strong ties to Roman-Catholicism. As Michael R. Ornelas (2004, 62) writes, "For the early American settlers who arrived in Texas, they imported attitudes that ranged from xenophobia against Catholics and Spaniards to racial prejudice against Indians and blacks." Much of this anti-Catholic sentiment permeated the sermons and religious writings of Protestant clergy and missionaries in Texas. Baptist minister Z. N. Morrell, describing his migration to Texas in 1834, gave this view of Mexico:

My mind was turned to Texas in the fall of 1834. Its government was then very much disturbed. This obstacle in the way, and the additional fact that the iron arm of Catholicism was stretched over the whole land of Mexico, then embracing the State of Texas, did not make it a very desirable field for a Baptist preacher, who had always been accustomed to express himself boldly and independently. Catholicism, "the man of sin," I considered as a sworn enemy to me as a Baptist. (1872, 20)

In Morrell's view, the "semi-savage" state of Mexican society was inextricably linked to the "tyranny of Catholicism" (32). Remedying this condition was Anglo-Protestant Christianity which Morrell insisted guaranteed "a good society" (viii). Conversely, rendering Catholicism as an enemy of what he understood as a good society reinforced the need to impose Anglo-Protestant ideals by whatever means necessary. Yet the shape this providential charge took was one of war and violent domination.

Appealing to a Biblical Warrior God

Those in United States favoring the use of violence often attenuated its terror effects by appealing to biblical authority. In 1847, near the end of the Mexican-American War, Rev. John McCarty, a United States army chaplain, preached a thanksgiving sermon at the National Palace in Mexico City. His sermon was based on one scriptural verse, 1 Sam 12:24: "Only fear the Lord, and serve Him with all your heart; for consider how great things He hath done for you" (McCarty 1847, 3). Addressing his audience as "my brethren of the Army," McCarty directed his military audience to acknowledge the "favoring Providence of the 'Lord of Hosts.'" Throughout his sermon, McCarty made an appeal to the warrior God of the Old Testament as the worthy recipient of their "praise and thanksgiving" (Lind 1980, 24–27; Miller 1973, 64–165). By invoking the God of hosts, McCarty placed the Mexican-American War within a larger cosmic and metaphysical conflict between the ultimate good and evil (Juergensmeyer 2003, 149). Moreover, he also consecrated the defeat of Mexico as a divine victory: "It can be shown to be the duty of a Christian people, and more so of the army of a Christian land, to offer thanksgiving to the great Ruler of Nations, for the victories by which He has crowned their arms" (McCarty 1847, 3). From this vantage point, the United States military assumed the position of ancient Israel, hence redefining the United States conquest of Mexico as the fulfillment of God's promise. Accordingly, McCarty construed the American war effort against Mexico as a "righteous cause" (4).

Warring Notions of Humanity

As for the violence inflicted upon the people of Mexico, McCarty (1847, 4) emphasized that the United States military gave full regard to "the laws of warfare recognized by the civilized and Christian nations." Here again, notions of magnanimity dissimulated the terrors of conquest. As McCarty described it:

> Never have the peaceful inhabitants of a theatre of hostilities had so little cause to complain of the treatment received from invaders and conquerors.... They have been better treated by us than their own armies; indeed we have been rather protectors than destroyers of the Mexican people. (9)

As his rationale suggests, underwriting the war effort stemmed from a paternal obligation to protect Mexico. For McCarty, the United States' superior moral position was clearly evidenced throughout the Mexican-American War: "Yes, we may thank God, with heartfelt satisfaction, that we were too American; have had too much respect for the rights of humanity, too much regard for our character, to come down to the low level of a Mexican soldier's notions of humanity, honor and civilization" (10). Polarized according to varying notions of humanity, Anglo-Americans represented a divine force of good, which, in turn, offered a moral justification for the violent seizure of Mexican territory (Juergensmeyer 2003, 165–66). McCarty often distanced United States conquest from the realm of human tragedy and trauma by providing a moral and theological logic for it:

> Estimating things in the light of Divine truth, the glory of our superior generalship and courage, of our splendid victories and wonderful success, is a small thing when compared with the glory resulting from the humanity, justice and generosity displayed in our warfare with this people. (1847, 10)

Although a harsh measure, warfare became the platform upon which the United States military was able to demonstrate superior Anglo-Protestant values to a morally deprived and religiously deficient Mexican society. Yet, revealed in McCarty's assessment of this public good was an Anglo-American Protestant impulse in which the bestowal of humanity, justice, and generosity to an "inferior" Mexican society was only achievable through warfare. Framing the United States war efforts as a humanitarian religious mission served to sacralize the violence thought necessary for improving Mexico.

The United States' Conquest as a Divine Mandate

McCarty proceeded in his sermon to provide a biblical understanding for war casualties. Reiterating his central theme of thanksgiving, he declared: "In offering our thanksgiving each of us should consider the goodness of his Heavenly Father, in his own preservation, not only from the violence of the enemy, but from the hand of disease" (1847, 11–12). He elevated the preserved life of the battle worn United States soldier to the otherworldly and the heavenly realm. Conversely, this was a cosmic-battlefield survival in which United States soldiers had been divinely protected from "the violence of the enemy" and "the hand of disease." Reimaging battle as a holy war elided the obvious reasons for Mexico's deployed violence, which primarily had to do with the defense of its sovereignty. For McCarty, war survival evidenced the soldier's alliance with the biblical warrior God. As he declared to his audience: "They should deeply consider and gratefully acknowledge, not their good luck and fortunate escape, which is but the religion of the atheist, but the sparing goodness of their Great Preserver, owning in the words of Holy Writ, 'God is the Lord, by whom we escape death'" (12). McCarty cited Ps 68:20 as inspiration for how the victorious United States soldier was to envision his survival. Implied in his reading of this verse was the view that the war efforts of a United States soldier were intrinsically good and inextricably tied to the warrior God of the Old Testament. This reading also perpetuated the portrayal of Mexico as an arch-nemesis of the United States, both on earth and in heaven. For McCarty, the soldier's escape from the perils of battle was too obvious a sign of God's favor upon the United States war efforts. He thus declared:

> Yes, my brethren it seems, that escape from the great dangers to which our officers and soldiers have been generally exposed would constrain the most irreligious gratefully to unite with the warrior Psalmist in the acknowledgement "the Lord hast covered our heads, and made us stand in the day of battle" [Psalm 140:7]. (12)

McCarty drew a parallel between the "warrior Psalmist" and the United States troops of the Mexican-American War. Their mutual service to a divine mandate justified the United States soldiers' literal appropriation of the psalmist's words (Renard 2012, 1–3). This common brotherhood also opened Ps 103:4 as a legitimate text for appropriation—in McCarty's (1847, 12) words, "And with him to call upon their souls 'to praise His Holy Name, who saveth our life from destruction and crowneth us with mercy and loving kindness.'" In marshaling these biblical texts, McCarty not only inspired the United States troops to view themselves as a continuation of biblical history, but also to safeguard the integrity of the United States' imperial mission.

In concluding his message, McCarty returned to his sermon's base text saying: "Let us regard the end for which we should now 'consider the great things the Lord hath done for us,' [1 Sam 12:24] in these deliverances and victories." A link between the great acts of Israel's warrior God and the United States' imperial mission in Mexico informed McCarty's hermeneutic. Indeed, all matters pertaining to the United States conquest of Mexico were achieved "by the help of the God of Battles" (12). McCarty's expansionist theology was rooted in the conquest narratives of the Old Testament in which the God of battles sanctions Israel's conquest of the land of Canaan. By appropriating this image of God, he relegated the United States fulfillment of its manifest destiny to the realms of war and violence. Hence, the victory of war against Mexico was a cathartic event that not only confirmed the United States as God's chosen nation but also as the standard-bearer of the public good. For this reason, McCarty assigned a civilizing mission to Mexico's postwar development, which included:

> Enlightening their religious ignorance and raising them from degradation to which they are reduced ... by extending the light and the blessings of our purer faith; so that by our Christian influence and example and by the intercourse between us, they may imbibe something of our free spirit and throw off the shackles of military and spiritual despotism. Believing that the Mexicans most need for their improvement, a purer exhibition of the Gospel of Christ. (13)

At the fore of this civilizing mission was the idealization of the Protestant ethic and Anglo-American individualism (Arieli 1964, 345–46). In contrast, the institutional constraints of the Catholic Church impeded Mexico's progress on the individual's will to realize his or her full potential (E. Johnson 1970, 237). The United States-Mexican War gave precedence to the notion that the ideal society could only occur when its citizens exercised individual autonomy. At least Mexicans would be able to acquire the "free spirit" of the Anglo-American Protestant and improve their society.

Thus McCarty (1847, 14) declared "that witnessing our superiority not only as soldiers, but as Christian men, they may honor our land, not only as free, enlightened and prosperous, but as blessed by superior means of Christian knowledge and piety, which are the foundation of all."

Civilizing the Texas-Mexico Border

For Anglo-American newcomers to the Texas borderlands ,the submission to a newly defined public good meant that they had to appropriate stigmatizing views about Mexican Catholic identity. In an 1853 article for the *Presbyterian Herald*, Rev. Hiram Chamberlain, a pioneer Presbyterian minister in Brownsville, Texas, made a negative comment on the Mexican Catholic presence in the Río Grande Valley. He asked: "If, however, as we believe, their system is wrong, and Protestants teach the true gospel of Christ, by which men must be saved, it may well be asked whether their system of action ought not to be reviewed?" The devaluation of Mexican identity emphasized religious differences that assumed Anglo-Protestantism's superior position. This inordinate value claim enabled unequal forms of social privilege and political access in the newly conquered Mexican territories.

In her book *Twenty Years among Mexicans*, Presbyterian missionary Melinda Rankin identified Mexican social decadence with despotic Roman Catholicism when she stated:

> Indeed, a pure Christianity had never penetrated these dark regions, as all the previous history of Mexico clearly proved. Upon the advent of the Spanish conquerors of Mexico, Roman Catholicism, with all its idolatrous rites, was substituted for paganism. Nothing withstanding the assumptions of the Roman system of religion, it proved fully as demoralizing, and which, besides its corrupting tendencies, ground down the poor inoffensive people under the most despotic bondage.... Its legitimate fruits were fully apparent by the moral degradation prevailing throughout one of the fairest countries upon the globe. (1875, 22–23)

This prevalent assessment of Mexican society not only heralded Anglo-Protestantism as the sole truth-bearer, but it also negated a significant feature of Mexican identity. Instead of fostering mutual notions of the public good, this wholesale negation of Mexican religious identity only served to exasperate Anglo-Mexican cultural conflict in the Texas borderlands region (Paredes 1993, 19).

For most ethnic Mexicans who remained in the newly conquered territories, the changed public good represented an Anglo-American regulated social space in which cultural strife rather than joint progress was the norm. Articles VIII, IX, and X in the Treaty of Guadalupe Hidalgo had secured the civil and property rights of ethnic Mexicans now under Anglo-American rule (Larralde and Jacobo 2000, 3). With the "Almighty God" as its witness, the United States government stipulated that annexed Mexican territory would be "incorporated into the Union of the United States" and that all ethnic Mexicans north of the newly marked border would have the "enjoyment of all the rights of citizens" (Klein 1905, 61). Though the treaty promised ethnic Mexicans the protection of their basic civil rights, the prevailing reality was an abiding racial antagonism that served to impede the social mobility of Mexicans-Americans (Menchaca 2001, 215).

In addition, throughout Texas the real estate market worked both legally and fraudulently against Mexican-American landownership (Montejano 1987, 53). The growing value of land prompted some to resort to the simple expedient of occupying a desired tract and violently expelling poor Mexican ranchers. The combination of economic pressure, title challenges, and outright theft led to significant Mexican-American land loss. Benjamin Johnson (2003, 33) estimates: "From 1900 to 1910 Hispanic-surnamed individuals lost a total of more than 180,000 acres in Cameron and Hidalgo counties."

Texas Ranger as the Sacred Warrior-Hero

The paramilitary group charged with the task of coercing Mexican ranchers off their lands was the Texas Rangers, which in borderlands Spanish was subversively rendered "*Los Rinches.*" A military unit during the United States-Mexican War, the Texas Rangers functioned as the military police of occupation, waging sporadic warfare whenever the need arose (Montejano 1987, 33–34). David Montejano explains, "The Rangers were not merely suppressing seditious Mexican bandits; in the large picture, they played the critical part in paving the way for the newcomer farmers" (116–26). Armed with a handgun, Winchester rifle and cartridge belt, the Texas Rangers secured the settlement of Anglo-American opportunists often with inhumane brutality. As Albert Bigelow Paine describes in his 1909 book, *Captain Bill McDonald, Texas Ranger: A Story of Frontier Reform:*

Early in 1836 Texas fought for and gained her independence, the only
State in the Union to achieve such a triumph. On the following year the
Texas congress recognized the Ranger Movement and authorized several
persons to raise Ranger companies to scour the country and annihilate
marauding bands. Indians and low class Mexicans ("greasers") often
consorted, and the work, desperate and bloody continued along the ever
widening and westering frontier up to within a period easily remembered to-day by men not beyond middle age. (130)

Echoing biblical notions of the holy war, the Texas Rangers served as the
region's quintessential warrior heroes. Like Israel's warrior-hero tradition,
they were mandated by the state to annihilate the border's primary nem-
esis, the Mexican bandit. As defenders of the public good, the Texas Rangers served as the archetypal protagonists in the hallowed meta-narrative of
the emergence of Texas.

The surge in Mexican land displacements gave rise to counter militant
movements among the ethnic Mexicans themselves. They transformed the
Lower Rio Grande valley into a virtual war zone between 1915 and 1917.
José R. Lopez Morin (2006, 19) describes this development: "The armed
insurrection by the border folk was their way of saying ¡Basta ya! (Enough
is enough) to the so called fortune makers in the Texas Border region." The
United States press and politicians branded their insurrection as "Mexican banditry" and eventually as a "Bandit War." Yet for the rebels it was
an attempt to regain control of their dispossessed lands in South Texas.
Their manifesto, "El Plan de San Diego," had the following political objectives: first, an uprising on February 20, 1915, by the Liberating Army of
Races and People (composed of Mexicans, "Negroes," Japanese, and Indians); second, an end to "Yankee tyranny"; and third, the creation of an
independent republic that would consist of Texas, New Mexico, Arizona,
Colorado, and California (Montejano 1987, 117).

Aimed at Anglo-American targets, the revolutionists destroyed houses
and farms, burned bridges, sabotaged irrigation systems, and derailed a
train twelve miles north of Brownsville (Danver 2011, 729). The Texas
Rangers were called upon to suppress the raids in the Valley region with
the natural inclination that all young ethnic Mexican males were suspect
(Morin 2006, 19). Appearing in the Mexican Review in 1915, the anony-
mous article "Light on Border Conditions" contains the following excerpt
from a correspondence between Sheriff and County Judge Emilio C. Forto
and United States Army Colonel H. J. Slocum:

From all reports (some from army officers whose testimony is probably available) a campaign of extermination seemed to have begun in those days. The cry was often heard, "We have to make this a white man's country!" It would not be difficult to establish the fact that many well-to-do natives of Texas, of Mexican origin, were driven away by the Rangers, who told them, "If you are found here in the next five days you will be dead." They were in this way forced to abandon their property, which they sold at almost any price. (20)

The late Texas historian Walter Prescott Webb, in his well-known book *Texas Rangers: A Century of Frontier Defense*, writes that the "orgy of bloodshed" caused by the Texas Rangers, local posses, and peace officers "has been estimated at 500 and at 5000, but the actual number can never be known" (1935, 478).[2] Rather than allaying the tensions on the border, the Texas Rangers did much to inflame them. Their policing tactics encouraged an abiding hostility among the ethnic Mexican population for Anglo-American authority. So deeply felt was the hostility that, as historian T. R. Fehrenbach writes, "even third and fourth generation citizens, who had never actually seen a Ranger, reacted with an instinctive phobia toward the name" (Samora, Bernal, and Peña 1979, 66).

The Texas Rangers and the Bible

It is extremely difficult to establish a link between the Texas Rangers and the Bible. After all, not every Texas Ranger viewed his service within the context of a holy war. Yet, as Brownson Malsch (1998, xiii) indicates, "some killed without mercy while others carried their Bibles with their guns." In 1874, Texas Governor Cook commissioned Leander H. McNelly as "Captain of Militia" (Cox 2008, 241). Captain McNelly, once a Presbyterian divinity student, and his volunteer militia company were dispatched to the Texas border where "in appearance and function they rode as Rangers" (242). His policing tactics were brutal and often inhumane. In his book, *The Men Who Wear the Star*, Charles M. Robinson (2001, 183) describes him as "soft-spoken and a sometime lay preacher, he nevertheless resorted to throat-cutting, lynching, and confessions through torture when they served

---

2. In B. Johnson's (2003, 34) view, the fragmentary nature of the surviving accounts and the discovery of skeletons even decades later suggest that a number in the low thousands is probable.

his purposes." As one charged with preserving the public good in Texas borderlands, McNelly embodied the ideal ranger warrior hero in which "he faithfully read the Bible for moral guidance" (Larralde and Jacobo 2000, 114), while at the same time "his prisoners were tortured and hanged without trial" (Franscell 2011, 24). In the metanarrative of Texas Ranger history, McNelly is mythologized into a "warlord and Christ figure: courageous and gentlemanly, utterly devoted to his men and his mission, a remorseless killer, and dead himself by the holy age of 33" (Draper 1994, 82). In this sacred history, he mirrors the biblical warrior-hero in the Old Testament who is divinely mandated to annihilate the ethnic other for the sake of the public good (Alexander 2013, 43). As a member of McNelly's rangers described in a letter to the mother of a fallen Ranger, the mission was "the annihilation of the Mexicans," for the "the liberty and the rights of mankind" (50).

Other Rangers were open about their Bible reading habits. For instance, John H. Rogers joined the Texas Rangers in 1882, rising to the rank of captain in 1892 (Harvey 2003, 46; Spellman 2003, 158). Off duty, he was an elder in the Presbyterian Church and president of his Sunday School class. Paul N. Spellman (2003, xi, 126–29) states, "His faith was open and unyielding, and he carried it on his sleeve as well as his pocket Bible." Essential to Roger's legendary ranger status was his commitment to the Bible. As Spellman describes it, "when the captain found himself on the trail on the Sabbath, he continued his long-standing habit of attending the closest church he could locate, often attending morning and evening worship there and voluntarily teaching a Bible class as well before moving on" (89). Contemporary to Captain Rogers was Texas Ranger Augie Old, a Methodist and, as former Ranger W. W. Sterling (1959, 376) characterizes him, a "deeply religious" man. Rogers and Old, in Sterling's words, "heeded the Biblical admonition to 'turn the other cheek' but between changes they would either shoot or knock the devil out of their adversaries." These Texan warrior-saints were a continuation of biblical history in which the divine mandate was to establish an Anglo-Protestant society. Their ties to sacred Scripture forever consecrate their legendary status and their extreme policing methods in preserving the public good in the Texan borderlands.

An Expansionist Bible: Concluding Comments

In the mid-nineteenth century, the Bible played a central role in the construction of a credible United States expansionist ideology (i.e., Manifest

Destiny). In mining the Bible for language, politicians, clergy, and military personnel exploited the themes of the Promised Land, the chosen people, and holy war to legitimate the state's violence against ethnic Mexicans. Hence, Manifest Destiny reveals less about a political ideology than it does about a particular hermeneutic in which the warrior-God figure of the Old Testament dictates meaning. Taking this figure literally provided the United States with a divine sanction to its declaration of war against Mexico in 1846. Violence and conquest are consecrated as necessary and holy acts, transcending into the celestial cosmic battle against good and evil.

The state-sanctioned violence in the Texas borderlands was fitted into biblical history in such a way that the United States became the natural heir of God's promise to Israel. Made permanent in this scripturalization of United States expansionism was Mexico as an earthly/cosmic force of evil. This immutable designation allowed for police groups like the Texas Rangers to transfigure themselves into biblical/mythological warrior-heroes. Ascribing mythical status to the Texas Rangers served to desensitize Anglo-Protestant society to the public displays of burned and beaten Mexican bodies throughout the borderlands region. They, along with other military and policing personnel, were subsumed under the United States' master narrative, making them God's chosen warriors and the standard bearers of the public good.

These historical strands in the fabric of the United States' master narrative have generally gone unquestioned, especially in light of the increasing militarization on the United States-Mexico border. The Mexican body continues to be a locus for state sanctioned violence and United States hero identity. Although this analysis of United States expansionism follows a particular constellation of ideas and assumptions, contemporary readers of the Bible cannot avoid the link between border enforcement and the pervading occurrence of human rights violations. The case made here is that this violence has a specific genealogy in which brutal and bloody violence against the Mexican population became biblically justified as a civilizing mission. In this biblical hermeneutic of violence, Anglo-Americans were the bringers of God's justice even though it meant the murder, dispossession, and conversion of the native Mexican people in this geographical area. The ramifications of this violence are still felt today in vicious border control tactics and references to the Bible that do not preach empathy with the border crossers.

Works Cited

Alexander, Bob. 2013. *Riding Lucifer's Line: Ranger Deaths Along the Texas-Mexico Border*. Denton: University of North Texas Press.

Arieli, Yehoshua. 1964. *Individualism and Nationalism in American Ideology*. Cambridge: Harvard University Press.

Bailey, Richard A. 2011. *Race and Redemption in Puritan New England*. Oxford: Oxford University Press.

Caballos-Ramírez, Manuel, and Oscar J. Martínez. 1997. "Conflict and Accommodation on the U.S. Mexican Border, 1848–1911." Pages 135–58 in *Myths, Misdeeds, and Misunderstandings: The Roots of Conflict in U.S.-Mexican Relations*. Edited by Jaime E. Rodríguez and Kathryn O. Vincent. Wilmington: Scholarly Resources.

Cass, Lewis. 1847. *The Mexican War Speech of Honorable Lewis Cass, of Michigan, in the Senate of the United States, February 10, 1847*. Washington: Office of Blair & Rives.

———. 1848. *The War with Mexico: Speech of Hon. Lewis Cass, of Michigan, in the Senate of the United States, March 17, 1848: On the Bill Reported from the Committee on Military Affairs to Raise for a Limited Time an Additional Military Force*. Washington DC: Printed at the Congressional Global Office.

Chamberlain, H. 1853. "Reports of Papists on the Río Grande." *Presbyterian Herald*. Type written transcript of article. William Stuart Reed Collection, Box C060. Austin Seminary Archives, Austin.

Cox, Mike. 2008. *The Texas Rangers: Wearing the Cinco Peso, 1821–1900*. New York: Forge.

Danver, Steven Laurence. 2011. *Revolts, Protests, Demonstrations, and Rebellions in American History: An Encyclopedia*. Santa Bárbara: ABC-CLIO.

Diener, Alexander C., and Joshua Hagen. 2012. *Borders: A Very Short Introduction*. New York: Oxford University Press.

Draper, Robert. 1994. "Twilight of the Texas Rangers." *Texas Monthly* 22:82.

Franscell, Ron. 2011. *The Crime Buff's Guide to Outlaw Texas*. Guilford: Globe Pequot.

Gibson, Charles. 1971. *The Black Legend: Anti-Spanish Attitudes in the Old World and the New*. New York: Knopf.

Graf, LeRoy P., and Ralph W. Haskins, eds. 1967. *The Papers of Andrew Johnson*. Knoxville: University of Tennessee Press.

Harvey, Bill. 2003. *Clifton and Shirley Caldwell Texas Heritage Series: Texas Cemeteries; The Resting Places of Famous, Infamous, and Just Plain Interesting Texans*. 5 vols. Austin: University of Texas Press.

Horsman, Reginald. 1981. *Race and Manifest Destiny: The Origins of American Racial Anglo-Saxonism*. Cambridge: Harvard University Press.

Johnson, Benjamin Heber. 2003. *Revolution in Texas: How a Forgotten Rebellion and Its Bloody Suppression Turned Mexicans into Americans*. New Haven: Yale University Press.

Johnson, Ellwood. 1970. "Individualism and the Puritan Imagination." *American Quarterly* 22:230–37.

Juergensmeyer, Mark. 2003. *Terror in the Mind of God: The Global Rise of Religious Violence*. 3rd ed. Comparative Studies in Religion and Society 13. Berkeley: University of California Press.

Klein, Julius. 1905. *Making of the Treaty of Guadalupe Hidalgo, On February 2, 1848*. Berkeley: University Press.

Larralde, Carlos, and José Rodolfo Jacobo. *Juan N. Cortina and the Struggle for Justice in Texas*. Dubuque: Kendall/Hunt, 2000.

Lawrence, Rev. A. B. 1840. *Texas in 1840: Emigrant's Guide to the New Republic*. New York: Allen.

"Light on Border Conditions." 1915. *Mexican Review* 2:20.

Limerick, Patricia Nelson. 1987. *The Legacy of Conquest: The Unbroken Past of the American West*. New York: Norton.

Lind, Millard C. 1980. *Yahweh Is a Warrior: The Theology of Warfare in Ancient Israel*. Scottdale: Herald.

Malsch, Brownson. 1998. *Lone Wolf Gonzaullas, Texas Ranger*. Norman: University of Oklahoma Press.

McCarty, John. 1847. *A Thanksgiving Sermon, Preached in the National Palace, City of Mexico, on Sunday, October Third, A.D. 1847: On the Occasion of a Public Thanksgiving for the Victories Achieved by the Army of the United States, in the Basin of Mexico, Under Command of Major-General Winfield Scott*. Mexico: Office of the American Star.

Menchaca, Martha. 2001. *Recovering History, Constructing Race: The Indian, Black, and White Roots of Mexican Americans*. Austin: University of Texas Press.

Miller, Patrick. 1973. *The Divine Warrior in Ancient Israel*. Cambridge: Harvard University Press.

Montejano, David. 1987. *Anglos and Mexicans in the Making of Texas, 1836–1986*. Austin: University of Texas Press.

Morin, José. 2006. *The Legacy of Americo Paredes.* College Station: Texas A&M University Press.

Morrell, Z. N. 1872. *Flowers and Fruits from the Wilderness: Thirty-Six Years in Texas and Two Winters in Honduras.* Boston: Gould & Lincoln.

Ornelas, Michael R. 2004. *Between the Conquest: The Early Chicano Historical Experience.* Dubuque, Iowa: Kendall/Hunt.

O'Sullivan, John L. 1845. "Annexation." *The U.S. Democratic Review* 17:7.

Paine, Albert Bigelow. 1909. *Captain Bill McDonald, Texas Ranger: A Story of Frontier Reform.* New York: Little & Ives.

Paredes, Américo. 1993. *Folklore and Culture on the Texas-Mexican Border.* Austin: CMAS.

Rankin, Melinda. 1875. *Twenty Years among the Mexicans: A Narrative of Missionary Labor.* Cincinnati: Chase & Hall.

Renard, John. 2012. "Exegesis and Violence: Texts, Contexts, and Hermeneutical Concerns." Pages 1–3 in *Fighting Words: Religion, Violence, and the Interpretation of Sacred Texts.* Edited by John Renard. Berkley: University of California Press.

Robinson, Charles M. 2001. *The Men Who Wear the Star: The Story of the Texas Rangers.* New York: Modern Library.

Rusk, Thomas J. 1848. *Speech of Hon. Thomas J. Rusk of Texas, on the Mexican War: Delivered the Senate of the United States, February 15, 1848.* Washington: Congressional Globe Office.

Samora, Julián, Joe Bernal, and Albert Peña. 1979. *Gunpowder Justice: A Reassessment of the Texas Rangers.* Notre Dame: University of Notre Dame Press.

Schroeder, John H. 1973. *Mr. Polk's War: American Opposition and Dissent 1846–1848.* Madison: University of Wisconsin Press.

Spellman, Paul N. 2003. *Captain John H. Rogers, Texas Ranger.* Denton: University of North Texas Press.

Sterling, William Warren. 1959. *Trails and Trials of a Texas Ranger.* Norman: University of Oklahoma Press.

Turner, Thomas J. 1848. *The War with Mexico Speech of Hon. T.J. Turner, of Illinois, in the House of Representatives, April 6, 1848.* Washington: Congressional Globe Office.

Webb, Walter Prescott. 1935. *The Texas Rangers: A Century of Frontier Defense.* Boston: Houghton Mifflin.

Weber, David J. 2003. *Foreigners in Their Native Land: Historical Roots of the Mexican Americans.* Albuquerque: University of New Mexico Press.

"How Long, O God? I Cry for Help": Habakkuk, Violence, and the Quest for a Just God in Honduras

Renata Furst

Resumen: El presente ensayo analiza la violencia en Honduras ocasionada por la conjunción de bandas armadas, narcotráfico, crimen organizado, una policía corrupta y una extrema pobreza. Esta violencia ha llegado al límite de ser indiscriminada y sin sentido. Las personas mueren en muchos casos sin saber por qué y las bandas o maras dominan en las ciudades produciendo víctimas en gran escala. El ensayo destaca la relación que se establece entre las maras y el fenómeno religioso, al punto que uno de los pocos modos de abandonar una mara es incorporándose a una iglesia evangélica ya que los integrantes de la banda aceptarán que se aparte de la organización si la persona manifiesta haber encontrado a Dios y su salvación. Toda esta situación es analizada y comparada a la luz de las palabras del profeta Habacuc en los capítulos1–2. En estas páginas Dios deja de ser un espectador pasivo de la violencia y aparece como un activo actor en el drama de la violencia. El ensayo muestra que en el texto Dios y Habacuc juegan papeles distintos; mientras el segundo está preocupado por la situación de violencia interna, Dios promueve la acción internacional de los caldeos, también violenta, para disciplinar a los habitantes de Judá. El artículo concluye señalando que es necesaria una lectura deconstructiva que deje en evidencia las verdaderas victimas de la violencia tanto en el texto de Habacuc como de las víctimas de la violencia en Honduras.

Over the last ten to fifteen years, Central America has rivaled and in some instances surpassed Colombia and Mexico as the most violent region of Latin America. In 2011, the United Nations Office on Drugs and Crime named Honduras the most violent country in the world (United Nations Office on Drugs and Crime 2011, 93). Rising violence is attributed to gang activity, drug cartels, native organized crime, inadequate or corrupt police, and poverty and its resulting social problems. Earlier in the twentieth century, violence in Central America was attributed primarily to the clash of political ideologies, but currently it is simply attributed to crime. This essay concentrates on the social violence experienced as uncontrollable and random in contemporary Honduras and examines it through the theological lens of Habakkuk, a book written during a time (605–597 BCE) when social violence peaked in Judah and the ancient Near East. More specifically, the essay discusses how violence affects the belief in a just world by looking specifically at the voicing and perception of victims, victimizers, and observers of violence in Habakkuk. I propose that the interactions among victims, victimizers, and observers in the textual world of Habakkuk shed light on how we need to think about gang violence in contemporary Honduras.

The presence of gangs in barrios in Honduras has greatly increased intentional and random violence, and much has been written about this type of violence (e.g., Brenneman 2012; Ganzevoort 2008; Aguiar, Vals, and Correia 2008; Zomeren and Lodewijkx 2009). This essay refers to some of these important studies, but overall it correlates Hab 1–2 to experiences of social violence in Honduras. It reads Hab 1–2 through the trauma of random violence. Further, it assumes that intentional, categorical, and calculable acts of violence become "random" in the perception of people when victims perceive violence as senseless and meaningless. Central to this investigation is the prophetic cry in Hab 1:2, because it articulates the need of victims to understand God's role in social violence. The prophet cries out: "How long, O God? I cry for help, but you do not listen! I cry out to you 'Violence!' but you do not intervene."[1] This outcry asks whether God is a passive observer or an active agent guaranteeing justice in the world. It still resonates today in societies such as in Honduras.

Habakkuk's question highlights the role of both the prophet and God as observers of violence. They focus on the victimizers, but the victims who are marginalized and live in the most fragile reaches of society are barely mentioned in the textual world of Hab 1–2. Hence, the observers of violence, the prophet and God, do not mention the poor, the widow, the orphan, or the stranger, so commonly referenced elsewhere in the Hebrew Bible. One needs to read Hab 1–2 against the norms established

---

1. Unless otherwise stated, all biblical translations are my own.

there so that one comes to see the victims in this textual world that is filled with violence.

The following essay is grounded in this basic insight. It examines the norms in Hab 1–2 that preserve a just-world belief by erasing the victims of violence and by highlighting the perspectives of the victimizers and the observers of violence. Social justice theories have shown that victims from inside a society, the so-called "in-group victims," threaten a belief in a just world more immediately than victims from other societies, the so-called "out-group victims" (Aguiar, Vals, and Correia 2008, 50). Thus, this study maintains that the total erasure of the in-group victims in Hab 1–2 enables the prophetic voice to affirm a belief in a just God while merely referring to other nations as victims of the Chaldeans (Hab 1:6–11). The discussion begins with a depiction of gang violence in Honduras, continues with a detailed examination of Hab 1–2 in light of Honduran violence, and concludes that reading of Habakkuk against its textual norms sheds light on just-world belief in God in Honduras.

Gang Violence in Honduras

Violence in Honduras comes from a multitude of sources: drug cartels, native organized crime, family violence, and institutionalized violence within government structures. Violence within and between gangs is very focused and purposeful. It establishes control over territories, goods, and members and instills fear in the nongang population. Violence is also a tool for creating identity and loyalty among new gang members. The populations living with violence and gang territories perceive violence as a *random* event. Yet importantly, violence perceived as random undermines people's belief in a just world guaranteed and supported by the presence of a just God.

What Is Random Violence?

Violence in the form of homicide does not discriminate. Every generation, social class, occupation, and political organization has its victims. In Honduras, this fact is expressed in the saying, "Cada familia tiene su muerto," or in English, "Every family has a dead member." Entire populations live in the midst of general and usually random violence. When violence is measured in terms of homicide, it collides with randomness and intentionality. The United Nations Office of Drugs and Crime states this fact:

The intentional killing of a human being by another is the ultimate crime. Its indisputable physical consequences manifested in the form of a dead body also make it the most categorical and calculable. (2011, 9)

Violence may be intentional, categorical, and calculable, but it becomes "random" when it is perceived to be senseless or meaningless. When violent death occurs, people in Honduras ask "Why was this person killed?" Often, they do not receive an answer, because institutions, such as the police and the courts of law, are unable to cope with the overwhelming violence engulfing the country. In this situation, lack of meaning threatens the personal and social perception that a just world is possible for both victims and by-standers or observers of violence. Martijn van Zomeren and Hein F. M Lodewijkx (2009, 223) explain, "Incidents of random, 'senseless' violence thus uniquely implicate observers in events because observers cannot blame the victim for his or her fate to protect their just world beliefs, and hence need to cope with this potential threat to self." People cope with this potential threat to self by blaming the victim: "Was he or she involved directly or indirectly with gangs?" "Did this person inadvertently step into gang territory?" "Perhaps the dead person unknowingly had a friend or family member who was involved with gangs, and this is 'payback' for a perceived threat to the gang?" "How can I avoid this to survive?" When there are no plausible answers, the threat to self, family, and society is perceived as uncontrollable, meaningless, and random.

Random violence is traumatic to survivors. "By using [the term *trauma*], we refer to shattering life events and we invoke the expectation that those involved suffer deeply and will be affected for the rest of their lives" (Ganzevoort 2008, 19). For survivors, random violence implies an upheaval in religious belief, social structures, and personal identity. Random violence impacts religious belief precisely because there is no longer a guarantor of justice in the world. The guarantor of a just world is the presence of God in the people's life. Theologically and morally, Habakkuk expresses this conviction in 2:4, "The just person shall live because of his or her faith," as well as in the opposite, "The one who pursues evil will be devoured by violence" (2:7–8). When meaningless violence impacts the life of a believer, it leads to questions about the disposition and character of God. Habakkuk articulates this dilemma: "How long, O God? I cry for help, but you do not listen! I cry out to you 'Violence!' but you do not intervene" (1:2).

Gang Culture, God, and Violence in Honduras

Gang culture is shaped by drug cartels, native organized crime, family violence, and institutionalized violence of government structures, but it is also fueled by poverty and limited access to education and a living wage. Street gangs (*pandillas*) existed in Honduras before the 1990s, but over the last fifteen to twenty years they have grown into sophisticated transnational *maras*. Various civil wars in Central America, especially in El Salvador, created large cohorts of immigrants fleeing the sociopolitical violence in the region. Many have become undocumented immigrants in North American cities, and their children eventually join gangs in United States cities for economic survival and a sense of belonging. Juan Fogelbach describes the link between United States and Central American gangs:

> The largest gangs in El Salvador, Guatemala and Honduras are M-18 and MS-13. Originally known as 18th Street, M-18 was formed in the 1960s by Mexican-American youth in the Rampart neighborhood of Los Angeles, California. The founders of the gang started M-18 because they were excluded from the Clanton Street gang. The gang grew by incorporating members of various races and ethnicities, including Central Americans as they arrived in large numbers in the 1980s. (2011, 420)

In the mid-1990s, United States authorities deported local gang members from Los Angeles to the countries that they or their parents had left to escape poverty and violence. These returning gang members brought with them the "sophistication" of United States gang culture, creating local "franchises" of the United States gangs (Brenneman 2012, 32). Fogelbach traces the internationalization of United States gang culture to its immigration policy:

> The passage of the Illegal Immigration Reform and Immigrant Responsibility Act facilitated the removal of many criminals and gang members from the United States. These deportees transplanted the MS-13 and M-18 gangs to Central America. Eventually, the gangs established 112 cells in Honduras, 434 in Guatemala, and 307 in El Salvador. (2011, 421)

In Honduras alone, an estimated 36,000 gang members are concentrated in urban areas (421). Violence has become so prevalent there that it threatens to overpower the government, creating even greater fragility in an already thin social fabric. Elsa Falkenberger and Geoff Thale comment on the phenomenon of gang violence from the perspective of public policy and law enforcement:

> Gangs and gang members are a serious threat to public safety in some communities both in Central America and in the U.S. However, the character and origin of youth gangs in Central America are not easily tackled or understood. They are shaped by both local and transnational factors, and entail social, as well as law enforcement issues. (2008, 46)

Yet while a considerable body of sociological research has targeted the reasons for gang proliferation and the impact on violence in Central America, the theological implications of gang culture have been explored only to a limited degree.

Gang Culture and God

Gang violence is meaningful and purposeful to members, because it establishes control over physical space and economic resources and membership through initiation rites. Violence, creating a group identity, enforces the laws of the group. Robert Brenneman describes a typical initiation rite for a young male, which gang members describe in theological terms:

> Pancho described his *bautizo* (baptism), the word the Central American gangs use for a jumping-in ceremony, as a memorable day in which he experienced a mixture of fear, curiosity, and excitement. The gang explained the ceremony to him, calling the beating he would receive from other gang members a warmup (*calentón*). The ceremony also included a reading of the thirteen rules of the MS-13. "Look man, I remember that day they beat me—but I mean a REAL beating—afterward everybody was like, 'Welcome to the barrio. Welcome to the barrio. Welcome to the barrio.' You know, the beating didn't matter to me because now I could call myself a gang member. After being beaten and kicked like that, they tattooed me. I had them put one on my leg." (2012, 68).

Brenneman's female gang members report that gang rape is part of the jumping-in ceremony, and continual sexual abuse is the price they pay for membership (102).

Violent initiation rites alternate shaming behavior with acceptance to create victims within the gang system who later become victimizers to those outside the gang. Gangs do not have to manufacture shame; its roots already exist in the broken families and poverty of the urban poor. Shame is activated and then assuaged in the initiation rites, so that potential members now belong to an important social structure beyond their precarious circumstances. Brenneman describes the motivation for gang membership:

> In sum, although the experience of shame is a deeply personal experience, the sources of shame can be traced to the institutions and policies that perpetuate endemic poverty, weak schools, and precarious family systems in the barrios of northern Central America. In effect, the concept of shame represents the intervening variable between these negative social phenomena and a small army of youth who have chosen to abandon traditional pathways to economic stability and respect in favor of the dangerous and frequently violent shortcuts offered by the gang. (2012, 107)

Gangs provide a sense of identity and belonging, but economically gang violence also gives access to wealth through extortion, the sale of drugs, and other criminal activity that would otherwise be beyond the reach of urban poor youth (94). Gang membership becomes less exciting and more burdensome as members age. Rather than guaranteeing safety or justice, membership creates greater uncertainty. Participation in violence between gangs creates enemies and a lifestyle of constant watchfulness. Gang members are targeted by other gangs to settle scores. They are also imprisoned, tortured, and executed by civil authorities in an effort to enforce a zero-tolerance policy. Other factors such as loss of faith in the gang's mission, the need to return to family, and a desire to settle down and begin a family are also factors that entice members away from gang culture. An exit strategy becomes all-important at this moment in a gang member's life. Yet violence in the form of the "morgue rule" is used to perpetuate membership. Brenneman (2012, 136) states: "*'¡Hasta la morgue!'* translated as 'All the way to the morgue!' or 'See you at the morgue!' is an affirmation, a slogan meant to underscore a gang member's lifelong identification with the gang."

Members leave their gangs via three exit routes. They abandon the gang, they become *calmados* or reservists, or they convert to evangelical Protestantism. According to Timothy Steigenga and Edward Cleary, the term *evangélicos*, as it is used in colloquial Spanish and by scholars throughout Central America, refers to a broad spectrum of Christian denominations.

> For the most part, scholars of Latin American religion and demographers have utilized the term *evangélicos* (evangelicals) to refer broadly to

a wide range of Protestant groups.... The term is used to include Classic Pentecostals, neo-Pentecostals, Historical (or Mainstream) Protestants, non-denominational Protestants, and in some cases even Seventh-Day Adventists. (2007, 7)

Steigenga and Cleary describe how evangelicals in Latin America define themselves vis á vis Catholicism: "They are, as they see it, part of the remnant 'true faith' which rejects the 'idolatry' of images, the special status of the priesthood, and the veneration of the Virgin" (49). This is expressed in the phrase: "*Soy Cristiano, no Católico*" ("I am Christian, not Catholic"). In Brenneman's (2012) research, the majority of conversions from gang culture move toward evangelical churches.

Yet simply walking away from the gang is no longer an option since 2004 because of increased enforcement of the morgue rule. *Calmados*, namely, those who opt for a "peaceful" life, settle down to a "normal" life, but they are still expected to participate in gang meetings and activities when called upon. Conversion is the safest means to escape the gang because of the respect that gang culture holds for God and the "things of God." Brenneman notes:

> Nobody gets out of the Mara Salvatrucha alive, they say. The only door that opens to them is that of the evangelical religious groups.... Many ex-gang members have found a place in churches and evangelical movements. In the mythology of the *mareros* (gang members) you don't touch those that have found God and his pardon. (2012, 155)

Conversion as an exit strategy highlights some aspects of the theological thinking underlying gang culture. Rites initiating young people into gangs emphasize hardening against pain, especially the pain of shame, whereas during the process of exiting a gang shame is expelled by crying (182).

Gangs establish spheres of influence by creating boundaries through violence. Within gang culture, God is perceived to have spheres of influence, which God defends with powerful wrath. Brenneman (2012, 158) traces this idea to a religious culture that socializes its members with the phrase, "*No escupas al cielo, o te cae encima*," which he translates as "Do not spit at the sky or it may fall on you." A more appropriate translation is "Do not spit at heaven, or heaven will come after you." Gangs therefore maintain respect for the things of heaven and monitor conversions to ensure that they are authentic. Brenneman describes the standards of behavior that ex-gang members must maintain: "Claiming to be a *cristiano*—regenerated, saved, and transformed as evangelical pastors believe a true convert must be—involves agreeing to a strict moralistic program that is starkly opposite to the lifestyle of the gang" (156). Backsliders are punished and even executed by the gangs to which they formerly belonged. More pragmatically, conversion from the gang to evangelical Protestantism ensures that gang members do not leave to establish a competing gang. Former members are no longer allowed to settle old scores within their gang or among former enemies.

Up to this point, we have primarily focused on violence *within* gang culture. In Honduras, barrios house the poorest people in society, namely, those who live outside the gang structure but within areas in which gangs operate. Thus, barrios are deeply impacted by the violence. Gangs are known to shut down entire neighborhoods threatening to kill their inhabitants. *Diario La Prensa*, a local newspaper describes the effects of gang violence as recently as in 2012:

> "They only gave us four hours to leave. They told us that we were protecting the 18 and for this reason we had to leave the house. If we did not leave, they would kill us," said Cesar, a former inhabitant of San Juan in Chamelecón, who left the place with his wife and four children.... They were expelled as others had been from the Barrio, because the MS 13 gang had connected them with the Barrio 18 gang. "There was nothing to think over.... We had to decide to save our lives or take our things. We saved our lives," he states helplessly. In the street where Cesar lived, eleven families had fled by the end of 2012.... Those who stay behind, remain silent. Their eyes reflect fear; they are terrified that they will say something that they should not ("Ellos también" 2013).[2]

---

2. The original Spanish text is as follows, which I translated into English: "'Solo cuatro horas nos dieron para salir, dijeron que estábamos protegiendo a los 18 y por esto teníamos que dejar la casa y si no nos salíamos, nos mataban,' cuenta César, un expoblador de la colonia San Juan, en Chamelecón, que huyó del lugar con sus cuatro hijos y su esposa. No había opciones. Fueron expulsados como otros del barrio porque miembros de la MS-13 los vincularon con la pandilla Barrio 18. 'No había nada que pensar. Solo agarramos la ropa que teníamos y nos fuimos.... Era la vida o las cosas y decidimos salvar nuestras vidas,' dice impotente. En el pasaje donde César vivía habían huido, hasta finales de 2012, 11 familias que se sumaron a las decenas que en otros sectores de la misma colonia también se marcharon. Los que han quedado guardan silencio. Sus miradas reflejan miedo, terror a decir algo que no deben."

Entire barrios are paralyzed by the *impuesto de guerra* (war tax) that gangs charge inhabitants for operating small businesses, using transportation, or simply having a home in the wrong place. People who do not belong to gangs are often abused, tortured, or murdered as violent illustrations of gang power and control. An article quoted by Brenneman describes a massacre of innocent people:

> On December 23, 2004, Chamelecón gained international notoriety overnight when armed men, ostensibly gang members, stopped a public bus and riddled it with gunfire from automatic weapons, killing twenty-eight passengers, most of them women and children. The perpetrators left a note indicating the crime was in response to the president's all-out war on crime. (189)

The note left on the bus and directed to the authorities stated, "We are not playing around. If you do not believe us, the blood of those who do not believe in us will flow" ("Masacre en Honduras" 2004). The innocent people on the bus were "collateral damage" chosen at random to make a political statement.

A recent cease-fire agreement between gangs seems to take into account the victims of violence, most of whom are related to the gang members. Roman Catholic Bishop Rómulo Emiliani, the mediator in the agreement, explained: "They are also tired of so much death. Hundreds and hundreds of their members have died. They are also worried about their families' safety, because family members are also dying. Now, they simply know that peace needs to come" ("Ellos También" 2013).[3]

Victims, Victimizers, and Observers

Boundaries between victims and victimizers in the barrios where gangs operate seem to shift constantly. Gangs seem to provide youths who are victimized by poverty, social conditions, and fragile family life with a social structure that allows them to shift from victim to victimizer for the sake of belonging. Who is cast in the role of observer? "Incidents of

---

3. The original Spanish text is as follows, which I translated into English: "Ellos también están hartos de tanta muerte. Han muerto cientos y cientos de sus integrantes y les preocupa también la seguridad de sus familias porque están muriendo también familiares de ellos y ahora simplemente saben que la paz tiene que llegar."

random "senseless" violence … uniquely implicate observers in events because observers cannot blame the victim for his or her fate to protect their just world beliefs, and hence need to cope with this potential threat to self" (Zomeren and Lodewijkx 2009, 223).

One could also ask who is most threatened by the presence of victims of gang violence. Sadly, in the case of Honduras, the response is an entire society living beside, with, and in spite of gang culture. In recent years, gangs have reached into middle and upper class neighborhoods, primarily through kidnapping and extortion.

Trauma and violence impact assumptions and systems that give meaning to the world, affecting not only life and physical well-being but also a sense of identity. This is true of both victims and observers of violence. Three basic assumptions shape the meaning that human beings give to their world and existence. R. Ruard Ganzevoort explains:

> The first is that the world is a meaningful and coherent whole, and not a basket of coincidences. The second is that the world is benevolent towards us and not inclined to do us harm. The third is that I am a person worthy of care and love. These basic assumptions are the foundations for our being in the world, for our social connections, and for our identity. (2008, 19)

Theologically, these assumptions are necessary for the belief in a just world to flourish in society. Yet for people living in urban poverty in Central America, violence and the trauma associated with family life in the barrios undermine the possibility of a belief in a just world.

Violence, Voicing, and Perception in Habakkuk 1–2

Violence in a textual world occurs through the portrayal of voices and perceptions in the text. The world of the text constructs encounters between layers of perception that are transmitted through the voice or discourse of narrators and characters (Rimmon-Kenan 1993). In this essay, "perception" is used instead of "point of view" to emphasize the visual, emotional, and intellectual processes involved in Habakkuk's vision. The words attributed to a speaker, (referred to as discourse field from now on) are normally marked by a quotation frame such as "God said to Habakkuk," followed by the citation. The cited words of the speaker are shown with quotation marks in English but do not exist in Hebrew. Thus, according to Cynthia Miller (1996, 226), reported speech embeds one speech event within another and is "an important narrative device by which a character may serve as a narrator of other speech events (previous, future, intended or hypothetical)." Awareness of this embedding allows readers to follow the interaction between the voices and perceptions of characters in the text.

Habakkuk 1–2 portrays an interaction between the prophet and God when local and international violence reached a high point in the ancient Near East. But is it a *truly* interactive exchange? Miller (1996, 235) defines dialogue in written texts as interactive reported speech mimicking conversation: "Conversation is fundamentally structured in terms of contiguous, alternating turns of talk, known as 'adjacency pairs.' The first pair-part of an adjacency pair produces the expectation of a relevant and acceptable rejoinder in the second pair-part." In Habakkuk, dialogue is *not* marked by quotation frames to indicate reported speech; instead, the character's discourse fields are juxtaposed, relating to each other through switched roles between speaker and addressee. I label the discourse fields of each speaker as follows:

> 1:2–4: Habakkuk's Quest for Localized Justice
> 1:5–11: God Speaks Through a Violent World
> 1:12–17: Habakkuk's Response: Where Are the Limits to the Victimizer's Violence?
> 2:1: Habakkuk's Stand
> 2:2–20: God Gives Voice to the Other Nations

The hierarchy of speech and perception for the entire text is set up in the opening verse: "The oracle [burden] which Habakkuk the prophet *saw*." The third-person narrator's description of Habakkuk's experience (an oracle, a speech event that describes a vision or perception), establishes the norms for the textual world through which readers will evaluate the speech and perception of each character. Schlomith Rimmon-Kenan (1993, 81) describes this process: "Put differently, the ideology of the narrator-focalizer is usually taken as authoritative, and all other ideologies in the text are evaluated from this 'higher' position." The narrator tells readers that the world of the text is situated in the context of a visual experience (חזה) that is transmitted by God and received by Habakkuk. According to Francis I. Andersen (2001, 91), "The verb and the cognate noun *ḥāzôn* have definite connotations of a visionary perception, such as would come to a prophet in a state of ecstasy. It would seem that such an experience often took the form of participation in the divine assembly."

A textual norm is established; the vision and everything voiced and perceived through it is revealed from heaven and therefore carries the highest
authority in the text.

Habakkuk's Quest for Localized Justice

The prophet's voice is the first source of action in the visionary experience
set up in the superscription, "How long, O God? I cry for help, but you do
not listen!" A reader "reads" into the text the speaker's identity based on
the second-person perspective and use of interrogatives. This grammati-
cal structure establishes a very personal appeal to God. The vocabulary
used in these verses also emphasizes their emotional appeal. According to
Andersen (2001, 110), the verb אֶזְעַק ("I have called out or shouted out")
is used in the Psalms and in Lamentations to emphasize the helplessness
of the speaker. Furthermore, Andersen raises the issue of the speaker's role
in a violent society: "The grounds of Habakkuk's appeal to Yahweh are not
disclosed. The note of lamentation is struck only indirectly if the misery
and suffering of v. 3a are the prophet's own" (911). The question is whether
the prophet is a victim or observer here?

Habakkuk's questions also raise the issue of God's role in the violent
world the prophet witnesses. The prophet explicitly characterizes God as
someone who is not involved but should be: "How long, O God? I cry for
help, but you do not listen!" (1:2). Habakkuk expects God to listen and
to respond in a way that provides help. Readers have often assumed that
God appears in the role of the guarantor of justice in a violent world. For
example, Andersen comes to this conclusion:

> There is no explicit appeal to God's compassion toward the pitiable,
> nor to his [sic] just anger toward the wicked, nor to his personal honor
> in keeping his promises. The language of v. 4, however, suggests that
> Habakkuk expects God to be concerned with justice. (2001, 111)

Even though the verses create an intense affective impact, the content of
the complaint remains generic.

In addition to the generic characteristic of the complaint, verse 2 does
not clearly portray the prophet as either victim or observer, because it does
not specify the victim by name, only referring to a general category of "the
just." This lack of specificity allows readers to read into the text. Andersen
(2001, 111) states, "The cryptic language does not show who the victim

is (the 'righteous one' in v. 4 is similarly general), whether the suppliant himself (as with Job and Jeremiah) or some unfortunate on whose behalf the prophet is making intercession." If the speaker is the victim, he or she calls out for justice, thus exercising his or her voice. On the other hand, if the speaker is a mediator for the victim, she or he is portrayed as someone who identifies with the trauma and accepts its reality in the world.

Practical theology provides insight into Habakkuk's questions. Ganzevoort describes identification with victims as the willingness to reread the tradition of the community:

> Usually … we refrain from that painful reading of the tradition. That does not mean we do not accept the reality of trauma in this world, but we see it as an individualized issue. This way we do acknowledge that some persons suffer from painful experiences, but we deny that their experiences and questions should be ours as well, let alone that their experience is in fact the central theme of our religious tradition. In fact, we treat them as the strangers to our world, the aliens that threaten our existence. (2008, 29)

Habakkuk does not particularize the identity of victims, as would be the case in the blaming strategy described by Ganzevoort. The speaker is not someone who protects the notion of a just world from the dangerous presence of victims and their stories but is someone who is willing to question why God is not acting in the traditional role of savior (29).

In short, in verses 2–4 the speaker portrays a world that disintegrates into violence and describes the violence as "devastation or lawlessness." Yet the underlying assumption is that God cares about injustice but delays intervention. On a personal level, this position translates as distress of someone who trusts, yet fears not being saved in time. The difficulty is that God's delayed response translates into greater and greater victimization of those whose existence is most fragile. In other words, Habakkuk describes a world on the brink of moral and physical extinction.

God Speaks through a Violent World (1:5–11)

God emerges from the role of silent addressee and observer by turning into the speaker. Thus, the prophet listens as God speaks, "Look over the nations and see, and be utterly amazed" (1:5). The speaker's identity is not revealed. Neither quotation frames nor the use of a proper name indicate the identity of the speaker (Miller 1996, 220–26). The standard strategy employed in narrative texts containing dialogue is that "the first person references to the speaker, the second person references to the addressee, and the third person singular or plural references to other participants" (Regt 1999, 43). However, these reference strategies are often inconsistent in poetic texts. Thus readers must identify God through content, vocabulary, and literary context that follow the prophet's complaint addressed to God. Furthermore, the speaker moves from the world surrounding the addressee (the prophet) to an international context, the rise and fall of the Neo-Babylonian Empire. Rainer Albertz reads this shift from a historical perspective:

> The late exilic Habakkuk redactor (HR) addresses his audience at the beginning of his book (Hab 1:5), commanding them to look at the astonishing and unbelievable work done "in their days" by Yahweh. What this refers to, as the following text makes clear, is the rise and fall of the Neo-Babylonian Empire, which convulsed the world in less than two generations! To portray its rise, HR drew on the descriptions of disaster (1:6ff, 14ff) with which the prophet Habakkuk had graphically warned the Judeans of the vast military superiority of the Neo-Babylonians, probably at the time of the battle of Carchemish (605 B.C.E.). (2003, 214)

God exhorts the addressee to perceive ("look at") a wider field of violence and allow the perception of his action to transform complaint into amazement.

Are these verses a direct response to Habakkuk's complaint? Is this a dialogue? In the strictest definition of a dialogue, they are not because there are no quotation frames signaling turn-taking. However, the verses are still interactive speech. Robert Longacre uses the concept of "repartee" to distinguish between these two types of reported speech at a deeper (notional) level. He writes, "Whichever term we use—repartee in referring to the underlying notional structure or dialogue in referring to the surface structure—the distinctive feature of the relations here considered is that they involve a sequence of speakers" (1983, 44). The first speaker is quoted and then the response of the addressee is reported. In other words, both participants take turns. Furthermore, the content affirms the interaction, because the speaker's vocabulary mirrors the prophet's. Andersen (2001, 139) notes: "The same verbs are used in God's response as in Habakkuk's prayer, and in the same poetic sequence." There is some discontinuity in the subject matter, domestic versus international violence, but the issue addressed is similar. Where is God in all of this?

Throughout God's speech, the theme of violence, with the roles of victimizer and victims is similar to Habakkuk's but in a new context. In this case, the focus is on the violent acts of the foreign Chaldeans who are specifically named as the most violent among the other nations. As the characterization of the victimizer increases in specificity (the nations, Chaldeans, a bitter and unruly people, "he"), so does the comparison of the Chaldeans and their armies to beasts of prey (leopards, wolves, eagle), "animals that will attack anything" in a rampage (Andersen 2001, 149). This nation (collective "he") derives law or justice and majesty from itself. It worships its own strength. The characterization of the victims of the Chaldeans, on the other hand, is minimal and almost impersonal. They are captives, heaped like grains of sand by a storm wind (1:9).

God's claim is that this manifestation of lawless strength is God's amazing work. God is no longer a silent observer but acts on the world stage through the violence of others. The nation working evil has mistakenly assumed that they are autonomous and their strength is their own. But their strength and destruction is aimed at the punishment of "kings and princes" (1:11). The reader must read into the text the identity of the unspecified victimized "kings and princes." This can be done by reading into these roles Habakkuk's indictment of the ruling class in 1:2–4. Victims who are lower on the social scale are not mentioned at all in the text. Chris Heard's deconstructionist reading of this text makes this point very emphatically:

> Curse the Chaldeans! The idea was to punish the guilty. The idea was justice. But this is not justice. The suffering of Judahite children for their father's sins is not justice. Now YHWH's announcement has me in a tizzy too! YHWH's exercise of justice by way of the Chaldean violence is going to hurt innocent children. We can't just let that go. The Chaldeans can't be allowed to get away with that. We must demand justice! (1997, 86)

Heard leaves out other victims, the women, the mothers of those children he is giving voice to. They are totally erased from the world of this text. Using the violence of one victimizer to "punish" another leaves "collateral damage" among those who are not mentioned in the text; they are the weakest and most vulnerable members of society. The ultimate victim is the one assigned to nonexistence in the textual world.

Habakkuk's Response:
Where Are the Limits to the Victimizer's Violence? (1:12–17)

Habakkuk's response contrasts God with the victimizing Chaldeans and the victims, whose status in creation is reduced to being objects of consumption. In this second person speech (1:12–17), the prophet layers the description of God's character with affirmations such as "from eternity," "holy," "immortal," and "rock" (1:12–3). In keeping with the previous emphasis on perception, the speaker draws attention to God's eyes and sight, characterizing them as too pure to endure the sight of evil (1:13). Yet this purity makes no difference. God is willing to tolerate and indeed to perceive increasing violence in spite of God's repugnance for it. "Why then do you gaze on the faithless in silence?" (1:13). At this point, God is the passive observer of injustice.

In the following verses (1:13–17), victimizer and victims appear at unequal levels of creation. Victims are reduced to the status of fish and creeping things, without self-rule, while the victimizer is characterized more fully as a successful fisherman, enjoying the fruit of his labor. The victimizer attributes numinous power to technology, the work of his hands; he "sacrifices to his net" and "burns incense to his seine" (1:16). The victims (are objects or means of consumption; human beings exist to provide his "generous portion" and "sumptuous repast" (1:16). These verses conclude with a question about the victimizer as murderer: "Shall he then keep on brandishing his sword to slay peoples without mercy?" (1:17). The prophet persistently questions the victimizer's limitless agency in this violent world. Where is the limit to violence when the victimizer is doing God's work? God is not fulfilling the role of guarantor, which is consistent with Habakkuk's description of God's character as "holy" and unable to "endure the sight of evil."

Habakkuk's Stance (2:1)

"I will stand at my guard post, and station myself at the rampart" (2:1). The voice of the prophet continues, but the prophet does not address God directly as discourse roles shift. Habakkuk is the speaker, but who is the addressee? The prophet or the people? Perception also shifts to the physical context of Habakkuk; from a view of the world as it is seen by God to the limited perspective of the *prophet* (e.g., Rimmon Kennan 1993, 78). This brings to mind a classic prophetic stance, the one which perceives beyond the limited views of one's social context, yet does not perceive as broadly as God. Toni Craven (2007, 419) notes the implication of the physical location of the guard post: "The watch post (2:1) calls to mind the role of the prophet as sentinel or lookout (see Isa 21: 6–12; Ezek 3: 16–21; 33: 1–9). As a watchman, Habakkuk functions as one who pays careful attention to what the wicked, the righteous and God do." This is also the attitude of someone, an observer of violence, or possibly a victim, who resolutely waits for a response from God, waits for the reestablishment of a just world.

God Gives Voice to the Other Nations (2:2–20)

Once again discourse roles shift so that God's voice is embedded within Habakkuk's discourse field by the quotation frame: "Then God answered me and said" (2:2). Now the prophet is the receiver of the vision, which the prophet is commanded to write down. God's perception of the world is recorded by the prophet for future reference, a perception that will also involve action: "For the vision still has its time, presses on to fulfillment, and will not disappoint" (2:2). The vision spills beyond the interchange between Habakkuk and God. Michael Floyd (2000, 143) comments from a historical perspective: "There were scribal groups with the prophetic desire to discern from those transformative events the patterns of God's involvement in their own time." Recording it ensures that readers outside the immediate exchange can access it. It raises the issue of the interaction between victims, victimizers, and observers of violence beyond the historical context of the text.

What is God's role? The content of God's response begins with the duality between the rash and the just, a theme already introduced by the prophet, in which the rash person is represented as proud, unstable, and greedily insatiable (2:4–5). Excessive greed aligns such a person with death, not life, in the effort to control the nations. The rash person's polar opposite is mentioned succinctly as a just person who lives with faith in God (2:4). At this point, it is important to pause and to ask whether or not this duality can be mapped into the victimizer-victim polarity. In other words, is the just person a victim here? The immediate context of these verses does not indicate it, but the reader is invited to construct this analogy when Habakkuk addresses God: "The wicked circumvent the just, this is why judgment comes forth perverted" (2:4). Finally, God agrees with Habakkuk's analysis of internal violence, while pushing the prophet to have some concern for other nations.

God's response continues with five "woes" attributed to the voice of other nations. The response is introduced by a quotation frame: "Shall not these take up a taunt against him, satire and epigrams about him to say?" (2:6). It embeds the voices of the nations in God's speech, which has in turn been embedded in Habakkuk's discourse field. The nations appear as another collective observer who are also victims, condemning the conduct of "he" who had gathered them up in his greed: "He who opens wide his throat like Sheol, and is as greedy as death. Who gathers for himself all the nations, all the peoples" (2:5). The victimized nations become the accusers who list the evils of the victimizing Chaldeans; they are greed, bloodshed, wrath, despoiling, shaming other nations, and idolatry. Inserted in these accusations are the means by which the victimizer is finally overcome; they are knowledge of God's glory spreading throughout the earth (2:14), retribution for crimes committed (2:16), and silence throughout the world at God's presence in the temple (2:20). The crimes of the victimizing Chaldeans are great, but the fruits of God's action go beyond retribution.

Casting other nations as victims of the Chaldeans, while historically accurate, also serves the textual argument. Why should the Judahites care about another nation's view regarding their victimizers? Other nations are the out-group whose culture and survival are not our (i.e., the in-group's) concern. Patricia Aguiar, Jorge Vals, and Isabel Correia (2008, 96) compare victimization between in-groups and out-groups stating: "People dehumanize victims of relevant out groups, not in an overt way but by a process of insensibility, i.e., by becoming indifferent to their suffering and needs. This insensibility facilitates the derogation or even the aggressive behavior toward out groups." Other nations are part of the out-group about which the Judeans are not concerned. God's decision to use the Chaldeans as punishment against Judah in 1:5–11 elicits Habakkuk's question: "Shall he [the Chaldean], then keep on brandishing his sword to slay peoples without mercy?" (1:17). The prophet is sensitized to the suffering of another out-group, who are the other nations, victims of the same violence. God has indeed expanded Habakkuk's concern for a just world.

How Just Is God's World?

Belief in a just world assumes that good and evil can be defined and that a power or authority exists that arbitrates between good and evil so that good overcomes evil. Victims can thus expect to be vindicated, and victimizers can expect punishment. The truly difficult position to hold vis-à-vis violence is that of the observer. When observers are not able to give meaning to violence, they are threatened by the experience of violence:

> Incidents of random "senseless" violence are threatening to observers because they involve situations where the victim cannot be blamed for his or her violent fate. Unlike situations in which victim blaming is possible, incidents of random, "senseless" violence appear like they could happen to anyone and represent a violation of just world beliefs.... Incidents of random "senseless" violence thus uniquely implicate observers in events because observers cannot blame the victim for his or her fate to protect their just world beliefs, and hence need to cope with this potential threat to self. (Zomeren and Lodewijkx 2009, 223)

In Hab 1–2, the reader is confronted with the interaction between two observers of violence: Habakkuk and God. Habakkuk's concern is with internal violence and the fact that victimizers are not punished. God's concern is focused on external international violence as a tool for eliminating violence internally. Furthermore, Habakkuk's concern originates with God's role as an apparently passive observer of the internal violence in Judah, but it progresses to even greater concern when God proposes to actively use the Chaldean's violence to eradicate violence. The out-group is used to punish the in-group.

Both the prophet and God, as observers of violence, focus on the victimizers. Yet the true victims, those who are marginalized and live in the most fragile reaches of the social scale, are barely mentioned in the textual world. Habakkuk 1–2 does not mention, for instance, the poor, the widow, the orphan, or the stranger. It takes an act of deconstruction to perceive the victims in the text. Instead of actively blaming the victim, the textual world preserves a just-world belief by erasing these in-group victims of violence and by focusing on the victimizer, as well as on the action or inaction of the observer. At the same time, by juxtaposing the prophet's perception and God's, the textual world highlights the viewpoint of another set of out-group victims, the nations that are "gathered up" like "fish of the sea" and "creeping things" (1:14).

How Long, O God, Will Violence Be Meaningless?
Concluding Comments

Violence may be intentional, categorical, and calculable, but it becomes random when victims perceive it as senseless or meaningless. Lack of meaning threatens the personal and social perception of victims and the belief that a just world is possible. Habakkuk 1–2 was used as a lens for interpreting the trauma of random violence throughout this essay. The prophet's cry, "How long, O God? I cry for help, but you do not listen! I cry out to you 'Violence!' but you do not intervene," articulates a victim's need to understand God's role in social violence. But this question remains, especially for the unacknowledged victims whose presence is erased in the textual world. Is God a passive observer or an active agent guaranteeing that a just world will ultimately prevail?

The notion of God working through violence appears both in Habakkuk and especially in the gangs and their surrounding religious culture in Honduras. Habakkuk's underlying premise is that there is a just world in which God will eventually intervene. Yet God's role as the guarantor of a just world is far more difficult to identify in the social research on gangs and the culture in which they flourish in Honduras. The notion of God working *through* violence appears both in Habakkuk and in Honduras. The statement used inside and outside the gangs, "Do not spit at heaven or heaven will come after you," speaks of a God who demands respect and enforces it through violent means. In Habakkuk, God uses the Chaldeans to violently discipline the Judahites and other nations, but the ultimate purpose is to reverse social injustice and much more. In other words, this prophetic text promises hope for a total world transformation. Conversely, in gang culture and even the culture surrounding gangs, transformation occurs only when people convert to a localized evangelical church. Thus, victims who belong to the in-group tend to be erased so that those who live with them are not threatened by their presence (Aguiar, Vals, and Correia 2008, 50). For Habakkuk and for Honduras, these victims are the most fragile people living on the margins of society. These are also the people who are most likely to view violence as a series of random events beyond their control, except through conversion to a localized church.

A reading of Habakkuk that discerns the roles of victim, victimizer, and observer in social violence highlights the very different perspective that a just-world belief brings to a violent situation. Just-world belief assumes an appropriate fit between people's actions and how the world responds to them; good will be rewarded by good and bad by bad in proportion to people's actions. According to Zomeren and Lodewijkx (2009, 71), "Generally the belief in a just world gives people a safe and secure feeling and sense of control over their actions and the consequences contingent upon these actions, making the world surrounding them predictable, manageable and a safe place to be." In Honduras, this is not true. People shift back and forth between the roles of victim and victimizer as they enter and exit gang culture. Observers not involved in gang culture are also potential victims. They try to avoid the victimization they witness, because survival is their highest priority. If they have any belief in a just world, their lives filled with random violence slowly diminish this hope. Thus potential victims who are observers of daily violence speak only with a muted voice: "Their eyes reflect fear; they are terrified that they will say something that they should not" ("Drama de Familias" 2013).

Habakkuk does not address such situations. In Hab 1–2, the prophet focuses on God who moves from being a passive observer to the active guarantor of justice. Although the text does not provide a solution to gang violence or the plight of victims in Honduras, it highlights the need for a prophetic voice. Habakkuk cries out in lamentation for Judah. Whose voice can cry out to God in Honduras? Is there a prophet to believe in a just world, who cries out to God?

Works Cited

Aguiar, Patricia, Jorge Vals, and Isabel Correia. 2008. "Justice in Our World and in That of Others: Belief in a Just World and Reactions to Victims." *Social Justice Research* 21:50–68.

Albertz, Rainer, 2003. *Israel in Exile: The History and Literature of the Sixth Century B.C.E.* Translated by David Green. StBibLit 3. Atlanta: Society of Biblical Literature.

Andersen, Francis I. 2001. *Habbakuk: A New Translation with Introduction and Commentary.* AB 25. New York: Doubleday.

Brenneman, Robert. 2012. *Homies and Hermanos: God and Gangs in Central America.* Oxford: Oxford University Press.

Craven, Toni. 2007. "Between Text and Sermon: Habbakuk 1:1–11." *Int* 61:418–20.

"El drama de familias desplazadas por maras en Honduras." 2013. *Diario la Prensa.* http://www.laprensa.hn/especiales/328425-273/el-drama-de-las-familias-desplazadas-por-maras-en-honduras.

"Ellos también están hartos de tanta muerte." 2013. *Diario La Prensa.* http://www.elheraldo.hn/alfrente/338532-209/ellos-tambien-estan-hartos-de-tanta-muerte.

Falkenburger, Elsa, and Geoff Thale. 2008. "Maras centroamericanas: Políticas públicas y mejores prácticas." *Revista CIDOB d'Afers Internacionals* 81:45–66.

Floyd, Michael H. 2000. "'Write the Revelation!' (Hab 2:2): Re-imagining the Cultural History of Prophecy." Pages 103–44 in *Writings and Speech in Israelite and Ancient Near Eastern Prophecy*. Edited by Ehud Ben Zvi and Michael H. Floyd. Atlanta: Society of Biblical Literature.

Fogelbach, Juan J. 2011. "Gangs, Violence, and Victims in El Salvador, Guatemala, and Honduras." *San Diego International Law Journal* 12:417–62.

Ganzevoort, R. Ruard. 2008. "Scars and Stigmata: Trauma, Identity and Theology." *Practical Theology* 1:19–31.

Heard, Chris. 1997. "Hearing the Children's Cries: Commentary, Deconstruction, Ethics and the Book of Habakkuk." *Semeia* 77:75–89.

Longacre, Robert E. 1983. *The Grammar of Discourse*. New York: Plenum.

"Masacre en Honduras: 28 personas acribilladas en ataque a un bus." 2004. *El Universo*. http://www.eluniverso.com/2004/12/25/0001/14/5A3170 627CF245B9BBF56552C577FE17.html.

Miller, Cynthia L. 1996. *The Representation of Speech in Biblical Hebrew Narrative: A Linguistic Analysis*. HSM 55. Atlanta: Scholars Press.

Regt, Lénart J. de. 1999. *Participants in Old Testament Texts and the Translator: Reference Devices and Their Rhetorical Impact*. SSN 39. Assen: Van Gorcum.

Rimmon Kenan, Schlomith. 1993. *Narrative Fiction: Contemporary Poetics*. London: Routledge.

Steigenga, Timothy, and Edward L. Cleary. 2007. *Conversion of a Continent: Contemporary Religious Change in Latin America*. New Brunswick, NJ: Rutgers University Press.

United Nations Office on Drugs and Crime. 2011. *Global Study on Homicide*. http://www.unodc.org/documents/data-and-analysis/statistics/ Homicide/Globa_study_on_homicide_2011_web.pdf.

Zomeren, Martijn van, and Hein F. M Lodewijkx. 2009. "'Could This Happen to Me?' Threat-Related State Orientation Increases Position Identification with Victims of 'Random Senseless' Violence." *European Journal of Social Psychology* 39:223–36.

THE CULTURE OF FEAR: ABOUT INTERNALIZED VIOLENCE IN ANCIENT NEAR EASTERN AND BIBLICAL LITERATURES

José Enrique Ramírez-Kidd

Este ensayo no se limita en la violencia física y visible sino que se enfoca en la violencia como forma de control sobre otros. Explora las condiciones sociales que crea la violencia como forma de perpetuar el modelo de sojuzgamiento que promueve la obediencia y sumisión al pueblo o la persona dominante. Señala el miedo como su principal arma y luego el autor expone dos formas de miedo: el miedo como parte de un clima cultural general y, el segundo modo, el miedo como parte de la psicología colectiva de una comunidad. El primero es analizado y expuesto en varios textos que ponen en evidencia esa cultura del servilismo y la sumisión. El segundo modo es presentado como más sutil y escondido en la conciencia colectiva de los pueblos sometidos. En este modo el sujeto sometido considera a su opresor como su benefactor y le reconoce prestigio y grandeza, características que contrastan con la pobre imagen que el vasallo tiene de sí mismo. A continuación el autor presenta una "semántica de la violencia" en los textos estudiados y señala que actualmente también poseemos tal semántica pero construida sobre dinámicas sociales y lingüísticas diferentes. En el final del ensayo el autor pone en evidencia que las formas de violencia ideológica y psicológica que encontramos en la Biblia no son muy distintas de las que padecemos en nuestra sociedad actual. Expone varios ejemplos de la actualidad social latinoamericana donde se pueden observar situaciones similares a las bíblicas. Al concluir, señala cómo la migración forzada, la pobreza y la violencia cotidiana en América Latina se ha tornado en algo habitual y aceptado.

Discussions concerning violence in the Hebrew Bible evoke images of physical and military brutality such as those described in the book of Joshua:

> When Israel had finished slaughtering all the inhabitants of Ai in the open wilderness where they pursued them, and when all of them to the

very last had fallen by the edge of the sword, all Israel returned to Ai, and
attacked it with the edge of the sword. The total of those who fell that
day, both men and women, was twelve thousand—all the people of Ai.
(Josh 8:24–25)[1]

Any person familiar with critical issues concerning the conquest narratives in the book of Joshua is aware of the fact that such texts are no more
than rhetoric that have no correlation with any historical events. They do,
of course, have much to do with violence, more specifically with intentional literary violence. Commenting on the battles of conquest narrated
in Joshua, Hubertus Halbfas notes: "The concern was not to address historical matters but rather to reflect on current situations. In a time of great
humiliation and powerlessness, these narratives redesign the past in order
to promote hope and motivation for the future. The strangest fantasies of
power were developed by those who had the least power and were victims
of violence and destruction" (Halbfas 2001, 132, my trans.).

Such extreme physical violence is associated not only with the people
of Israel as a group, but also with key biblical figures like Moses, Samuel,
David, and Elijah. For instance, we read in the Hebrew Bible:

Moses said to them: "Put your sword on your side, each of you…. Kill
your brother, your friend, and your neighbor." (Exod 32:27–28)

Then Samuel said, "Bring Agag king of the Amalekites here to me."…
And Samuel hewed Agag in pieces before the LORD in Gilgal. (1 Sam
15:32–33)

David struck the land, leaving neither man nor woman alive. (1 Sam
27:9)

Elijah said to them, "Seize the prophets of Baal; do not let one of them
escape."… And Elijah brought them down to the Wadi Kishon, and killed
them there. (1 Kgs 18:40)

It is important to underline that none of the above texts include a word
of censure or condemnation from the narrator. In contrast, 2 Sam 11:27b
states, "But the thing that David had done displeased the LORD."

---

1. All biblical quotations are taken from the NRSV.

My interest in this contribution is not the physical expressions of violence but rather the social conditions that violence constructs as the cultural and symbolic environment for the life of a community. Fear is an extreme form of violence which has often more lasting and destructive effects than concrete forms of violence. It is in this sense a form of internalized violence that makes ruling over others a simple and practical political exercise. I focus on violence, not in the sense conveyed by the German term *Gewalt*, which connotes the use of force against someone, but in the sense of *Zwang*, which expresses the use of coercion. I thus refer to the noun "violence" in the sense of "power to control others," even in the absence of direct physical actions of violence. The Latin term *potestas* (control) also conveys this kind of meaning for the word *violence*.

Much of the Hebrew Bible reflects literary motifs typical of the vassal literature characteristic of the ancient Near Eastern political context. In the Hebrew Bible, however, this literature was produced in a context in which Israel/Judah represented the weaker party in diplomatic relationships of clear asymmetrical power. Even more important, much of this literature functioned to symbolically compensate for the material and military incapacity to retaliate against colonial overlords. This dynamic is evident in Isa 60:

> Foreigners shall build up your walls, and their kings shall minister to you; for in my wrath I struck you down, but in my favor I have had mercy on you. Your gates shall always be open; day and night they shall not be shut, so that nations shall bring you their wealth, with their kings led in procession. For the nation and kingdom that will not serve you shall perish; those nations shall be utterly laid waste.... The descendants of those who oppressed you shall come bending low to you, and all who despised you shall bow down at your feet; they shall call you the City of the LORD, the Zion of the Holy One of Israel. (Isa 60:10–14)

This passage illustrates how the social conditions created by violence turn into internalized violence in which those suffering from it conform to the dominating power.

In other words, military violence is not only the means whereby conquerors acquire political dominion over vassals. It also constructs a cultural milieu that makes it possible for vassals to deal symbolically through literature and other forms of imaginaries and representations with conditions of domination. Thus, violence results from a material and symbolic environment that significantly diminishes material and psychological potential of those living in such circumstances to the advantage of the overlords. It is important to clarify that the creation of such a social milieu should not be understood as materialized evil; it is not a Joker hidden in a bunker planning evil plots against Gotham City.

The creation of such conditions is not accidental, nor is it always the result of the conscious actions of a particular individual or group. The consequences, however, are very real for people experiencing them. To put it another way, the issue is not whether or not monsters are real. The issue is that human fear is real. As a mental creation, monsters are an external expression of that which is the real fear. Monsters are one possible expression of fear among many others in particular contexts. Yet what is relevant, from my perspective, is the need to consider the historical conditions that create the need for monsters. I thus approach the subject of violence not by focusing on its concrete material expression but on the social milieu created by violence. Violence creates cultural conditions that promote obedience and submission.

In this essay, I explore the phenomenon of internalized violence. I begin with a discussion on the pedagogies of violence as apparent in the books of Judith and Tobit. I continue the focus on internalized violence and its effects on dominated people in a more detailed analysis of the violent power of fear as part of the general cultural climate and the general collective psyche, as depicted in ancient Near Eastern and biblical texts. I conclude with a few general comparative remarks about internalized violence present in contemporary Latin America.

Pedagogies of Violence

The German writer, Wolfgang Borchert (1921–1947), who lived through World War II wrote about violence in this poem: "When the war was over, a soldier came home. He had nothing to eat. Then he saw a man who had a piece of bread. He killed him. You cannot simply kill a man, the judge said. Why not, asked the soldier" (1949, 317). The situation described in this poem is not that different from situations depicted in various ancient Near Eastern and biblical texts. Biblical literature moves between cosmology and eschatology, and warfare is at the very core of these topics in which primal struggles give way to final combat, as beginnings and endings are defined in battle. The same pattern is found in the history of Israel. A quick look at the linguistic map of terms demonstrates that physical violence was familiar in the world behind the Bible. The language of warfare, essential to biblical imagery, is associated with persons (the official, chief, enemy, hero, foe, adversary, warrior, spy), instruments (sword, spear, armor, armies, weapons, enemy, shield, arrow, host, chariot), activities (to battle, to combat, to make war, to fight, to besiege, to subdue, to overpower, to shoot, to rape, to violate, to force, to burn, to kill, to destroy), techniques (to ambush, *herem*, to siege, to spy out, to conspire, to make a plot, to form a conspiracy, to be allied together), psychological disposition (hostility, hostile disposition, to be an enemy, to be in state of conflict, to torment), as well as many other terms related to warfare (oppression, power, strength, triumph, warfare, battle, strength).

From the Egyptian exodus to the Maccabean wars, the song is always the same: "I will sing to Lord, for he has triumphed gloriously. The LORD is my strength and my might.... The LORD is a warrior; the LORD is his name" (Exod 15:1–2). Historically and geographically, the lasting resonance of violence in the Hebrew Bible may be explained in part by Palestine's location as both a battleground and a buffer zone for the empires at the time and by the fact that the Hebrew Bible in its final form is a product of exile.

This dynamic also appears in biblical books of the Hellenistic era. The books of Judith and Tobit are from the Hellenistic period, portraying Jews as living under the threat and domination of empire. They also depict various ways to express violence. The book of Judith describes the military advance of king Nebuchadnezzar's general, Holofernes, toward the countries of the West. Carey A. Moore (1985, 144–45) notes that the original author depicts the threat that the Babylonian army represented for the region. Accordingly, Holofernes set out to "smother the whole western region with their chariots, cavalry, and picked infantry" (Jdt 2:19), "cut ... through Put and Lud and plundered" (2:23), "razed all the walled towns along Wadi Abron" (2:24), "occupied ... Cilicia and slaughtered all who" (2:25), "set their tents on fire and plundered" (2:26), "set fire to all their fields, destroyed their flocks and herds, sacked their towns, stripped their plains, and put all their young men to the sword" (2:27), and "demolished all their sanctuaries and cut down all their sacred poles ... so that all ... should worship Nebuchadnezzar alone ... and ... should call upon him as god" (3:8) (see Moore 1985, 135–36). In other words, the Babylonian army did not make a "perfunctory, show-of-strength march through the West: they were bringing death and destruction to all who resisted" (144). The surrounding nations responded in kind:

Therefore, they send him envoys to sue for peace and say, "We, the servants of the great king Nebuchadnezzar, lie prostrate before you. Treat us as you please. Our buildings, all our land, every wheat field, the flocks and herds, all the sheepfolds of our encampments—they all yours! Treat them as seems best to you. Our towns and their inhabitants are your slaves. Come and treat them as you fit (lit: as is good in your eyes)." (136)

A second example from the book of Tobit shows how psychological impact of violence is experienced even in the absence of actual warfare.

I also buried any whom King Sennacherib put to death when he came fleeing from Judea in those days of judgment that the king of heaven executed upon him because of his blasphemies. For in his anger he put to death many Israelites; but I would secretly remove the bodies and bury them. So when Sennacherib looked for them he could not find them. Then one of the Ninevites went and informed the king about me, that I was burying them; so I hid myself. But when I realized that the king knew about me and that I was being searched for to be put to death, I was afraid and ran away. Then all my property was confiscated; nothing was left to me that was not taken into the royal treasury except my wife Anna and my son Tobias…. And my neighbors laughed and said, "Is he still not afraid? He has already been hunted down to be put to death for doing this, and he ran away; yet here he is again burying the dead!" (Tob 1:18–20; 2:8)

This passage demonstrates that the exiled Jews had become accustomed to seeing their fellow Jews killed and thrown into the streets of Nineveh as easily as they had become accustomed to the cold of winter. It was not good, but it had become part of the landscape. Unburied bodies signaled the brutality of the masters, but they were also evidence of the extent to which this pedagogy of terror had penetrated the consciousness of the exiled people. Fear had become a kind of "psychological skin." This fear discouraged rebellion and produced slow and passive adaptation to the unjust order prevailing in society. Exiled Jews had learned to respond with automatic fear. The abandonment of their sisters and brothers who were killed and thrown into the street reflected the spirit that prevailed in the community. They had become indifferent to the grave physical and military violence surrounding them.

In short, the book of Tobit illustrates, as Yves Michaud (2007, 3–8) explains so clearly, that violence can be either direct or indirect, massive or disseminated, destined to hurt or to destroy someone, whether in terms of a person's physical wholeness or psychological health. Such violence afflicts his or her possessions, or it generates symbolic affliction. Thus, violence is not only an act that is committed actively and brutally, but it also finds expression in how those acts are perceived and judged. Yet the meaning of the term "violence" is often limited to physical violence, reducing it to material actions or to the immediate visible effects of those actions. Violence is not always so plainly evident. Chaos and disorder, minimizing life or making it impossible to sustain life, are also conditions of violence. The books of Judith and Tobit demonstrate that a culture of fear was not only a constant of daily life under imperial domination. Even so, the books of Judith and Tobit also illustrate a way out of this fear. They make the culture of fear the subject of serious theological reflections.

The Violent Power of Fear

We thus need to understand that violence appears in various ways, including less visible ways that are nonetheless powerful expressions of deeply instilled fear. These expressions include two prominent forms of fear. They appear in the general culture, and they are part of the collective psychology.

Fear as Part of the General Cultural Climate

The geopolitical context of ancient Near Eastern societies has been described as the "Club of the Great Powers." The three elements of diplomacy, trade, and warfare shape their game of political chess (Cohen and Westbrook 2000, 15–27). When armies were not actually marching, letters were constantly exchanged. Ancient Near Eastern empires created and sustained their power among vassal populations by relying on another important method to maintain their power. They built a culture of fear. A good example of this method is the famous phrase in Jeremiah about the evil coming from the north. Edward Lipinski (2003, 441) explains that this expression does not have any mythological connotations but reflects "a simple fact of experience: the enemies of Israel and Judah, be they Assyrians, Aramaeans or Babylonian" who came from the north.[2]

---

2. In Jer 6:22–24, an oracle against Judah (see also 4:6; 6:1–22; 10:17–22), the enemy from the north was Babylon. Jeremiah 50:41–43, an oracle against Babylon, depicts an interesting situation. Whereas in Jer 6:22–24 Babylon is the evil from the

The strategy of fear has been popular through the ages, as for instance, evidenced by Machiavelli's political treatise, *The Prince*. Machiavelli argues that the secret of power resides in love and fear, the two foundational powers moving people. He explains: "Upon this a question arises: whether it be better to be loved than feared or feared than loved? It may be answered that one should wish to be both, but, because it is difficult to unite them in one person, it is much safer to be feared than loved" (1984, 24). Precisely in this sense, force and threat were essential elements of ancient Near Eastern empires. Guided by means of political propaganda, they engendered fear and demanded "love." Fear in the political context of ancient Near Eastern societies was not equivalent to the individual-subjective definition of the term common to the psychology of our modern Western societies. The former assumes epistemological categories not developed in Western culture before the Renaissance. I refer to one of the most important political expressions of that fear: political obedience. As T. Jacobsen explains in a classical work on the culture of the ancient Near East: "The individual stood at the centre of ever wider circles of authority which delimited his [*sic*] freedom of action" (Frankfort et al. 1954, 217). Jacobsen quotes a hymn that describes the coming of a golden age characterized as an age of obedience: "Days when one man is not insolent to another, when a son reveres his father, days when respect is shown in the land, when the lowly honor the great, when the young brother … respects his older brother, when the older child instructs the younger child and he (the younger) abides by his decisions" (217). Jacobsen further comments: "But obedience to the older members of one's family is merely a beginning. Beyond the family lie other circles, other authorities: the state and the society. There is the foreman [*sic*] where one works, there is the bailiff who oversees agricultural works in which one takes part; there is the king. All these can and must claim absolute obedience" (217).

It is clear that in this "Club of the Great Powers," the "biblical lands" were one of the weakest links in the chain. This is made evident in the Amarna letters, the diplomatic correspondence of the region during the late Bronze and early Iron periods. The mayor of Tyre Abi-Milku wrote the following letter to pharaoh:

---

north, in Jer 50:41–43 Babylon herself awaits a foe from the north. Even the might of the great empires was, in fact, fragile.

To the king, my lord, my god, my sun: a message of your servant Abi-milki (of Tyre): Seven times and again seven times I prostrate myself at the feet of Your Majesty–I, the dust under the sandals of Your Majesty. My lord is the sun (god) who rises over all the countries, day after day, according to the ordinance of the sun god his gracious father, whose sweet breadth gives life and which craves when he is hiding, who makes the entire country rest under the protection of his mighty arm; who thunders in the sky like the storm god so that the entire country trembles at the sound of him.…. This is the message of a slave to his master after he had heard what the kind messenger of the king said to his servant upon arriving here, and felt the sweet fragrance that came out of the mouth of Your Majesty toward his servant. Is not the entire world happy when it hears the kind messenger who comes from the very presence of my lord? Also the entire country was in awe of my lord when he heard about. You are the sun that rises above me and the wall of bronze that towers around me. And for this very reason and on account of the mighty arm of Your Majesty, I rest secure. This is what I have still to say to the Sun, my father, Your Majesty: When will I see Your Majesty face to face? (Oppenheim 1967, 123–24; EA 147)

The repeated expressions of political servility illustrate of the ideology of obedience that responds to the cultural milieu of fear described earlier. The mayor declares absolute devotion and servility to ensure the continued protection of his overlord. Political servility is thus common in the Amarna letters. For instance, one letter states: "I am a servant of the king and a dog of his house" (Moran 1992, 132; EA 60). It indicates that the speaker of this sentence accepts his or her low position, even comparing his or her position to a dog, when he or she talks about the king. Other examples are:

"As I have placed my neck in the yoke that I carry, may the king, my lord, know that I serve him with complete devotion." (310; EA 257)

"Who am I, a mere dog, that I would not grant a request of the king, my lord?" (301; EA 247)

"How, if the king wrote for my wife, how could I hold her back? How, if the king wrote to me, put a bronze dagger into your heart and die, how could I not execute the order of the king?" (307; EA 254)

All of these texts thus show that the ancient Near Eastern leaders and their vassals employed skillfully, openly, and repeatedly literary-rhetorical expressions that responded to the overarching culture of fear. They never dared to question the sociopolitical and military structures of power.

Fear as Part of the General Collective Psychology

Another less visible way in which violence permeates cultures of fear is that it makes peace a condition contrary to well-being. The Hebrew Bible promotes various strategies that make this kind of violence acceptable in the collective psyche of subjugated populations. Echoing a familiar literary image, 1 Kgs 4:25 describes the reign of Solomon in terms of safety and wellbeing: "During Solomon's lifetime Judah and Israel lived in safety, all of them under their vines and fig trees." Yet, in the book of Judith, the conditions for peace have changed, and safety is only found through absolute submission: "Treat us as you please…. Treat them as seems best to you … as is good in your eyes" (Jdt 3:2–4). The narrator sums it up in verse 4: "All that we are and all that we have is in your hands." In contrast to 1 Kings, then, the book of Judith implies that safety can be obtained only when the people recognize that peace requires handing over of their entire material possessions to the divinity and by extension to the subjugating king.

This position appears again much later in Machiavelli (1984, 24) when he explains: "Men forget more quickly the death of their father than the loss of their patrimony." So why would a community hand over voluntarily its entire material wealth? It is important to understand that the book of Judith imagines submission to have taken place in response to the fear created by the propaganda of Nebuchadnezzar's might even before any military action had taken place. In fact, the actual destruction and conquest of the land was only a last resort for the conquerors, because they preferred their enemies to surrender voluntarily so that the land did not have to be destroyed in order to force the population into submission. Stephanie Dalley (2006, 420) acknowledges this military strategy of the Assyrian empire when she states: "For the Assyrians expended much effort to persuade foreign people to submit willingly, to spare themselves the expenses of destructive campaigns." The account of Sennacherib's incursion in Palestine and siege of Jerusalem described in 2 Kgs 18–19 illustrates this tactic. Physical violence was necessary only when a vassal did not exhibit the proper conduct vis-à-vis the master. The induction of fear was thus essential and served as an effective means of political control.

The internalized submission becomes even more obvious in the juxtaposition of beneficence and fear toward ancient Near Eastern kings.

An example appears in the Ode to Senusert I: "He is terrible, smashing foreheads.... Yet he is full of sweetness. Citizens love him more than their own selves" (Foster 1995, 132–33). Another example appears in *Lipit-Ištar*'s poems (A Praise Poem of Lipit-Estar, 43–61): "I am he who makes an abundant crop grow. I am a river of plenty ... I am a lion in all respects, a source of great awe for the soldiers" (Black et al. 2004, 309–10). The king is portrayed as the great giver of food, natural plenty, and military power. As the bringer of peace and abundance, he has to be revered and feared.

The following sequence of texts further illustrates that a vassal submits appropriately by appealing to both the beneficence and the greatness of the master in contrast to a vassal's miserliness. Images of might, destruction, and terror reigning down on the king's enemies maintain a level of fear and threat that ensure the proper submission of the vassal. Three ancient texts stand out as extreme cases of this fear-induced attitude toward the emperor. First, in the Assyrian Annals from Shalmaneser III the voice of the master begins the poem:

> I approached the cities.... They attacked me to do battle. With the exalted might of the divine standard which goes before me and with the fierce weapons which Assur, my lord, gave to me, I fought and defeated them. I felled their fighting men with the sword, rained down upon them destruction as the god Adad would, piled up their bodies in ditches, filled the extensive plain with the corpses of their warriors and with their blood I dyed the mountain red like red wool. (Grayson 2002, 16; Annals of Shalmaneser, 40–51)

Second, another poem comes from the Asiatic Campaigns of Ramses II. It starts with the voice of the scribe:

> Then the great princes of every land ... were dismayed and afraid, and the terror of his majesty was in their hearts.... They despoiled themselves of their own goods, being charged with their annual dues, with their children at the head of their tribute, in praise and homage to his [name] Ramses II. So every foreign country was in humility under the feet of this good god. (Pritchard 1969, 257; The Asiatic Campaigns of Ramses II, 21–23)

Third, a text from the Amarna Letters illustrates the voice of the servant:

> To the king, my lord, my Sun, my god, the Sun from the sky: Message
> of Yidya, your servant, the dirt at your feet, the groom of your horses. I
> indeed prostrate myself, on the back and on the stomach, at the feet of
> my king, my lord, 7 times and 7 times. I am indeed observing the orders
> of the king, my lord, the son of the Sun, and I have indeed prepared food,
> strong drink, oil, grain, oxen, sheep and goats, before the arrival of the
> troops of the king, my lord. I have stored everything for the troops of the
> king, my lord. Who is the dog that would not obey the orders of the king,
> my lord, the son of the Sun? (Moran 1992, 352; EA 324)

It is difficult to determine how much of what is recorded in these texts is
mere rhetoric and what expresses actual situations or feelings. The coex-
istence of communal laments and imprecatory psalms suggests that the
wounds suffered under the "nations" lie just underneath the surface of
many biblical books and texts, including Obadiah, Nahum, eschatological
texts, and the oracles against the nations. The three texts illustrate vividly
that ancient Near Eastern cultures of fear required subordinate vassals to
express with great rhetorical flourish their willingness to accept and to
uphold political inequities and hierarchies imposed by the dominating
power. With their expressions of rhetorical obedience, they hoped for so-
called peace.

Accordingly, forms of fear that were usually part of the general cultural climate and part of the general collective psychology are less visibly
identifiable, but they have always been powerful markers of violence. They
were effective means of making subjugated populations and their leaders
compliant and complicit in imperial structures of violence in its internalized and explicit varieties.

Semantics of Violence

As explained previously, military and physical violence on behalf of
empires occurred occasionally, sometimes only in the form of annual
military incursions into the dominated region. Yet the rhetoric of fear
was central in the world of the dominated, which had a lasting effect. It
resulted in propaganda shaping the symbolic world and defining values
and beliefs that were internalized and constructing collective and personal worldviews. Submission was next. This dynamic appears in ancient
Near Eastern and biblical texts. It also affected the portrayals of God. In
the Bible, people's relationship with God was placed into a covenantal
relationship that demanded their undivided obedience and loyalty. It

trained the Israelites to accept conquering armies and their imperial leaders, the kings and emperors of Egypt, Assyria, Babylon, and Persia. It also meant that the actions of the biblical God lack mercy and grace. In fact, divine actions engender violence not only upon Israel's enemies but also on Israel when it disobeys its God. Biblical literature is an impressive document of the semantics of violence, widely found in other ancient Near Eastern texts.

When we compare the historical-cultural dynamics of violence and war in the ancient Near Eastern and biblical literatures with our contemporary contexts, important differences become visible. The intellectual revolution that took place in the eighteenth century CE created a fundamental change in contemporary collective cultural perspectives, and so it is possible for modern scholars to point out the shortcomings of biblical rhetoric without fear or hesitation. For instance, no longer do today's readers interpret concepts such as hell through the prism of medieval imagery but rather in light of the modern-scientific worldview. Accordingly, today's hell is recognized in the miseries of urban life, prisons, mental hospices, gulags, or even in psychological illness and depression.

Contemporary scholarship has also led to a better understanding of the ideological role that violence plays in religion and politics. Our better understanding of ideology has impacted the study of biblical texts. The current discussion about of the inherent violence of monotheism, its premises, and its implications in the wider context of an intercultural dialogue is a clear example of this discussion. Modern scholars read the Bible and find forms of violence where earlier generations of readers saw nothing disturbing.

For instance, in pre-eighteenth century Christian interpretations, the figure of Cain represented the incarnation of evil and rebellion against divine power. Yet with the rise of the French Revolution at the end of the eighteenth century CE, the understanding of this biblical character changed dramatically. During the age of absolute monarchy in Europe, the acceptance of divine will and royal will was seen as two sides of the same coin. Citizens were enjoined to accept political decisions, no matter what they were, as part of the divine will. It meant that Cain's curse by God had to be accepted as God's judgment. Yet, with the triumph of the French Revolution, a feeling of social rebellion emerged that validated the figure of Cain. He was no longer seen as the incarnation of the sinner but as a hero suffering under unjust tyranny ordained by God (Ramírez 2009, 34–37; Liptzin 1985, 17–18).

Regina M. Schwartz explains this development when she reflects on the logic of scarcity as exemplified in God's condemnation of Cain's sacrifice. She writes:

> What would have happened if God had accepted both Cain's and Abel's offerings instead of choosing one, and had thereby promoted cooperation between the farmer and the shepherd instead of competition and violence? Cain kills in the rage of his exclusion. And the circle becomes vicious: because Cain's sacrifice is cast out, Abel is murdered and Cain is cast out. We are the descendants of Cain because we too live in a world where some are cast out, a world in which whatever logic of scarcity made that ancient story describe only one sacrifice as acceptable—a scarcity of goods, land, labor, or whatever—still prevails to dictate the terms of a ferocious and fatal competition. There will always be losers. (1997, 3–4)

Schwartz explains that the logic of scarcity continues in the blessing of Jacob and the exclusion of Esau. She writes: "There is not enough divine favor, not enough blessing, for both Jacob and Esau. One can prosper only at the other's expense. And again the Outcast becomes murderous" (3–4). In her interpretation of Gen 4, Schwartz depicts the fraternal rivalries in a central role in which sympathy accumulates for the older brothers, including Cain, and the character of God is overruled. The story becomes an anti-imperial approach in contrast to pre-eighteenth century conventions. This approach must be considered as a radical innovation, because it sides with the cursed brother over against the God doing the cursing.

In other words, the literary motif of fraternal rivalry became central in interpretations of Gen 4, and exegetes have identified this motif throughout the Hebrew Bible. To them, it illustrates the inner struggle of the communities behind the texts and their discontent. Modern interpreters do not "find God" in this tale anymore. Rather, they view God as a literary character with which the original communities and writers conveyed their particular understandings of God. Today, we uncover the ancient ideologies embedded in the biblical texts, but few scholars believe in them. Our semantics of violence is too different from the ancient one to sound credible and authoritative anymore.

Violence in Latin America Today

The situation in the examined ancient Near Eastern and biblical texts is so obviously similar to the political situations in contemporary Latin America that there is no need to make any particular effort to contextualize it. Two examples from the recent political history of our continent illustrate how violence creates a culture of obedience and submission. They come from Nicaragua's and Haiti's political history. Both countries suffered brutal and most oppressive dictatorships under Anastasio Somoza D. (1925–1980) and François Duvalier (1970–1971). The dictatorships resulted in civil wars and political riots in the effort of overthrowing them. The misery faced in the aftermath of these events was tremendous and has made many people in those countries conclude that the situation under those regimes "wasn't really that bad." From the perspective of the subsequent conditions of poverty and international isolation, many Nicaraguans and Haitians started to say that the dictatorships were a sort of "golden age" for their countries. This position was devastating for the future political history of both countries.

The prevailing logic in our world opposes the conquerors and sides with the defeated. In this asymmetrical context, justice is no longer a right, but a favor, a gift, even a concession. The conquered cannot take their humanity for granted, but they must constantly bargain for it. Violence acquires a new dimension that is not always physical but always inhuman. It reduces a person's humanity, because this person does not perceive herself or himself as having a chance to live as a human being. In the words of Urs Bitterli (1991, 126–27): "The encounter between people of different cultures was replaced by a father-child relationship.... Unable to take any initiative of their own in the 'Reducciones,' the Indians were condemned to a life of big kids, never knowing the true joys of childhood."

Yet in the surreal worlds of our societies, the line between life and death is not clear anymore. Fernando Vallejo's novel on the violence of drug cartel warfare in Colombia, *Our Lady of the Assassins*, describes an accident that at first glance seems illogical. A car hits a pedestrian at full speed but does not kill the pedestrian. The conclusion is immediate: "It didn't kill him because he was already dead" (2001, 116). The threshold between life and death can be found already here in our midst:

Manrique[3] is where Medellin ends and *comunas* begin, or vice versa. It is what they call the gates of hell although one does not know if it is the entrance or the exit, if hell is the one that's round here or the one that's round there, going up or going down. Whether up or down, at all events

---

3. This is the area in the city of Medellín, Colombia, where the novel takes place.

Death, my godmother, prowls these skirts absorbed in her work without
turning her nose up at anybody. (116)

Vallejos's novel resembles Dante's visit to hell where he passes through the
gate of hell that bears the inscription: "Through me is the way among the
lost people.... Leave every hope ye who enter!" (Alighieri 1952, 4). But
eyes adjust to darkness and learn to live there as if darkness was a normal
condition, as for instance beautifully depicted in the "Allegory of the Cave"
in book 7 of Plato's *Republic*. In contexts of continual violence civil life is
not disrupted but is replaced by a world where the death toll is calculated
by the hour.

Another example comes from the writing of Uruguayan writer and
political activist Eduardo Galeano. He observes that during the military
dictatorships of Brazil in the 1960s, the first death from torture was a
national scandal. When ten died, it barely made the news, and when
fifty were murdered, it was accepted as normal. He explains that, "the
machine teaches one to accept horror as once accepts the cold of winter"
(1996, 87).

In contexts of prolonged war, as in Colombia, what is produced is not
the disruption of civil life's own dynamic. Rather society turns into a world
in which civil life's own dynamic is substituted by another: a surreal world
in which the number of deaths per day increases and goes unnoticed, as
for instance in Honduras or Juárez. People adapt their psychological and
symbolic worlds by turning a surreal world into the real world. Life is
lived in a culture of violence even when an individual does not experience
violence in a concrete way. Violence comes through low intensity warfare
and the pedagogy of utter exhaustion. The repeated and constant presence of these indirect ways of violence results in structural violence that
is perceived as normal. There is a bargaining, a reduction, and regression
of humanity.

María Socorro Entrana describes this regression of humanity in the
context of poverty, as the concrete expression of the culture of violence:

Indigence, extreme poverty, usually undermines the confidence of those
who experience it. This psychological suffering is more scathing than
physical suffering. It is a feeling of impotency, psychic collapse, a lack
of faith in one's own abilities, the intimate feeling that one can do nothing; self-esteem collapses, disillusionment grows, in the well of passivity.
(2001, 84)

In short, the culture of violence undermines the people living in it. They cannot imagine anymore that peace and justice are available to them. Obediently, they submit and live in quiet despair, passively waiting for change that they believe is out of reach.

Violence as a Way of Life: Concluding Comments

This essay analyzed violence as a cultural and literary expression as found in ancient Near Eastern and biblical texts as well as in recent Latin American history. A selective study of the ancient literatures suggests that imperial politics of domination does not always resort to military action. Demonstrations of military power become only necessary when a subjugated people does not accept its subjugation. Such resistance calls for extreme measures in the form of military destruction and occupation. In most instances, however, actual conquest was carried out through much less costly and complicated means. It included diplomacy and political ideology as political weapons based on fear and intimidation of the indigenous population. It also required unequivocal obedience. Many ancient near Eastern and biblical texts indicate that violence generated the conditions for obedience in automated responses. They were based on internalized and taken-for-granted fear that permeated the general culture. The pedagogy of fear was a form of violence. It produced efficient submission of large numbers of people. This strategy of domination and conquest is still prevalent in the political cultures of contemporary Latin America, based in security regimes and military movements that engender fear and political submission. Displacement, poverty, and a culture in which violence is no longer perceived as unusual is the consequence. They become normal ways of life.

Works Cited

Alighieri, Dante. 1952. *The Divine Comedy.* Translated by Charles Eliot Norton. Chicago: Chicago University Press.

Bitterli, Urs. 1991. *Die "Wilden" und die "Zivilisierten." Grundzüge einer Geistes-und Kulturgeschichte der europäish-überseeischen Begegnung.* München: Beck.

Black, Jeremy, Graham Cunningham, Eleanor Robson, and Gábor Zólyomi. 2004. *The Literature of Ancient Sumer.* Oxford: Oxford University Press.

Borchert, Wolfgang. 1949. *Das Gesamtwerk*. Hamburg: Rowohlt.

Cohen, Raymond, and Raymond Westbrook. 2000. *Amarna Diplomacy. The Beginnings of International Relations*. Baltimore: Johns Hopkins University Press.

Dalley, Stephanie. 2006. "Ancient Mesopotamian Military Organization." Pages 413–22 in vol. 2 of *Civilizations of the Ancient Near East*. Edited by Jack M. Sasson. 2nd ed. Peabody: Hendrickson.

Entrana, María Socorro. 2001. *Pobreza*. Madrid: San Pablo.

Foster, John L. 1995. *Hymns, Prayers and Songs: An Anthology of Ancient Egyptian Lyric Poetry*. WAW 8. Atlanta: Scholar Press.

Frankfort, Henri, H. A. Groenewegen-Frankfort, J. A. Wilson, and T. Jacobsen. 1954. *Before Philosophy*. Baltimore: Penguin Books.

Galeano, Eduardo. 1996. *Días y noches de amor y de guerra*. Madrid: Alianza Editorial.

Grayson, A. Kirk. 2002. *Assyrian Rulers of the Early First Millennium BC II (858–745 BC)*. The Royal Inscriptions of Mesopotamia: Assyrian Periods 3. Toronto: University of Toronto Press.

Halbfas, Hubertus. 2001. *Die Bibel. Erschlossen und kommentiert*. Düsseldorf: Patmos.

Lipinski, Edward. 2003. "Sāpôn north." Pages 435–43 in vol. 12 of *Theological Dictionary of the Old Testament*. Edited by G.J. Botterweck, H. Ringgren , H. J. Fabry. Grand Rapids: Eerdmans.

Liptzin, Solomon. 1985. *Biblical Themes in World Literature*. Hoboken, NJ: Katv.

Machiavelli, Nicolò. 1984. *The Prince*. Translated by W. K. Marriot. Chicago: Chicago University Press.

Michaud, Yves. 2007. *La Violence*. Paris: PUF.

Moore, Carey A. 1985. *Judith*. AB 40. New York: Doubleday.

Moran, William L. 1992. *The Amarna Letters*. Baltimore: Johns Hopkins University Press.

Oppenheim, Leo A. 1967. *Letters from Mesopotamia: Official, Business and Private Letters on Clay Tablets from Two Millennia*. Chicago: Chicago University Press.

Pritchard, James B., ed. 1969. *Ancient Near Eastern Texts Relating to the Old Testament*. 3rd ed. Princeton: Princeton University Press.

Ramírez Kidd, José E. 2009. *Para comprender el Antiguo Testamento*. San José: Editorial Ubila.

Schwartz, Regina M. 1997. *The Curse of Cain: The Violent Legacy of Monotheism*. Chicago: Chicago University Press.

Vallejo, Fernando. 2001. *Our Lady of the Assassins.* Translated by Paul Hammond. London: Serpent's Tail.

PART 2
READING BIBLICAL TEXTS IN AMERICAN CONTEXTS

Denouncing Imperialism:
An Argentine Rereading of the
Tower of Babel (Gen 11:1–9)*

Pablo R. Andiñach

Resumen: El presente ensayo parte de considerar que las lecturas corrientes de la narración de la Torre de Babel (Gen 11:1–9) han omitido un aspecto importante de su mensaje. Normalmente se concentran en el texto como fundante de la división de lenguas entre los pueblos, y como un castigo por la pretensión de buscar ser "como Dios." Sin embargo este trabajo, que asume la condición polisémica del texto, muestra que hay una profunda denuncia del imperialismo en sus líneas. Se analiza el uso ideológico del nombre Babel, con el que se hace un juego de palabras con la palabra balal, cuyo sentido es "confusión." Desde el poder opresor se pretende poseer la llave de los Dioses pero el texto lo ridiculiza señalando que lo que hay confusión. Lo mismo sucede con el lexema shem/sham que juega con el doble sentido de "nombre" y "lugar [allí]" para poner en evidencia que la pretensión de ser famosos ("hacernos un nombre") culmina ubicándose en un lugar donde hay humillación para el poderoso. Pretende tener fama y poder y logra vergüenza y debilidad. Hacia el final, se analiza la situación de vivir en un contexto donde el idioma no es el propio. La lectura tradicional entendió la diversidad de lenguas como una maldición, mientras que nuestra lectura es que la única lengua confundida es la del opresor. De esa manera, la diversidad es riqueza y cada lengua es una oportunidad más de mostrar la capacidad creadora de los pueblos que las hablan.

The story of the tower of Babel in Gen 11:1–9 has usually been read from the perspective of the colonizers. This viewpoint has a long tradition, and

---

* I want to express my gratitude to Larisa Grams and Ignacio Benítez for their help in translating and correcting my English. I also thank my coeditor, Susanne Scholz, for her invaluable help in getting this essay into its final form.

it is certainly not uniquely affiliated with the Hebrew Bible. For instance, the Roman writer, Virgil, identified with the forces of empire when he wrote in the first century BCE:

> Roman, it is for you to rule the nations with your power,
> (that will be your skill) to crown peace with law,
> to spare the conquered, and subdue the proud. (Virgil, 6.851–853 [Kline]).

In his poem, Virgil articulated eloquently the doctrine of imperialism. Such imperialism has prevailed throughout the ages and continues to plague us today. It has also held sway over interpretations of Gen 11:1–9. Consequently, many readers know that this biblical tale wants to explain why humans speak different languages. Wanting to be "like God," humans disobey God. As a result, God punishes humanity so that we would never again unite against God. Most commentaries follow this interpretative logic and neglect the possibility that the narrative might, in fact, deal with a completely different explanation about the origins of the various languages.

The existence of so many languages has certainly always invited explanations, and Gen 11 gives a mythical one. Since it is a myth, the story offers more than any literalist interpretation will ever be able to articulate. The mythic nature of Gen 11 makes it polysemeous. I am an Argentinian Bible scholar, living in the postdictatorship era in my country, and I want to propose an interpretation that uplifts a reading perspective that goes against the grain of the empire-friendly approaches that have dominated the interpretation history of Gen 11:1–9. My reading exploits the polysemeous qualities of this tale, allowing me to read it from the side of the oppressed and the colonized, from those who suffer under empire even today. In other words, my interpretation challenges the imperial interpretation history of Gen 11:1–9, and, as such, it rejects Virgil's defense of empire. I present my argumentation in four sections. The first section makes a case in support of an anti-imperial approach to the biblical narrative under consideration. The second section elaborates on the importance of recognizing the Tower of Babel story as a theological construct. The third section explains how the writers of Gen 11:1–9 challenged empire with their etymological sophistication. The fourth section discusses the symbolic significance of the confusion of the languages for an anti-imperial interpretation. A conclusion sums up the main points.

An Anti-imperial Approach to Gen 11:1–9

My reading of Gen 11:1–9 as a story that denounces imperial oppression is grounded in the Argentinian and Latin American experience of having lived under powerful empires. It has made us sensitive to symbols, words, and ideas whose richness invites many readings, including anti-imperial ones. Usually, oppressed people prefer symbols that express their feelings for two reasons. First, symbolic language is ambiguous, which imperial authorities find difficult to tolerate. Second, symbols and myths have often been used to share feelings among oppressed peoples. They speak and understand symbolic and mythic language, because it assumes the ability to read between the lines, to be well-versed in a hermeneutics of suspicion, and to address indirectly situations of grave injustice so that the powerful do not realize how much the oppressed people know about the politics of their situation and the possibilities of resisting it.

I posit that oppressed people share those sensibilities and interpretation abilities throughout time. Whether we look at the oppressed Israelites, people dominated by the Roman Empire during Virgil's time, or at the millions of oppressed people today, their dire situations are similar in the sense that they face imperial structures of domination. For instance, millions in the so-called "South" live under economic violence imposed by empires from the North. There are workers in factories like the "maquila," who receive paltry salaries for their long days of work. There are micro-farmers who are pushed to produce coca leaves, because the market value of those leaves is much higher than coffee beans. Coca leaves are turned into drugs and sold through illegal channels in Europe and the United States. All the while, the small farmer receive only a minor fraction of those profits, which mainly go to large drug dealers. Then there are the big banks that control most of the money in Argentina. Usually headquartered in the United States or Europe, these banks normally transfer profits back to their country at the end of their fiscal year. Yet if it is a bad year for them, the banks ask and receive help from the Argentine Central Bank, because they tell our government that they "want to keep the bank open" and not lay off employees. However, when the same institutions make money, they send the profits to their home countries, and the people of Argentina do not receive anything from them. This is what it means to live under empire.

When I use the term *empire*, I refer to an entity that is not limited to one country but to a complex infrastructure that spans the globe today.

For instance, since the 1960s we speak of United States American imperialism; it was then that the United States appeared to be the new superpower as the world entered into the Cold War, a war between the Northern
Atlantic world, led by NATO, and the USSR. In the midst of this "war,"
millions of people in Latin America suffered under military regimes,
extreme economic liberal policies, and the persecution of popular movements reacting against these powers. Today, we live in a globalized world.
We have discovered that imperialism is an economic structure of enormous military, political, and cultural dimensions. Gigantic transnational
banks and corporations dominate it. More importantly, these corporations
do not only oppress people from the South but also poor and working-
class people in their various home countries. Consequently, many people
who are marginalized in the so-called "first world," such as in France, the
United Kingdom, and the United States, not to mention smaller countries
like Greece, Spain, and Ireland, have come to realize that they too are victims of the neoliberal economic system. The Occupy Movement, as well as
United States American and European workers who lost their jobs or even
homes understand now that the empire's interests are not their own. I hope
that for many people in the North this situation makes them recognize
that in most of countries in the South neoliberal laws and practices have
been the normal behavior of banks and corporations during the last two
centuries. Without a doubt, average United States American or European
families have better tools at their disposal than poor or low-class Latin
American families. However, after the recent decades of neoliberalism,
few people deny that the IMF and the World Bank protect the wealth of a
small minority of rich people, who do not hesitate to destroy jobs, homes,
and lives of ordinary people. They have done so in the South, and with
some adaptations to new conditions they continue doing so even in the
North. They are currently implementing the same destructive policies in
northern countries as they have been doing in our countries. Although the
situation is not new, for the first time the poor in the North are suffering
the same oppression as their partners in the South. Thus, my reading of
Gen 11:1–9 offers an anti-imperial interpretation that sides with the colonized people on the planet anywhere.

Reading Gen 11:1–9 as a Theological Construct

I am not interested in discussing the historical origins of this mythic tale
for three main reasons. First, since Gen 11:1–9 is a myth, it is not a histori-

cal report about events as they occurred in the past. It is part of the primordial stories in Gen 1–11 that are not strongly bound to any particular historical context. Obviously, the Tower of Babel story was produced in a particular sociohistorical time period, but due to its mythical character we can only speculate when it might have been composed. The writers left us with a tale that contains strong theological and ideological interests that still resonate in the present era of colonial oppression. The differentiation between history and myth must be kept in mind when we read the story of the Tower of Babel. Because it is a myth and not history, it contains an abundance of theology.

Second, Gen 11 is part of the Jewish and Christian canon. One of the characteristics of any canonical text in any religion is that the community that recognizes the narrative as canonical sees in its words a message beyond the original context. Such a community believes that the text deserves to be preserved, because it carries an essential message for future generations. To such a community, the text is more than a historical record of the past. Sometimes it is respected as a record of historical events, theologies, and experiences, but it is valued as a text that illuminates the present and the future welfare of the community that holds it in high esteem. Each generation has the task of rereading the text from within their situations and for finding meaning in it. Such a text is a theologically meaningful communication from past generations handed over to future generations. This process guarantees theological continuity and innovation at the same time.

Third, another important theological point explains the significance of rereading Gen 11:1–9 as a challenge to imperial oppression and not as a historical tale. A myth is always a story that presents itself as history. In fact, people who nurture and keep these stories assume them to be historical. One condition for understanding a myth is that it is read as a "real story" that is not only fiction, even if it is known that it is fiction. A historical reading of a myth is thus a misunderstanding of a myth's literary genre and purpose. When interpreters read history into myth, they miss the theological point of the tale. For instance, the story of the crossing of the Red Sea in the book of Exodus articulates the power of the Israelite God who has dominion even over the waters of the sea. That myth affirms that God created the sea and has the power to close or open the waters as it pleases God. The theological message is that God has more power than the Egyptian Empire. In short, Gen 11:1–9 does not depict a historical event. Rather, it is a literary construct that, as it was composed in the past, continues to contain a serious anti-imperial theology.

Challenging Empire with Etymological Sophistication

The writers of Gen 11:1–9 challenged imperial oppression not only by making profound theological claims about God siding with oppressed and dominated peoples, but also with their etymological sophistication. They developed and included literary constructions that played with words and names to indirectly and subtly challenge the Babylonian Empire. This etymological sophistication is not unique to the narrative in Genesis but also appears in other cases, such as in the naming of Moses (Exod 2) or Samuel (1 Sam 1:20). It is certainly pronounced in the name of Babel and contributes to the development of an anti-imperial interpretation.

In the Akkadian language, the city of Babel is called *bab-il*, which means "the door of God." It is the short form of *babilani*, which in one word stands for "the door of the gods." This longer form is not found in the Hebrew text. In its plural form, it was passed down to the Septuagint where it is translated as *Babulon* or *Babulonus*, turning from there into the English "Babylon" and the Spanish *Babilonia*. Interestingly, the Septuagint does not contain a short form for this city name; it is always translated as *Babulon*. Because Akkadian is a Semitic language, Hebrew writers would have unquestionably known of the Akkadian name *bab-il*. We can thus expect that they used the Akkadian name in Hebrew to present a wordplay, because this name has strong ideological and political implications in Hebrew.[1] They invite playing with imperial and anti-imperial possibilities of meaning.

When a city is named in Akkadian as "the door of the gods," the meaning of this name endorses the empire. It signifies that the inhabitants of this city have found the door to heaven, that they experience a direct and exclusive relationship to their gods, and that they are in charge of granting access to their gods on the merit of being inhabitants of a city that offers "the door of the gods." It indicates that those who name their city in this way proclaim that the gods are with them and not with the inhabitants of other cities. They affirm that their gods have chosen them. In other words, the name of the city, "the door of the gods," suggests that the inhabitants of

---

1. Clare Amos (2004, 9–10) notes that "these people may think that they can *make* something, including a *name* for themselves," reveling the relationship between the building of a city and the construction of an identity is based in the power and the submission of other people under cultural homogeneity and unity.

Babylon are on the side of the gods. They have access to the divine home by virtue of living in Babel.

This arrogance is denounced with the recurrence of the lexeme "there" (*sham*) and "name" (*shem*). In verse 2, they settled "there" (*sham*) where, according to verse 4, they will make themselves a "name" (*shem*). Then in verse 7, their plan changes when "there" (*sham*) their language is confused by God, and from "there" (*sham*) they will be "scattered abroad," according to verse 8. The summary in verse 9 explains that the city will be called a "name" (*shem*), "because there" (*sham*) God "confused" them and from "there" (*sham*) they were "scattered over the face of all the earth." In the end, God's action made the place (*sham*), intended to be the location of the city's name (*shem*), the place for confusion and humiliation. Severino Croatto (1997, 356) affirms this linguistic observation when he explains: "The lexeme *sham* ('there') is not just a literary form. In fact, it could be omitted sometimes. But the combination of *shem* ('name') produces an effect on the sense: in that place (*sham*), where a city is being built, they look for fame and reputation, but the only remains at the time will be a name of a city called *confusion*."[2]

Yet, obviously, the storytellers are not explicit about their understanding of *bab-il*. Thus, in verse 9, the etymological meaning of Babel does not derive from the Akkadian *bab-il* but from the Hebrew root *balal*. This root has the basic meaning of "confusion" and also appears in nouns such as *tebalul* (darkness, obscurity) and *tebel* (confusion, violation of divine order). The etymological sophistication of the Hebrew writers obfuscates their challenge to imperial theology and conceals it with Hebrew terminology as if imperial language were uninvolved. They protected themselves and others from imperial persecution.

For the Israelites—a people who had a city with a terrene name, as Jerusalem means "the city of peace" or "the peaceful city"—to think of Babel as the "door of the gods" was highly pretentious. As victims of a powerful economic, military, and political system, they knew where the "real" power was, and as done by colonized peoples in all ages, they generated disguised wordplays that reveal the origins of oppression. Oppressed peoples anywhere have always denounced their oppressors. Once they understand the origins of their oppression, they develop discourses to

---

2. The English translation is based on my own translation of the original Hebrew text.

challenge it. In stories, jokes, and wordplays, they unmask the strategies of their oppressors. When we apply this insight to the Tower of Babel, the storytellers knew that most Babylonians believed that they and their authorities held the true key to their gods. Yet the Israelites knew this is a lie and that the "door of the gods" was propaganda, a marketing ploy to legitimize Babylonian power and domination. To the Israelites who lived in oppression, the name "Babel" undoubtedly stood for imperial power. They knew that the empire under which they suffered proclaimed to the world that it owned the key to the heavens and that their authority and power was granted by the Babylonian gods requiring submission and obedience. To own the key to "the door of the gods" was equivalent to having divine power, and so the Babylonians believed to have the gods on their side. However, to the Israelites who had to submit to daily state violence, it was clear that the top of the big and tall ziggurat was empty. They knew there was no door to the gods on top of that tower. In fact, they declared in Gen 11:1–9, against the Babylonian claim, that only "confusion" prevailed on top of it.

In short, the biblical writers connected the etymological origin of Babel with the Hebrew root of *balal* not because they did not have enough knowledge of Akkadian or Hebrew. Rather, their etymological explanation communicated that they rejected any *religious* reasoning about their political, economic, and cultural oppression. While the Babylonians proclaimed to be the owners of the world because of their special and intimate relationship with their gods, the opposite was the case from the oppressed people's perspective. The Babylonian Empire was not appointed by the gods on the basis of a key fitting perfectly into the door to the divine throne. Rather, the power of the empire was built on military, political, economic, and social oppression and domination, also legitimized by imperial theologizing.

I observe a direct correlation to contemporary imperial ideologies of oppression. To this day, oppression and violence against poor people are justified on the basis of divine blessings that are called "manifest destiny," "the axis of evil," or "the theology of prosperity." This kind of theological discourse asserts that God blesses the rich with their richness while punishing the poor with their poverty. We suffer from this kind of distortion in the biblical faith. People who believe in Christ as their only savior are pushed to add to their faith—as if it were intimately related—a faith into capitalism and Western culture as the best and only way of saving the world from inevitable final destruction. Western leaders are promoted as the only capable ones to rationally govern the world. When biblical faith is preached in this way, it becomes an ideology endorsing particular political projects. In Latin America, during the 1960s and 1970s, people were subjugated to brutal dictatorships that posed as Christian and claimed to oppose the "materialism" and "atheism" of the socialist and communist people (Bruno and Andiñach 2001). These regimes killed thousands of people, most of them peaceful workers, farmers, poor people, students, leaving thousands more without fathers, wives, husbands, daughters, and sons. They forced Argentinians to create the neologism of the "disappeared people" so that we could name all of those who were kidnaped and killed without leaving any signs of their existence. I propose that the Hebrew writers told the Tower of Babel story to challenge this kind of imperial theology. They told this narrative pretending that the people built a tower, had the key of the door to heaven, were like God, and presided over life and death, but in truth everybody knew all of it was a lie that nobody believed.

However, the city name of *balal/babel* is not the only wordplay in the text. There is also irony when verse 5 reports that God "descended" to see the work of the Babylonians, as if God even cared how they had built the city and the tower with the goal of reaching the heavens (Berlin and Brettler 2002, 29). The story reveals that the intent of reaching the heavens is not just impossible but an ideological instrument to overwhelm the spirit of the oppressed people. It aims to humiliate them even more. According to the ironic pattern in the text, the builders of the tower were not merely confused but also scattered around the world. They suffered the same punishment that they, as the empire, had brought upon peoples.[3] The Judahites remembered what happened with the Samaritans (2 Kgs 17:5–6) and how they had been disseminated throughout the empire. They also recalled what had happened to themselves and how the Chaldeans had sent them all over the world (2 Kgs 24–25). These examples indicate that the writers of Gen 11:1–9 used the Tower of Babel narrative as a weapon that counterattacked imperial ideology at its core. It challenged its religious-ideological assertions. Since the Israelites had neither real weapons nor political power, they told a story that expressed their strong conviction that their God was stronger than any Babylonian imperial tower and certainly more powerful than any Babylonian god in need of towers or

---

3. Alejandro García Santos in two long and strong articles shows how the focus of this story is most the scattering of the people than the diversity of languages (1989, passim; 1990, 185–87).

cities. Thus, when the tale is read from the perspective of the colonized and the oppressed, the building of a city and a tower illustrates the weakness of the imperial gods of Babylon. Towers and cities merely hide the low performance of the Babylonian gods as instruments of oppression that the victims of oppressive regimes will never recognize.

The Symbolic Significance of the Confusion of Languages

I assert that the storytellers chose the confusion of the languages to denounce imperial dominance. It demonstrates their precise understanding of the dynamics between oppressors and the oppressed. They knew that language serves as a superior tool to divide and to classify people into "otherness." Thus, Gen 11:1–9 illustrates that language and words are always central, present, and powerful in every structure of domination even though empire has deep and extensive economic, military, and political dimensions. Language makes sure that these dimensions stay in place.

To clarify what is going on in Gen 11, it is worthwhile to mention the famous dialog between Alice and Humpty Dumpty in which they discuss how words work in Wonderland:

> "When I use a word," Humpty Dumpty said, in rather a scornful tone, "it means just what I choose it to mean—neither more nor less." "The question is," said Alice, "whether you can make words mean so many different things." "The question is," said Humpty Dumpty, "which is to be master—that's all." (Carroll 1999, 57)

In other words, choices over vocabulary relate to power. The understanding of terminological power games is central to understanding imperial power in general. In an anti-imperial interpretation, the significance of verse 1 should not be underestimated. It dreams of one language for all peoples when it states that "the whole world spoke the same language and the same words." The story suggests that once upon a time all peoples spoke the same language; then something unexpected happened, which transformed the unified situation into chaotic language plurality.[4]

---

4. Note that the narrative is not taking into account that in the previous chapter—chapter 10—there already are different peoples and a strong geographical distribution, and these take for granted the existence of a variety of languages. This incongruence could affect an historical narrative, but it has less or no effect in a mythical narrative

However, when this story is read with anti-imperial lenses, the change does not refer to the creation of language plurality. Rather, it means that one language, namely, the language of the empire, was banned, because, since that day, builders stopped building the city and the tower. Accordingly, in an anti-imperial reading, God uses the multiplicity of languages to limit imperial powers.

Another aspect is related to Israel's lived experience as a foreign nation that is forced to survive in a country whose language is not familiar to them. In Babylon, the Israelites had to speak the language of the empire, itself not a simple issue but a situation fraught with ideological and political implications. For instance, in Latin America, it is common among groups that do popular readings of the Bible to highlight this particular point in Gen 11:1–9. In most of our countries, the native populations were subjugated through violence, executed by the sword as well as culturally and socially oppressed. The abolition of the languages of the native peoples was always one of the most important tools to establish domination. The conquerors knew that if they could condemn the native language and ban its use, they would destroy the heart of the identity of the people. Without a clear identity, it is very difficult to organize resistance against the oppressors. Thus, the Tower of Babel story presents an important challenge to most local native communities in Argentina. White biblical scholars often try to understand why native people find in this story a mirror of their experiences.[5] Meanwhile, native people like to read the Bible within their historical experiences of losing their land, being forced to repress their language, and being ashamed of their cultural marks. They claim that Gen 11:1–9 and other texts, such as Neh 9:36–37, describe their current experiences as if they were written for them.

Thus, terminology and word choices are crucial even today. For instance, what is the meaning of the word "democracy" in American political discourse? The United States government, arguing that it promotes "democracy," has supported almost all of the military regimes in Latin America during the twentieth century. Furthermore, what is the meaning

---

(Birch et al. 1999, 64; Childs 1993, 120), where the author refers to the Mesopotamian background of the text and interprets it as a "form of divine displeasure," a distortion which can also be expressed in a nonchronological way of presenting facts.

5. One example is the work by Juan Manuel Ekó Ekó Ada (1991). The author presents a reading from his African experience as belonging to a people oppressed by European conquerors.

of human rights to United States politicians when their country imprisons people in the Guantánamo Bay Detention Camp, which is a de facto concentration camp, while the prisoners lack access to lawyers, the rule of law, or any other civilized legal protection basic to any other Western country? It reminds me of my own country when the Argentinian people suffered imprisonment in jails like Guantánamo Bay during the last dictatorship that ended in 1983. Since then, we have lived in a stable democracy despite many political, economic, and social problems. Yet, we would be horrified if something like Guantanamo happened in our country today. People and social movements, and I believe even right-wing parties, would oppose and protest if the Argentinian government detained people and locked them up into such an inhumane prison camp. What is the meaning of the words "freedom" and "liberty"? In Argentina, we always raise this question when these terms are used to question ideas about the so-called free market or when corporations and banks mention these words—freedom and liberty—while they swallow up small competitors. What is the meaning of "corruption" when the word is applied to countries of the South but not to the European Union that is made up of countries in which we now "discover" fraud, lack of information, and corruption by bribes? Why do some politicians claim freedom for Cuba but not for Saudi Arabia? Who decides the meaning of words such as "democracy," "human rights," "freedom," and "corruption"? The answer is that imperial ideology defines and limits the meaning of these and similar words. Military, political, economic, and cultural oppression goes hand in hand with them.

A people like the Judahites, who proclaimed that their God created the cosmos from the divine word, could not ignore the value and power of language and words. They knew that language and words are vehicles for power and domination. There are many examples in the biblical canon to illustrate this point. For instance, one impressive case appears in the dialogue between the official of Sennacherib and Eliakim, the son of Hilkiah, a representative of Hezekiah, king of Judah. The local officers ask the officials: "Please speak to your servants in the Aramaic language, for we understand it; do not speak to us in the language of Judah within the hearing of the people who are on the wall" (2 Kgs 18:26). Both sides are depicted as being aware of the power of language and words. In this case, the conqueror decides to use language that undermines the confidence of the people of Jerusalem in its leadership. Another example appears in Neh 13:24 where Nehemiah denounces that "half of their children spoke the language of Ashdod, and they could not speak the language of Judah."

It is clear that for the Judahites language was very important, and they understood the political and social implications when one language was preferred over another.

The significance of languages is still a delicate matter revealing who has power and who does not. In international settings, languages are always a sign of power forcing "thought" upon the nations whose languages are not spoken. The dominant culture defines the language not only for itself but also for the oppressed. The language of the oppressed is viewed as vulgar and rustic, as not suitable for good literature and poetry or any kind of sophisticated scientific thought and work. Most importantly, the imperial system declares that the language of the oppressed does not work as appropriate communication with God. For instance, American missionaries teach English hymns and songs (classic Protestant hymns) to Third-World native people, because these songs are "truly" spiritual in contrast to local poetry, rhythms, and melodies. Another example of internalized colonial values occurs when Argentine pastors insist on Western or what we call "white" liturgies and practices in native Christian communities, because "they need to become civilized."

Oppressed people are forced to learn the language of the colonizers. They speak the language of empire. Of course, there is always a difference between acquiring general knowledge of the sciences and a second language. The new language will always be spoken with an accent and with difficulty. The accent reveals the condition of the oppressed. It shows that the native person belongs to another people as a foreigner, an alien, an immigrant. People can hide or reproduce different cultural characteristics, such as clothing, food, or architecture, but as soon as they speak a word in the second language, they expose themselves as newcomers. The biblical people knew about this sensitive condition. For instance, they address it in Judg 12:6, which mentions how the pronunciation of one particular word reveals tribal or national origins. It can be that easy. Thus, an anti-imperial reading of the Tower of Babel story rejects the imperial dream of one language as a desired goal. It cherishes, nurtures, and celebrates the diversity of languages. This is an anti-imperial move.

Taking God's Side with the Oppressed and Colonized: A Conclusion

No single text has the power to prevent empire from happening. The story of the Tower of Babel is not an exception. We should not think that the Judahites from the Persian Period believed that writing a story would dispel the power of the people who kept them in humiliation and poverty. In a different way, because they lived and suffered oppression, the Israelites created this story to denounce the injustice of their oppressors. At the same time, Gen 11:1–9 states that God rejects world domination of one people over the rest of the world. The narrative teaches that the God of Israel takes the side of the colonized and the poor. It denounces Israelite captivity and proclaims to the oppressed that God is with them. This kind of storytelling happens when people realize their oppressive situation and when they see more clearly the cultural and economic origins of their situation. Therefore, the discourse of oppressed people, conscious of their oppression, is direct and sharp. In the case of Gen 11, the greatness of the story's theology consists in the fact that it is sees beyond the understandable anguish produced by the oppressive situation. The story wants to overcome the tendency of contextualizing imperialism. It denounces it in this myth teaching, that, in fact, God rejects all forms of past and future imperialism. Placed within Gen 1–11, the Tower of Babel story depicts reality in a deep and complex way, but it deplores imperialism and its abuses in *every* time and place.

When Gen 11:1–9 is read in this way, the tale condemns violence perpetuated by imperial powers. Most importantly, the narrative does not blame the violence on the diversity of languages. Rather, its message is that any language is worthy of and suitable for communication, because the diversity of languages is *not* a consequence of humanity's sin but God's way of stopping imperial structures of domination. While empire defines God in service of its imperial power as it tries to convince ordinary people that God is with the empire and blesses imperial ideas and practices, the victims of empire view God as a dynamic actor who works on behalf of their liberation. In this sense, then, the story is powerful, a real "myth," as it tips the balance in favor of the oppressed.

Works Cited

Amos, Clare. 2004. "Genesis." Pages 1–16 in *Global Bible Commentary*. Edited by Daniel Patte. Nashville: Abingdon.

Berlin, Adele, and Marc Zvi Brettler, eds. 2002. *The Jewish Study Bible*. New York: Oxford University Press.

Birch, Bruce, Walter Brueggemann, Terence E. Fretheim, and David L. Petersen. 1999. *A Theological Introduction to the Old Testament*. Nashville: Abingdon.

Bruno, Daniel, and Pablo R. Andiñach. 2001. *Iglesias evangélicas y derechos humanos en la Argentina (1976–1998).* Buenos Aires: La Aurora.

Carroll, Lewis (Charles Lutwidge Dodgson). 1999. *Through the Looking-Glass, and What Alice Found There.* New York: Dover Publications.

Childs, Brevards. 1993. *Biblical Theology of the Old and New Testament: Theological Reflection on the Christian Bible.* Minneapolis: Fortress.

Croatto, Severino. 1997. *Exilio y sobrevivencia: Tradiciones contraculturales en el Pentateuco; Comentario a Génesis 4:1–12:9.* Buenos Aires: Lumen.

Ekó Ekó Ada, Juan Manuel. 1991. *La torre de Babel: Signo de libertad en el plan salvífico de Yavé; Génesis 11:1–9.* Diss., ISEDET, Buenos Aires.

García Santos, Alejandro. 1989. "Génesis 11:1–9: Crítica literaria y de la redacción." *Estudios bíblicos* 47:289–318.

———.1990. "Análisis de la forma de Génesis 11:1–9." *Communio* 23:167–207.

Virgil. 2014. *The Aeneid.* Translated by A. S. Kline. London: Poetry in Translation.

Biblical Interpretation as Violence: Genesis 19 and Judges 19 in the Context of HIV and AIDS

Cheryl B. Anderson

Resumen: El presente ensayo estudia la violencia ejercida en el acto de interpretar las Escrituras y en la actitud de las iglesias hacia las personas portadoras del VIH o quienes han desarrollado SIDA. Analiza Génesis 19 y Jueces 19 para mostrar cómo el modo de interpretación bíblica influencia nuestra comprensión de los problemas de la sexualidad en nuestros días. Se señala que debemos distinguir entre la violencia visible y la invisible; la primera es la que todos podemos observar pero la segunda es la violencia que se oculta debajo de la primera y que está en los orígenes de la violencia visible. En ese sentido, el alto nivel de infectados en una determinada población, en este caso la afro-americana, es comprendido como la violencia visible que revela la realidad de una violencia cultural y estructural ejercida sobre esa comunidad. La causa profunda de esa condición es la pobreza y la falta de equidad social y económica. Aplicado a la iglesia, esto revela que la inequidad de trato hacia la mujer hace que esta no pueda imponer prácticas de sexualidad seguras en su casa aun cuando sea consciente de la infidelidad de su pareja. Luego de analizar los textos bíblicos mencionados concluye que el VIH/SIDA presenta un desafío para los métodos de interpretación bíblica en el ámbito académico y para la práctica tradicional de comprensión de la Biblia en la comunidad de la iglesia.

Thirty years have passed since the human immunodeficiency virus (HIV) that leads to AIDS (acquired immunodeficiency syndrome) was discovered. Yet there are over 50,000 people who are newly infected with the virus each year, and we know that the disease disproportionately affects African Americans.[1] African Americans are 12–14 percent of the United States

---

1. Current statistics on HIV infections in the United States and the affected popu-

population, yet 44 percent of all new infections are within that community. An African American man is seven times more likely to be HIV positive than a white man, twice as likely as a Latino man, and ten times more likely than an African American woman. However, comparably high statistics exist for African American women: when the most recent statistics for women are considered, African American women are twenty times more likely to be infected than white women and five times more likely than Latinas. In general, though, the most affected population is the gay and bisexual community (across all racial/ethnic groups). Although they only constitute 2 percent of the United States population, men who have sex with men (MSM) are 63 percent of all new infections.[2] Therefore, we can conclude that HIV and AIDS raise issues of race/ethnicity (African Americans), gender (women), and homosexuality (or male same-sex relationships).[3]

Usually, Christian churches consider an individual's HIV-positive status to be primarily a matter of his or her sexual behavior even though other methods of transmission exist.[4] From this perspective, an individual is solely responsible for his or her HIV status, and an infection is presumed to be solely the consequence of sex outside of the traditional heterosexual marriage—either promiscuous heterosexual behavior or condemned homosexual behavior. Correspondingly, then, the HIV pre-

lations can be found at the website of the Centers for Disease Control (CDC) at www. cdc.gov/hiv. The latest year for statistical analysis is 2010.

2. The term "MSM" is used by the CDC to identify "behaviors that transmit HIV infection, rather than how individuals self-identify in terms of their sexuality" (Center for Disease Control and Prevention, n.d.).

3. Considering these issues separately does not negate "intersectionality," i.e., the recognition that any person can experience marginalization based on one or all three of these identity markers. For example, a white homosexual male has privileges based on race but has disadvantages based on sexual orientation. Similarly, an African American lesbian would have disadvantages based on all three: race/ethnicity, gender, and sexual orientation. Intersectionality is acknowledged but will not be explored fully in this brief study.

4. HIV is transmitted through an exchange of bodily fluids, and such exchanges can also occur during intravenous drug use and breastfeeding. By referring to "Christian churches" or "the church," I do not ignore the diversity of Christian traditions that exist in the United States. Nevertheless, I am arguing that there has been a consensus in the tradition itself concerning the treatment of racial/ethnic groups, women, and the issue of homosexuality. Some particular denominations may have moved away from some of the traditional perspectives presented here, but the positions described here are still upheld as the historical and authoritative ones by conservative ecclesiastical bodies.

vention methods that traditional Christian churches have advocated are to abstain from sex until married, to be faithful in marriage, and, if those fail, to use a condom—an approach that is commonly known as "ABC." Yet, from a different mode of inquiry, one that is grounded in the epidemiological patterns of HIV infections, it is clear that those who are disproportionately impacted are also those who are marginalized in society.

For example, the medical doctor Paul Farmer finds that disease prevalence is related to social, political, and economic inequities such as poverty and gender disparities. He bases his findings on his extensive work with poor populations in Haiti and other countries (2001, 59–93; 2005).[5] He refers to those inequities as "structural violence," and that violence is directly related to disease prevalence (Farmer, Connors, and Simmons 2011). Applying Farmer's analysis to the HIV patterns in the United States, then, we could expect that the disproportionate infection rates for African Americans, women, and the gay community are related to social, political, and economic inequalities (structural violence). Consequently, I suggest that the church consider the impact of these inequalities when developing its stances on HIV and AIDS.

Farmer's concept of structural violence is related to another theoretical framework that was developed by the Norwegian theorist, Johan Galtung. Although Galtung is himself associated with the field of peace and conflict studies, his research applies to the broader range of human dynamics (1969). Galtung's foundational question was why permanent peace could not be achieved. He recognized that nations can attain peace but that eventually another conflict seems to be inevitable. As shown in the diagram on the following page, he maintained that visible conflict, such as war (direct violence), was just the end result of invisible cultural and structural violence (2004). In other words, even when direct violence (war) does not exist, the harmful attitudes (cultural violence) and social-economic processes (structural violence) that fuel conflict remain. It stands to reason, then, that permanent peace will only be achieved when the underlying harmful cultural and structural patterns are eliminated.

Galtung's analysis is helpful, because it provides the theoretical basis for Farmer's work on disease prevalence. Putting the work of the two scholars together means that the existence of high HIV and AIDS rates

---

5. For more on the work of Paul Farmer, visit the Partners in Health website at www.pih.org.

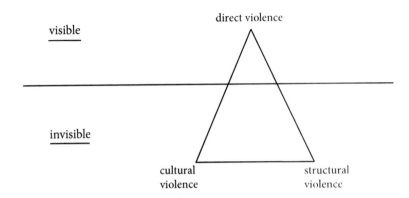

can be regarded as the visible harm (direct violence) caused by invisible and inequitable cultural and structural patterns (cultural and structural violence). It stands to reason that we will not be able to lower these high rates without addressing the underlying inequalities that fuel the situation.

According to Galtung (1990, 291), "cultural violence" refers to "those aspects of culture, the symbolic sphere of our existence—exemplified by religion and ideology, language and art, empirical science and formal science (logic and mathematics)—that are used to justify or legitimize direct or structural violence." In other words, if religious values foster inequities, they become part of the cultural violence that justifies social and economic inequities (structural violence), and, collectively, they legitimize actual harm (direct violence). As a result, understanding cultural violence must become a Christian responsibility in the age of HIV and AIDS. The pandemic challenges both traditional practices of the church and scholarly methods of biblical interpretation to transform religious doctrines and biblical hermeneutics so that they do not privilege anymore the *mythical norm*, that is, the perspective of the privileged, white, male, and heterosexual person. This essay outlines the serious needs for implementing such changes in a discussion on Galtung's theory of violence and in an analysis of exegetical approaches to two biblical narratives, Gen 19 and Judg 19.

The Church and Patterns of Inequity: Applying Galtung's Theory of Violence

We can see how Galtung's theory works by considering the church's traditional stance on women. The church has traditionally held that women need to be subordinate to men in the home (men are to be the heads of their households) and in the church (by discouraging or banning the ordination of women), thereby advocating an inequitable relationship between men and women. In Galtung's terminology, the ecclesial position that women should be subordinate to men justifies women being paid less than men for equal work in the marketplace (structural violence). Both of these forms of violence have contributed to women being economically and socially dependent on men. Such dependence becomes especially problematic in the context of HIV and AIDS, because the wife's dependent status means that she is unable to negotiate safer sex practices at home, even when she is aware of his infidelity. Therefore, marriage is a risk factor for women globally. For example, in sub-Saharan Africa, more women than men are HIV positive. Ultimately, then, women experience harm in the form of higher rates of HIV infections (direct violence) that is the result of both cultural and structural violence.

Furthermore, some Christian churches have privileged European Americans (whites) over African Americans (blacks) by condoning slavery and limiting the full participation of black people in the life of the church and its leadership (cultural violence).[6] That privileging of whites serves to justify our current disparate sentencing laws. These laws place heavier penalties on the use and possession of drugs used by African Americans (crack cocaine) than on those drugs used by whites (powder cocaine) (structural violence). As a result, there is a higher incarceration rate for African Americans, which in turn is associated with higher HIV infection rates (direct violence).

The dynamics of Galtung's theory also work concerning the gay and transgender community. Because the church promotes compulsory heterosexuality, heterosexuals are privileged over homosexuals (cultural violence), and such privileging justifies the acceptance of laws that deprive these persons of legal protections concerning housing, employment, or their committed relationships (structural violence). Consequently, many LGBTQ persons have greater difficulties in meeting their basic needs, and sometimes in order to survive they engage in high risk behavior such as drug trafficking and sex work. Because high risk behavior increases the

---

6. I have in mind the incidents leading up to the founding of the African Methodist Episcopal and the African Methodist Episcopal Zion churches but the effects linger. See, e.g., Brooten 2010.

likelihood of HIV infection, rates are correspondingly higher in this community (direct violence).

Stated succinctly, the premise of this essay is that inequitable Christian practices are part of the cultural attitudes concerning women, racial and ethnic others, and the gay community that contribute to social, legal, and economic inequities against them (structural violence). Both of these dynamics have allowed HIV (direct violence) to thrive in these groups. Thus Galtung's theory is especially helpful in two ways. First, his theory allows us to see HIV infections as the result of broader institutionalized dynamics and not just as individual behavior. Second, his theory forces us, as people of faith, to examine our policies and practices of privileging one group over another. For it is such privileging that creates inequities of dominant over subordinate, and we know that the subordinate group ultimately will become more susceptible to disease. Consequently, as Christians, we must face how we contribute to the construction of "isms"—racism, sexism, and heterosexism.[7] Such constructions privilege whites over racial/ethnic groups (racism), men over women (sexism), and heterosexuals over homosexuals (heterosexism). Such privileging is harmful, because it creates dominant and subordinate distinctions (cultural violence) that translate into broader social dynamics (structural violence), and these dynamics lead to high HIV rates in these groups (direct violence), as seen in the statistics above.

It is not hard to make the connection between the various "isms" and the doctrines and practices of traditional Christianity. I argue elsewhere that there is a *mythical norm* that reflects the perspectives and realities of the affluent white, heterosexual male, and that this norm has become equated with what is considered "*the* Christian tradition" (Anderson 2009, 3–29; see also Lorde 1984). There are two important implications of the mythical norm for this study. First, such a norm automatically constructs distinctions between the dominant group and others: those who are not white (black), not heterosexual (homosexual), and not male (female). Furthermore, because those who reflect the attitudes of the mythical norm hold a privileged position, those who are "Other" necessarily hold a subordinate position in society. Since we know that dominant/subordinate hierarchies are related to cultural and structural inequalities and that these

---

7. For the sake of brevity, the term "homosexuality" is used in this study, but it is used as a comprehensive term that covers the range of gender identities and sexual orientations beyond the traditional man/woman and heterosexual/homosexual binaries.

inequalities contribute to higher HIV infection rates, we should expect that the "other" groups (African Americans, women, and the gay community) would be disproportionately impacted by the virus. And they are. The problem, however, is that these marginalized groups, disproportionately affected by the disease, are not the ones determining *the* Christian approach to HIV prevention. Individuals and institutions representing the mythical norm do. As a result, HIV infections continue to occur without an effective and compassionate response from the church.

The second implication of the mythical norm is that this norm determines not only what constitutes Christian traditions and practices. It also determines the meaning of biblical texts, especially those concerning women, homosexuals, and non-Israelites (other racial/ethnic groups). I contend that using the mythical norm as a point of reference helps us to see how readings of biblical texts reinscribe the "isms" of racism, sexism, and heterosexism. In the following section, we will see how Gen 19 and Judg 19 have been interpreted to reinforce patterns that, whether obviously or not, privilege some (white, heterosexual males) over "Others."

Two Narratives Involving Sexuality, Gender, and Race/Ethnicity: Genesis 19 and Judges 19

Before analyzing the two biblical stories, I will briefly summarize them both. In Gen 19:1–11, Lot lives in Sodom, and he invites two divine men (angels) to stay at his home for the night before they continue their journey the next morning. At first the men object, but Lot insists, and eventually they go to his home. That evening Lot serves a feast, and they eat. Before Lot and his guests lie down for the night, the men of Sodom, both young and old, surround the house. They question Lot about the men who arrived, saying, "Bring them out to us, so that we may know them" (Gen 19:5).[8] Lot begs them to not "act so wickedly," and he offers instead his two young daughters "to do with them as you please." The crowd rejects the offer and is about to "deal worse with Lot" than with the strangers, when the two guests pull Lot inside the house, shut the door, and strike with blindness the men who are outside.

Although the women are spared in Gen 19, the woman is not spared in the other story. In Judg 19:1–31, a Levite living in Ephraim has a

---

8. Unless otherwise noted, all biblical quotations are from the NRSV.

concubine (secondary wife) who is from Bethlehem in Judah. For some reason, she leaves the Levite and returns to her father in Bethlehem. There is some scholarly speculation as to why the concubine left. On the one hand, J. Cheryl Exum (1993, 176–84) sees an implication that the secondary wife was somehow unfaithful ("she whored against" the Levite), but in the patrilocal marriage of that time, it could just mean that she dared to leave her husband. On the other hand, Pamela Tamar-kin Reis (2006, 129) argues that the concubine left, because "she whored for" the Levite, meaning that he was prostituting her.

Four months after the concubine left, the Levite goes to Bethlehem "to speak tenderly to her and bring her back" (Judg 19:3). During the visit, the concubine's father and the Levite eat and drink, and, when he wants to return home, the father insists that the Levite remain day after day. Finally, the Levite and the concubine leave on the evening of the fifth day. As it grows dark, they are near Jebus (Jerusalem), but the Levite refuses to sleep in a town of foreigners. He prefers to continue on to Gibeah or Ramah, towns that are within Israelite territory. When they reach Gibeah, the sun is setting, but no one offers them hospitality. Finally, an old man, who set-tled in Gibeah but is originally from Ephraim, speaks with the Levite and invites him and those with him to stay in his home. While the Levite and his host are enjoying themselves with food and drink, the men of the city, "a perverse lot," surround the house and demand that the Levite be sent out so that they "may have intercourse with him" (Judg 19:23). The old man responds, "No, my brothers, do not do this vile thing," and he offers his young daughter and the concubine instead, saying: "Ravish them and do whatever you want to them, but against this man do not do such a vile thing" (Judg 19:24). The crowd refuses to listen, and the Levite seizes his concubine and puts her out with them. The men "wantonly rape her and abuse her all through the night until morning," and as dawn is breaking, they let her go. She falls down at the door of the house, and the Levite finds her there in the morning, "with her hands on the threshold" (Judg 19:27).

There are obvious reasons for considering these two texts together: both involve hosts who are resident aliens in a town and take in two male strangers (Gen 19) or one male stranger (Judg 19). Townsmen who demand to have sex with the stranger surround the homes of the hosts, but the hosts refuse to turn their guests over to the crowds. Similarly, both hosts offer their daughters instead of the male guest. This essay uses the two narratives to show that even academic interpretations privilege those who fit the mythical norm and, correspondingly, marginalize those who do not. Rather than being a comprehensive analysis of scholarly work on these stories, this essay will demonstrate how patterns of biblical interpretation have contributed to the marginalization of racial/ethnic groups, women, and the gay community.

Traditionally, Gen 19 and Judg 19 have been interpreted to condemn homosexuality. In fact, the terms "sodomy" and a "Sodomite" for male same-sex activity are based on the Gen 19 narrative, and the condemnation of such activity is thought to be supported by the divine destruction of Sodom and Gomorrah (Gen 19:12–29). Consequently, some interpreters have seen a connection between sexual sin and punishment (Dawson 2007, 147). From this perspective, both stories share key elements. For instance, the men who want to have sex with the male visitor are characterized as "a perverse lot" (Judg 19:22), and, in both narratives, the host begs the men "not to act so wickedly" (Gen 19:7 and Judg 19:23). Such an interpretative emphasis is also supported with references to biblical laws such as in Lev 18:22 and 20:13, which refer to same-sex relationships, and Rom 1:1–18 which refers to same-sex relationships as "unnatural." Furthermore, interpretations from this perspective have maintained that "marriage between a man and woman is the normative form for human sexual fulfillment, and homosexuality is one among many tragic signs that we are a broken people, alienated from God's loving purpose" (Hays 2003, 82). Clearly, such interpretations affirm heterosexuality and condemn homosexuality. As a result, they privilege heterosexuality over homosexuality (heterosexism).

There is still another reading of Gen 19 and Judg 19 that does not support heterosexism, but it remains problematic for a different reason. This reading contends that homosexuality is not the subject of these stories for two reasons. First, both narratives condemn the violent act of gang rape and could not have referred to homosexuality as an orientation, because that understanding did not exist until the modern era (the nineteenth century) (Jordan, 1997; Halpern, 1990). Second, these interpreters point out that, if the guests were harmed, the hosts would be forced to violate ancient cultural norms of hospitality, as mentioned in Matt 10:11–15 and Luke 10:10–12. Finally, these interpreters explain that the gender paradigm in antiquity required men to always be dominant. Thus, they stress that since male-male relationships meant that one man was penetrated and so became subordinate (the female position) to his male partner, such subordination was considered to be "unnatural" for males (Brawley 1996; Rogers 2009). Such a reading, then, does not support using these texts to condemn homosexuality as an orientation in today's context.

As stated previously, my purpose here is not to provide a comprehensive analysis of these two narratives, and neither is it to determine which one is the stronger argument on the issue of homosexuality. Instead, I want to show why both of these interpretations are problematic, especially in regard to the treatment of women. Whether focusing on the condemnation of homosexuality or the significance of hospitality, both interpretations ignore the reprehensible treatment of women in these texts.

It seems obvious that the biblical narratives suggest that it is better to rape a woman than a man. Both hosts, striving to protect their male guests from harm, offer women to the crowd outside the house even when those women are their own daughters. Furthermore, biblical laws can be construed to support this assertion: if two men have sexual intercourse, the penalty is death (Lev 20:13), but if a man has sexual intercourse with an unmarried virgin, the penalty is simply that he can pay a fine and marry her (Exod 22:16–17 and Deut 22:28–29). The necessary conclusions have to be that biblical hospitality offers no protection to women and that a woman's body should be subject to male control.[9] Although their analyses of homosexuality may be different, both interpretations seem to agree (if only by silence) that women should be subordinate to men. As a result, these readings of Gen 19 and Judg 19 privilege men over women (sexism), albeit unintentionally, and therefore make sexism part of the religious values that shape cultural violence.

A third way of interpreting the problem in Gen 19 and Judg 19 focuses on the tribal/ethnic differences in the narratives. In Gen 19, Lot is related to Abraham (Gen 11:27, 31). He is therefore an Israelite and a resident alien (ger) in Sodom. Similarly, in Judg 19, the old man who invites the Levite is from Ephraim, living in Gibeah, the territory of the Benjami-

---

9. More helpful readings concerning women have been proposed. For instance, Toesing (2000, 69) notes that "women, children, and the environment were the collateral damage in the war to root out the wickedness of men." Similarly, Reis (2006) suggests that Judg 19 is not about hospitality but demonstrates the negative consequences of Israelite males failing to protect the women in their care. From my vantage point, the significance of these two readings of Gen 19 and Judg 19 is that they question how women are treated in the texts, thereby addressing a gap of the usual readings.

nites (Judg 19:16). Taking these differences into account, the argument has been made that the offering of hospitality by resident aliens was a cultural offense that triggered the hostility of the townsmen. More specifically, some interpreters maintain that the offer was perhaps an offense to the residents, because the hosts, as resident aliens, offered hospitality instead of the citizens of the respective towns (Sodom and Gibeah) who should have offered it. Consequently, the townsmen were dishonored (Matthews 1992; Boswell 1980).[10]

Another possible explanation is that the townsmen tried to challenge Lot's honor as a lowly resident alien by dishonoring him or his guests with a same-sex rape. Apparently, the gender logic of this approach is that if the townsmen rape the host or his male guests, the raped males will be forced into the "feminized," that is, the subordinate position. This position then would affirm the dominant status of the townsmen. Similarly, the townsmen in Judg 19 are willing to rape the Levite's concubine, because, by violating a woman who is associated with him, the Levite is dishonored indirectly (Stone 1995; Carden 1999).

Still another approach to Gen 19 acknowledges that the men of Sodom wanted to humiliate Lot and the strangers by gang rape. Yet this acknowledgement also asserts that the attempt to gang rape the male visitors would "unlawfully seek to punish men who have done them no harm." Consequently, this approach to Gen 19 describes the men of Sodom as "barbarians" and "without human moral worth."

> The men of Sodom show themselves to be outside of civilization—they are barbarians who know no shame. In a culture in which honor is the highest value, the Sodomites are the antitype of human moral worth. (Hendel 2010, 84)

The labeling of a group as "barbarian" and without "human moral worth" sounds familiar. Randall Bailey (1995) suggests that the labeling of a group as sexually deviant is one of the strategies used to distinguish the Israelites from their ancient Near Eastern neighbors. The problem with

---

10. A slightly different, but related, interpretation is that when the townsmen ask "to know" the visitors in Gen 19, the phrase is understood to simply express a desire to become acquainted with the visitors and to be assured that the visitors are not a threat. See Morschauser (2003); Pirson (2012). Such a reading, however, is not widely followed.

such a strategy, he writes, is that it dehumanizes those who are depicted as having practiced sexual taboos, and, once that is done, "other acts of Israelite oppression or devaluation of these people are readily sanctioned, condoned, and accepted by the reader, both ancient and modern" (137). Applying Bailey's assessment, we have to consider who the townspeople were (Sodomites and Benjaminites) and why there may be an interest in depicting them as sexually deviant. A possible rationale for the depiction in Gen 19, for instance, might be that Sodom and Gomorrah are in Canaan, the land that the Israelites sought to occupy (Lyons 2009). Similarly, the book of Judges has a narrative thesis that underscores the need for a king by pointing out the increasing chaos that results from having everybody "do what is right in his own eyes" (e.g., Judg 21:25). Yet, overall, Judges is part of the Deuteronomistic History (DtrH), which is associated with the Davidic monarchy. This fact may explain why Gibeah and the Benjaminites are portrayed unfavorably. Redactors in the DtrH tradition supported the establishment and continuation of the monarchy but not with a king from among the Benjaminites. Given that Saul, the first king, is a Benjaminite (1 Sam 9:1), there may be at play a subtle devaluing of Saul and his legacy, in favor of David. Yet none of the previous interpretive possibilities explore *why* the townspeople might be viewed negatively, and so they leave sexual labeling as a dynamic without critical exploration.

If the dynamic of sexual labeling remains unexamined, it can also be used against other groups. Bailey, an African American, contributes significantly to this understanding when he connects negative sexual stereotyping in biblical texts with the negative sexual stereotyping of the African American community. He states: "As a member of the Black African diaspora, I have lived my life as an outsider in a society that has used sexual stereotyping as a means of sanctioning its racist practices in oppressing my people" (1995, 124). In other words, biblical texts can be and have been used to privilege one group over another. Although the Israelites are represented as the privileged group in the biblical texts, in the contemporary era, European Americans have arrogated that privilege to themselves. As a result, differences that were ethnic or tribal in Gen 19 and Judg 19 have been used to support racial and ethnic differences today. Accordingly, the biblical stories provide the framework for racial and ethnic hierarchies (racism) that have been used to advance notions of white superiority over other racial and ethnic groups. In such cases, religious values foster inequities that contribute to cultural violence and are related to structural and direct violence.

Conclusion

Without a doubt, the HIV/AIDS pandemic presents serious challenges to both traditional practices of the church and scholarly methods of biblical interpretation. Church leaders need to understand that HIV infections are the result of individual behavior, but that behavior is shaped by socio-economic realities. Furthermore, according to Galtung's theory, those realities are marked by inequalities of race/ethnicity, gender, and sexual orientation that the church, with its traditional doctrines, has helped to create. Consequently, the church has undermined the effectiveness of its approach to HIV prevention: to abstain, to be faithful, and, as a last resort, to use a condom ("ABC"). Women who are subordinate to men do not control their own bodies, and, given the prevalence of rape in our culture, they cannot always abstain from sex. Similarly, the church condemns homosexuality and often refuses to observe marriage equality, even in the states where it exists. Therefore, same-sex couples are not given the opportunity to be faithful in marriage. Finally, churches do not usually support condom use, whether for the purpose of contraception or HIV prevention. As a result, the church not only contributes to the very inequities that make infections more likely, but it also condemns one of the truly effective prevention methods that would make infections less likely.

On the whole, the HIV/AIDS pandemic challenges the church to reconsider its adherence to the mythical norm—privileged, white, male, and heterosexual—for its doctrinal standards. In a context in which those who are disproportionately affected by HIV are not white, not male, not heterosexual, and not rich, there is a stark discrepancy between those who develop doctrinal standards and those who are affected by them. We need to acknowledge that God's people represent a broad range of humanity, with different perspectives and different realities, and that God's love extends to all of them. The divine desire for human flourishing is not limited to those who fit the mythical norm.

As for biblical scholars, the HIV and AIDS pandemic challenges us in two ways. First, as shown earlier, scholarly treatments of Gen 19 and Judg 19 have reinforced the mythical norm, whether intentionally or unintentionally. By condemning homosexuality or by not raising questions about the treatment of women and the racial and ethnic Other, many interpretations reinforce the traditional stance that is white, male, and heterosexual. Consequently, the pandemic forces the recognition that scholarly inquiry is not as objective as we once thought. Second, by reinforcing the mythical norm, biblical readings also reinforce cultural inequalities (cultural violence) that justify social and economic inequalities (structural violence), and, subsequently, they result in high infection rates for certain groups (direct violence). In other words, biblical interpretations have direct consequences, and those consequences can be harmful. Thus interpreters must consider how their readings of biblical texts contribute to the conditions that result in the direct violence of over 50,000 new HIV infections in the United States each year.

Works Cited

Anderson, Cheryl B. 2009. *Ancient Laws and Contemporary Controversies: The Need for Inclusive Biblical Interpretation*. New York: Oxford University Press.

Bailey, Randall C. 1995. "They're Nothing but Incestuous Bastards: The Polemical Use of Sex and Sexuality in Hebrew Canon Narratives." Pages 121–38 in vol. 1 of *Reading from This Place*. Edited by Fernando F. Segovia and Mary Ann Tolbert. Minneapolis: Fortress.

Boswell, John. 1980. *Christianity Social Tolerance, and Homosexuality: Gay People in Western Europe from the Beginning of the Christian Era to the Fourteenth Century*. Chicago: Chicago University Press.

Brawley, Robert L., ed. 1996. *Biblical Ethics and Homosexuality: Listening to Scripture*. Louisville: Westminster John Knox.

Brooten, Bernadette J. 2010. *Beyond Slavery: Overcoming Its Religious and Sexual Legacies*. New York: Palgrave Macmillan.

Carden, Michael. 1999. "Homophobia and Rape in Sodom and Gibeah: A Response to Ken Stone." *JSOT* 82:83–96.

Center for Disease Control and Prevention. n.d. "HIV among Gay and Bisexual Men." CDC.gov. http://www.cdc.gov/hiv/group/msm/index.html.

Dawson, Richard M. 2007. *Flame of Yahweh: Sexuality in the Old Testament*. Peabody, MA: Hendrickson.

Exum, Cheryl. 1993. *Fragmented Women: Feminist (Sub)versions of Biblical Narratives*. Valley Forge: Trinity Press International.

Farmer, Paul. 2001. *Infections and Inequalities: The Modern Plagues*. Berkeley: University of California Press.

———. 2005. *Pathologies of Power: Health, Human Rights, and the New War on the Poor*. Berkeley: University of California Press.

Farmer, Paul, Margaret Connors, and Janie Simmons, eds. 2011. *Women, Poverty, and AIDS: Sex, Drugs and Structural Violence.* Monroe, ME: Common Courage Press.

Galtung, Johan. 1969. "Violence, Peace, and Peace Research." *Journal of Peace Research* 6:167–91.

———. 1990. "Cultural Violence." *Journal of Peace Research* 27:291–305.

———. 2004. *Violence, War, and the Impact on Visible and Invisible Effects of Violence.* Polylog: Forum for Intercultural Philosophy. www.them. polylog/5/fgj.en.htm.

Halpern, David. 1990. *One Hundred Years of Homosexuality and Other Essays on Greek Love.* New York: Routledge.

Hays, Richard B. 2003. "The Biblical Witness Concerning Homosexuality." Pages 65–84 in *Staying the Course: Supporting the Church's Position on Homosexuality.* Edited by Maxie D. Dunnam and H. Newton Malony. Nashville: Abingdon.

Hendel, Ronald S., Chana Kronfeld, and Ilana Pardes. 2010. "Gender and Sexuality." Pages 71–91 in *Reading Genesis: Ten Methods.* Edited by Ronald S. Hendel. New York: Cambridge University Press.

Jordan, Mark D. 1997. *The Invention of Sodomy in Christian Theology.* Chicago: Chicago University Press.

Lorde, Audre. 1984. "Age, Race, Class, Sex: Women Redefining Difference." Pages 114–23 in *Sister Outsider.* Freedom, CA: Crossing Press.

Lyons, William John. 2009. "Sodom, Sodomite." Pages 313–14 in vol. 5 of *New Interpreter's Dictionary of the Bible.* Edited by Katherine Doob Sakenfeld. 5 vols. Nashville: Abingdon, 2006–2009.

Matthews, Victor H. 1992. "Hospitality and Hostility in Genesis 19 and Judges 19." *BTB* 22:3–11.

Morschauser, Scott. 2003. "Hospitality, Hostiles, and Hostages: On the Legal Background to Genesis 19:1–9." *JSOT* 27:461–85.

Pirson, Ron. 2012. "Does Lot Know about *Yada*?" Pages 203–13 in *Universalism and Particularism at Sodom and Gomorrah: Essays in Memory of Ron Pirson.* Edited by Diana Lipton. Atlanta: Society of Biblical Literature.

Reis, Pamela Tamarkin. 2006. "The Levite's Concubine: New Light on a Dark Story." *SJOT* 20:125–46.

Rogers, Jack. 2009. *Jesus, the Bible, and Homosexuality: Explode the Myths, Heal the Church.* Louisville: Westminster John Knox.

Stone, Ken. 1995. "Gender and Homosexuality in Judges 19: Subject-Honor, Object-Shame." *JSOT* 67:87–107.

Toensing, Holly. 2005. "Women of Sodom and Gomorrah: Collateral Damage in the War against Homosexuality." *JFSR* 21:61–74.

How to Read the Bible in the Belly of the Beast: About the Politics of Biblical Hermeneutics within the United States of America

Susanne Scholz

Resumen: Este ensayo nos muestra como la violencia experimentada en los Estados Unidos gran parte de la población—mujeres, hombres y niños-es ayudada y promovida por la hermenéutica bíblica dominante. Esto se ve reforzado porque la principal corriente de investigación bíblica que se utiliza en los Estados Unidos no establece la relación con la violencia interna en la sociedad; no solo no habla de ello sino que en ocasiones la avala. En realidad, esta investigación está sostenida por métodos exegéticos y estrategias de lectura que alejan el sentido de la Biblia de las diversas formas de violencia que abundan, sean estas la pobreza, la condena a muerte, la violencia policial o la violencia sexual. La pregunta es cómo esta complicidad exegética con las actuales formas de violencia ha venido a ser tan ampliamente aceptada en los Estados Unidos. Este ensayo presenta la discusión sobre el contexto cultural e histórico de la principal corriente de exégesis y su confianza en principios hermenéuticos que aunque aspiran a la objetividad, universalidad y a la neutralidad, es cómplice de la sociedad violenta. El ensayo también ilustra la complicidad exegética al examinar una selección de interpretaciones actuales de Jueces 21 elaboradas en Estados Unidos; de ese modo se identifican tres principales estrategias de lectura en diversos comentarios bíblicos. Al finalizar, el ensayo considera los desafíos de lo político para la hermenéutica bíblica en los Estados Unidos a través de proponer una sociología de la hermenéutica bíblica como un camino de resistencia a la violencia en este país.

The contemporary United States of America is a violent society, not only historically as a former slave society or politically as a past and present warring nation in the world, but also internally toward its own citizens.

Deeply entrenched in neoliberal, technocratic, and market-driven notions about the public good, this society allows economically challenged citizens and noncitizens to experience staggering violence in their lives. Economically cushioned citizens and the wealthy echelon of United States society barely know about the extent of this violence because of their marginal contact with poor and economically struggling people in their country. Many systemic societal structures facilitate the class-segregated way of life. The popularity of gated communities, the difference between private and public schooling, the considerable geographical distances to be bridged between impoverished and well-to-do neighborhoods in urban and rural towns, cities, and communities, and the general absence of public spaces reinforce the clustering of people of the same background.

The situation is topped by the "American Dream," a culturally ingrained notion about social mobility in the United States. Since social mobility is believed to be merit-based, a person's economic prosperity is understood to be independent of social class or circumstance of birth. The American Dream ideology legitimizes profound economic disparities in a country in which almost 30 percent of US-American children live in households with an income below 60 percent of the national median income of $31,000 annually (Ingraham 2014). Or to put it differently, according to the United States Census Bureau 45.3 million people lived in poverty in 2013. This means that 14.5 percent of the total population is officially recognized as poor ("Poverty" n.d.). To be counted as living in poverty, an adult person makes less than $11,490 or is part of a family of four making $23,550. Single mothers struggle the most; one third or 15.6 million of such households are classified as poor. This number is even worse for black single mothers; 42.5 percent of them live in poverty (Gongloff 2014). In other words, poverty is highly gendered and racialized while the American Dream ideology regards sociopolitical, economic, and cultural structures as insignificant for social mobility. It blames economic distress on an individual's unwillingness to work hard.

Violence is, of course, not limited to class issues. Importantly, the United States has the largest number of prisoners when compared to any other developed country. Nicole Flatow (2014) reports that "more than 1.57 million inmates sat behind bars in federal, state, and county prisons and jails around the country as of December 31, 2013." Or, as CNN states, 6.9 million Americans are in prison, on parole, or on probation. If the correctional system were counted as a city, it would constitute the second largest in the United States after New York, a fact that outrages even conservative politicians like Newt Gingrich who are usually in favor of the "law and order" approach (Gingrich and Van Jones 2014). In addition, the prolific and disproportionate use of the death penalty against poor people and members of racial and ethnic communities in the United States adds lethal violence into the mix (for details, see "Know the Facts about Capital Punishment," n.d.). Increasing militarization of the US-American police force across the country has escalated even further the violence inflicted upon the population. As Frances Weaver (2014) reports, "many small-town police departments now boast the same weaponry once wielded by United States military units in Afghanistan—including tanks with 360-degree rotating turrets, battering rams, and automatic weapons. Those weapons are today deployed against Americans suspected of crimes in their own homes." Mixed with racism and classism, police brutality is mostly experienced in racially and economically challenged communities, as the police murder rate of black unarmed men in Ferguson, Cleveland, New York, and other cities demonstrates (see, e.g., Juzwiak and Chan 2014). Simultaneously, the so-called middle class has been disappearing since the 1970s (Lazonick 2013; Dorfman 2014). Unquestionably, the US-American population experiences a formidable extent of violence today.

I posit that the internal violence experienced by so many people—women, men, and children—is aided and abetted by the biblical hermeneutics dominantly practiced in the United States. Mainstream Bible scholarship does not make connections to internal US-American violence; it is silent about it, sometimes even endorsing it. In fact, it is grounded in exegetical methods and reading strategies that distance biblical meanings from the various forms of violence plaguing the country, be it poverty, the death penalty, police brutality, or sexual violence. The resulting complicity with violence within US-American society instructs the public that the Bible, correctly read, is removed from the hurt, suffering, and pain in people's lives. When Bible interpreters engage with contemporary forms of violence, their work is seen as less erudite, academic, and authoritative than readings that distance contemporary concerns from the exegetical task.

The question is how this exegetical complicity with contemporary forms of violence has become so widely acceptable in the United States. This essay offers answers to this question in several sections. It features a discussion on the historical-cultural background of mainstream US-American exegesis and its reliance on hermeneutical principles aspiring to objectivity, universality, and value-neutrality of meaning that are complicit with violence in US-American society. The essay also illustrates the exegetical complicity by examining selected contemporary US-American interpretations of Judg 21; it identifies and elaborates on three reading strategies found in the commentary literature. Finally, the essay proposes a sociology of biblical hermeneutics as a way to read the Bible in resistance to the violence in the United States.

About Mainstream Bible Exegesis and Violence within the United States

If one were to ask well-meaning persons living in the United States about the Bible and its meaning, many would respond that the primary purpose of the Bible is to strengthen and nurture one's Christian or Jewish faith. They would also explain that the Bible is meant to be related to one's personal life as it can help those believing in the Bible to lead better lives and to deal with life's challenges in accordance with God's will. They might also add that biblical texts are historical documents from a distant past, although not everything mentioned in the Bible is historically accurate. Most likely, such persons combine a "PPS" hermeneutic with a historical hermeneutic. The former is a reading strategy that seeks to identify personal, private, and sentimentalized meanings in the Bible whereas the latter usually advances simplified versions of historical criticism. It subscribes to the idea that the Bible was written by people of a distant past and that it is the task of interpreters to reconstruct the Bible's original meaning as its human authors intended it to be understood. In both cases, the reading of the Bible is unrelated to worldly affairs and kept apart from larger sociopolitical, economic, cultural, and religious considerations about society.

The renowned biblical scholar Elisabeth Schüssler Fiorenza has written much about biblical hermeneutics. For instance, she classifies the two just mentioned approaches as belonging to the religious-theological-scriptural and the critical-scientific-modern paradigms. In her view, the former paradigm "obscures the power relations and interests at work in biblical texts and interpretations" (2009, 66) as it finds truth in literal readings of the Bible. People reading within this paradigm often assert the Bible's inerrancy, believing that God's word is directly accessible in the Bible. In contrast, the critical-scientific-modern paradigm has developed in the European context of the Protestant Reformation, the Renaissance, and the so-called Enlightenment as a challenge to ecclesial control and authority. It subscribes to a scientific-positivist epistemology that demands objectivity, disinterestedness, and value-neutrality "in order to control what constitutes the legitimate, scientifically established, true meaning of a text." The adherence to these proclaimed standards makes this paradigm "patently *kyriocentric* and *Eurocentric*" (68); it is based on an interpretive positivism also favored by literalist biblicism. Both marginalize or even eliminate "discourses and struggles for justice, radical equality, and the well-being of all" (2007, 243). They are grounded in confessional, individualistic piety or in the antiquarian notion of the "hard sciences" that promote biblical exegesis as a linguistic, technical, and antiquarian enterprise.

Schüssler Fiorenza also explains that, as an academic field, biblical studies developed from "religion" to "science." By this she means that since the eighteenth century biblical exegesis, emerging like other scientific fields, has contributed to the hegemonic-academic legitimization of structures of domination, including sexism, racism, heterosexism, colonialism, nationalism, class privilege, ableism, and ageism. In other words, the field of biblical studies has successfully communicated an ethics of interpretation that socializes readers "into the ethos of 'pure,' value-detached, positivistic scientism" (1999, 198). Since this ethos is also characteristic of the literalist-pietistic reading strategy, readers value, often unconsciously, "the ethos of empire: submission, violence, and exclusion" (2007, 6). This ethos stands in sharp contrast to what Schüssler Fiorenza calls "a scriptural ethos of radical democracy" (7). It advances a conceptualization of biblical studies as an academic enterprise within a democratic context; it evaluates "academic research, religious rhetoric, and public discourses as to their function in maintaining global exploitation, injustice, and violence" (27). Average readers, however, do not usually expect that such a critical-democratic positioning ought to be the driving motivation for their readings of the Bible. They are surprised when they hear that the Bible could and should be interpreted as a challenge to neoliberal, technocratic, and market-driven principles promoted in contemporary US-American society.

That the average Bible reader knows little about these hermeneutical distinctions is not only related to a general unfamiliarity with current Bible scholarship but also to important political-exegetical developments in the twentieth century. Among them is the fact that the academic field of biblical studies has its roots in German theological studies. Until perhaps thirty or forty years ago, most Bible scholars of non-German origins travelled to German theology departments to study with Bible professors there.[1] Many of them studied with the influential German professor in Old Testament Studies, Gerhard von Rad (1901–1971). This scholar's standing in the field remains undisputed. One year after the death of von Rad, in 1972, W. H. Schmidt published an article with a title that says it all: "Old Testament *before and after* Gerhard von Rad" [emphasis added] (1972, 1). In 1973, Rolf Rendtorff affirmed that von Rad's work constituted a major break, primarily due to the "decisive methodological breakthrough" (lit. *die grundlegende methodische Neuorientierung*) in the discipline of Old Testament studies (1973, 21).[2] In 1978, James L. Crenshaw also stated that von Rad's "influence has been keenly felt throughout the entire discipline of Old Testament studies. It would be difficult to find an Old Testament scholar anywhere who is not indebted to Gerhard von Rad in one way or another" (1978, 15).

All of them acknowledge the extraordinary significance of von Rad's work, but Rendtorff further specified the moment of von Rad's "decisive methodological breakthrough" (1973, 21). It occurred with the publication of "The Form-Critical Problem of the Hexateuch," first published in 1938. Rendtorff explained that von Rad had developed his ideas more fully "after the profound break [*tiefen Einschnitt*] of the Second World War." Thus, "the years from 1946 to 1953 constituted [von Rad's] most productive writing period in his career." Rendtorff expounded, "During these years he produced numerous studies with profound methodological considerations, in which he reflected upon and evaluated his works of earlier years methodologically and so developed the foundation for his scholarship forthcoming in the next decades" (27). In short, von Rad's work has long been recognized as influencing post-Holocaust Bible students and scholars, many from Germany and from across the globe. What is not usually acknowledged is the fact that von Rad laid the foundation for his research during the pinnacle of the Nazi era in 1938, the year of the *Reichspogramnacht*,[3] continuing to articulate his methodological views as soon as it became possible after World War II (Scholz 2010).

---

1. The center of academic learning is, of course, related to the fact that key ideas about the function of universities related to nineteenth-century notions about universities as articulated by German academics. For a brief discussion about the influence of German universities on American institutions of higher education in the late nineteenth century, see Stone 2015, 1–9, esp. 4–6.

2. This and the following quotes are my translation of the original German.

3. For historical explanation of *Reichsprogramnacht*, see, e.g., "Kristallnacht" n.d.

This fact is important because German Bible scholars, including Gerhard von Rad, have been not only the driving force but also staunch endorsers of historical criticism. They have promoted this method as the key for objective, universal, and value-neutral text analysis. Generally, historical critics pride themselves for avoiding the "traps" of context specificity, and, as producers of what they believe to be scientific exegesis, they regard their historical work as context-independent. Originally, this hallmark of historical criticism empowered scholars to challenge religious authorities. As a result, early historical critics were refused academic teaching positions, and some of them faced heresy trials at the end of the nineteenth century. During the Nazi era, the insistence on historical criticism as a context-free method also had political implications. Gerhard von Rad's methodological agenda withstood the contextualizing Nazi hermeneutics (see Weber 2000; Heschel 1994; Osten-Sacken 2002). His insistence on a context-free method enabled him to reject the contextualizing Nazi hermeneutics while standing in the epistemological tradition of German academia.

In a nutshell, then, von Rad's methodological choice represented an intellectual form of resistance to the Nazi regime. His historical-critical reading of the Hebrew Bible rejected the Nazi hermeneutics as nonscholarly propaganda and simultaneously proclaimed its loyalty to modern scientific epistemology. Von Rad's success over the Nazi hermeneutics generated the ongoing popularity of his work and of historical criticism. In fact, his hermeneutics proved so convincing to post-Holocaust biblical studies that the context-free study of the Bible, grounded in historical criticism, has become the norm ever since.

Yet the method's proclaimed disconnection from its interpretative context masks the fact that it, too, is a context-based approach. That is, historical criticism helped von Rad resist the political and ideological structures of domination prevalent within his 1930s and 1940s context. However, more than seventy years later, his approach is still largely employed without awareness of its intrinsic context-specificity. The epistemological ethnocentrism of historical criticism is still coined as epistemological universality although historical criticism's presumed a-contextuality is the very characteristic of the specific context from which it emerged. Von Rad did not elaborate on his reasons for using historical criticism as a (conscious or unconscious) strategy to reject Nazi-ideology, and his students and students of his students followed his approach without asking meta-level questions about the contextuality of their teacher's work. In fact, even today many historical critics still do not recognize the inherited German, white, male ethnocentrism that shapes their rejection of contextualized Bible interpretations.

The question arises how German biblical scholarship would look like if it took into account its positionality. This issue is not limited to the German-European context although it has already been discussed on the relative margins of biblical studies elsewhere, including in the United States (e.g., Boer and Segovia 2012; Felder 1989). If one considers the internal US-American violence as a context, the question then is how to read the Bible under conditions that neoliberal, technocratic, and market-driven notions have fostered in this society. One response seems clear. Von Rad's preference for historical criticism, as he developed it in resistance to the Nazi regime, cannot be simply transferred into another context of a later era. Different hermeneutical convictions than those advanced by historical critics, such as von Rad, are required to resist contemporary structures of domination within the United States. The current popularity of the antiquarian and a-contextualizing use of historical criticism suggests that this method does not offer an effective resistance strategy in today's United States. Rather, it fits right into the overall silent acquiescence to the pervasive US-American violence, as mainstream biblical scholarship accommodates structures of domination, sometimes even contributing to them.

The next section details how the US-American exegetical complicity excuses, overlooks, and excuses violence in women's lives in the United States. An analysis of selected commentaries of Judg 21 illustrates that interpreters rely on various hermeneutical arguments to minimize, marginalize, and ignore the violence in the narrative, in this case the experiences of the disappeared and sexually violated women from Jabesh-Gilead and Shiloh. The proclaimed ethos of value neutrality and positivistic scientism aligns comfortably with the depicted violence, foregoing any kind of protest or resistance to it.

Complicity with Sexual Violence in US-American Interpretations of Judges 21: A Selective Analysis

When US-American commentaries on Judg 21 are examined for their responses to the sexual violence mentioned in the biblical text, the interpretations turn into harmful and dangerous materials. Rarely if ever do they consider the perspective of the mass-abducted women of Jabesh-Gilead or Shiloh, and they do not reflect upon the women's family members, their mothers, fathers, sisters, brothers, or friends left behind. Instead, commentators read the biblical tale from the dominant perspective of the male characters, even when they criticize their violent actions. To the interpreters, the women are collateral damage in a situation already filled with gross violence, murder, and war.

The following analysis is limited to a sample of US-American commentaries on Judg 21 published since 2000.[4] The analysis suggests that the ethos of "pure," value-detached, positivistic scientism makes the selected interpretations complicit with situations of physical and sexual violence today. They read like bystander reports that passively support violence against women. In this sense, then, biblical interpretations and the institutions in which they are produced, taught, and studied, such as in churches and synagogues, seminaries, and departments of religious studies, indirectly endorse past and present abuse and killing of women and girls. By not opposing such violence in Judg 21, the commentaries argue as if they abided by the idea that biblical and contemporary women are expendable in cultures of violence.

Three reading strategies are prominent in contemporary commentaries on Judg 21, although not every strategy appears in every commentary. One of the reading strategies emphasizes the historical distance between the so-called biblical times and the contemporary era. Another strategy accepts the violence as a lesser evil to arrive at the larger good, which is the survival of the tribe of Benjamin, and a third strategy articulates various explanations that merely name the violence as rape, use anthropological concepts to minimize the violence, or address the dilemma of an absent God. It needs to be noted that contemporary interpretations of Judg 21 usually mention several strategies simultaneously, but at the same time they emphasize one strategy more than others.

Reading Strategy 1: A Historical Argument, or Abduction and Forced Marriage Was Okay Back Then

A popular reading strategy stresses the historical distance between the events in Judg 21 and the contemporary era. Interpreters explain that the narrative comes from a distant past filled with customs, habits, and conventions that conflict with contemporary notions about morality or jus-

---

4. For a survey on the interpretation history from antiquity to the twentieth century, see Gunn 2005, 243–75.

tice. For instance, John Goldingay (2011, 162) explains that "in reacting to what happens to the girls from Jabesh and from Shiloh, we do need to allow for some cultural differences," because, as he imagines it, "for all we know, the girls from Jabesh and Shiloh may have been happy ever after." Other commentators, too, pursue a historical argumentation to make sense of Judg 21. The series Understanding the Bible Commentary stands in this reading tradition as well. Accordingly, series editors Robert L. Hubbard Jr. and Robert K. Johnston explain that, "as an ancient document, the Old Testament often seems something quite foreign to modern men and women," but "the purpose of the commentary series is to help readers navigate this strange and sometimes forbidding literary and spiritual terrain" (2012, ix). In fact, the series aims "to break down the barriers between the ancient and modern worlds so that the power and meaning of these biblical texts become transparent to contemporary readers" (ix).

The question is how this interest in breaking down "the barrier between the old and modern worlds" plays out in the reading of Judg 21. The commentary's title on the biblical passage is short and simple: "§30 Israel Preserved Intact (Judg. 21:1–25)" (Harris, Brown, and Moore 2012, 402). In other words, J. Gordon Harris, Cheryl B. Brown, and Michael S. Moore find the story "bad" (402), but they assure us that eventually "everyone lived happily ever after" (406). Thus, Harris, Brown, and Moore acknowledge that the solution in Judg 21 is "not kosher" (405), but it helps the male Benjaminites to live happily ever after. The commentators also clarify that the Benjaminites use two strategies to solve their predicament. The first "solution" requires them to "kill every male and every woman who is not a virgin" and "every woman who is a virgin (four hundred women) they take to the camp at Shiloh in Canaan" (404). Since the men do not reeive enough women, they pursue a second "solution [which] yielded them two hundred wives, just what was needed" (405). The phrase, "just what was needed," hints at the interpreters' reading perspective. They timidly approve that the men take only what they need, not more and not less; theirs is a measured action to survive the earlier blow. Merely reiterating the biblical tale, the three interpreters do not criticize the women's abduction or wonder about the women's or their relatives' situations. The silence about the women's fate suggests that they side with the violent men of Benjamin. After all, the title of their interpretation emphasizes that in the end Israel is "preserved intact."

Some hesitation, however, shines through the commentary when Harris, Brown, and Moore write about Judg 21:23: "Each man caught one [woman] and carried her off to be his wife: There is great irony here, because the Hb. expression for 'to marry' is 'to take a wife.' In this context, it takes on new meaning; for that is exactly what the Benjaminites were instructed to do" (2012, 287). It is not entirely clear what they mean by "great irony"[5] or "new meaning." Do they suggest that ancient Israelites did not usually equate marriage with abduction although here marriage is equated with abduction? Or do they excuse the male Benjaminites, because the men did what they were expected to do? In any case, the interpreters tell the story from the perspective of the male Benjaminites although they do not say so openly.

Another observation needs to be made as the commentary series claims to "break down barriers" between the past and the present but then fails to do so. For instance, the interpreters do not explain that the events depict what nowadays is classified as sex trafficking. They also do not show any outrage or concern for the women and their families, and they do not even explicitly oppose the abduction. Instead, they endorse the narrative's apparent goal to "preserve" Israel even though women are forced into marriages against their will. At best, then, it is unclear how this interpretation breaks down the gap between the "old" text and contemporary readers. It seems to rest comfortably in the ongoing silence about violence against women.

Reading Strategy 2: The Lesser of Two Evils, or the Abduction of Women Saves a Lost Tribe

The idea that this story is about a historically problematic moment of a distant past is also part of other commentaries. In some of them, however, another reading strategy is prominently featured. It has to do with the survival of the Benjaminite tribe that faces extinction if they do not find women for procreative purposes. Accordingly, Victor H. Matthews (2004, 198) maintains that "the narrative in Judg 21 is dominated by the dilemma of finding suitable wives for the 600 surviving Benjaminite warriors." He is also interested in making a historical-literary link between the mention of Jabesh-gilead in Judg 21 and Saul, who, as a war leader, relieves the siege of Jabesh-gilead by the Ammonites in 1 Sam 11:5–11. To Matthews,

---

5. Another commentator, Barry G. Webb (2012), stresses the "irony" in this tale (495, 505, 507) that "wrestles" with the problem of the tribe becoming "extinct" (405).

then, "the marriage between the surviving Benjaminites and the 400 virgins of the oath-breaking city of Jabesh-gilead are thus the ancestors of Saul's rejuvenated tribe" (199). In other words, Matthews insinuates that without the abduction of the women there would have not been King Saul. So the stakes are high, and the "novel legal loophole" devised by the Israelite elders provided a solution to the Benjaminite tribe, even if it was "callous" (199–200). It necessitated the women to be "so cavalierly and brutally treated." Although it led to the physical rape of the women and their families' financial loss, eventually "the tribes return home" after the problem is solved and the "battle lust deflated by these forced nuptials" (200). Women and families of Jabesh-gilead and Shiloh pay a heavy price, as Matthews emphasizes, but it also guarantees a future Benjaminite king over all of Israel.

Other commentators, too, emphasize the eventual benefit of murder, rape, and "marriage." Rob Fleenor and Mark S. Ziese (2008, 291) assert that the story is about the "Provision for the Lost Tribe (21:1–25)." They explain that the "ultimate disappearance" of the Benjaminite tribe is the central problem, and so in Judg 21, the Benjaminite men must find "wives for the survivors" (292). In other words, in this commentary the abduction of the women of Jabesh-Gilead and Shiloh turns into an unavoidable necessity as the men need wives for their procreative future. Interestingly, the commentators chastise the Israelites for having been "foolish" enough to vow not to marry their daughters to the men of Benjamin, as if, so the commentators note, these men were a "pagan group" (293). Without hesitation, then, Fleenor and Ziese side with the violent and warring men and justify this stance by blaming the other Israelites for a vow that characterizes marriage with the male Benjaminites as a "spiritual contamination" (293).

At the same time, Fleenor and Ziese also highlight that the Israelites only pretend to be concerned over "corruption" (293). After all, so they explain, the entire book of Judges describes corruption after corruption among the Israelite tribes, and so the other tribes are not much better than the Benjaminites. Fleenor and Ziese do not further explore the general Israelite corruption but proceed with a short depiction of the events, stating:

> The Israelites send an overwhelming force of 12,000 to slaughter the Gadite town of Jabesh-Gilead, ostensibly for their non-participation against the Benjamites.... The men of the city will be sacrificed to repopulate Benjamin. Entire families are destroyed, but 400 virgin girls are

preserved as wives for the Benjamite remnant. To restore Benjamin to its status as a tribe, the other tribes host a reconciliation ceremony at Shiloh. As part of the reconciliation, the remaining Benjamites are presented with the 400 survivors of Jabesh-Gilead as wives. (294–95)

This terse summary uplifts the violent events to solve the Benjaminite "problem" as a matter of fact. All Israelites are implicated in the events as all Israelites "host a reconciliation ceremony at Shiloh." Yet as the first abduction does not bring in enough wives, Fleenor and Ziese clarify that "the remaining [200] survivors of Benjamin" did not have any "wives." The commentators then state that the shortage of wives forces the men to go to Shiloh "to abduct virgin female worshipers during an annual celebration." The abduction includes "rape," but the commentators hasten to stress that the women are made "wives according to the Law" (296). As Fleenor and Ziese sense the difficulty of this explanation, they add a note that historicizes further the abduction as legal in biblical times:

> The Mosaic Law made the provision of marriage for a female rape victim. In a patriarchal society, a rape victim is treated as damaged goods and considered unmarriageable. God insightfully prevented women from societal ostracism by forcing the attacker to marry his victim and pay a fine to the girl's father. (296)

In other words, Fleenor and Ziese turn God into the originator of the legal idea that a rape victim-survivor would be better protected from "societal ostracism" by marrying the rapist. However, they overlook that biblical or "Mosaic" laws were probably not actually practiced and applied law. This omission enables them to classify the storyline in Judg 21 as disturbing to contemporary sensibilities but as acceptable in Israelite society. They declare, "It is a command that certainly seems strange and even cruel by modern standards, but within the sociological context of the ancient world God is intending to provide for the victim and minimize her consequences" (296).

In short, Fleenor and Ziese remind us that the abduction and forced marriage of women was legal in ancient Israel and even divinely sanctioned (see, e.g., Scholz 2005). Interestingly, Fleenor and Ziese also explain that the law was collectively "misapplied" as a justification for marriage. In their view, "the law is misapplied at a community level in order to justify rape as a guarantor of marriage. A fifty-shekel payment to the girl's father legitimizes the union, and everyone is able to comfortably sidestep the vow made at Mizpah" (296). Even when they have a chance to criticize the action of the Benjaminite men, they merely state matter-of-factly:

> Hiding in the vineyards in the hills around Shiloh, the 200 remaining Benjamites wait for the young female worshipers to make their appearance. In action reminiscent of the Roman history tale, *The Rape of the Sabine Women*, the soldiers kidnap the young women and force them into what is at least a coerced marriage. (296)

At least a coerced marriage is better than only rape, so they argue. The comparison with the Roman story brings to light that, according to Fleenor and Ziese, Judg 21 could be classified as a tale about rape, but then it is more than that. It is a about "coerced marriage." Alas, they do not explain the meaning of coerced marriages or what contemporary readers are supposed to do with this statement that regards a biblical story about coerced marriage better than a Roman tale of rape.

Even in their final comments, Fleenor and Ziese observe only that the "narrator critiques both the passivity and the deliberate evil that causes the innocent to suffer" (297). Not mentioning any specifics about "the innocent" who suffer, Fleenor and Ziese do not sympathize with the murdered villagers, and they do not protest the abduction of the women forced into marriage against their will. In the end, readers are expected to accept that this "provision" for the Benjaminites ensures the tribe's survival until David will be king, uniting Israel and bringing righteous leadership to the Israelites (297). To the commentators, the women experience serious violence, but it is for the greater good, the survival of the tribe of Benjamin.

Reading Strategy 3: Rape as a Matter of Fact, Anthropological Classifications, and an Absent God

Yet even less religiously conservative commentators keep the focus on the men and their predicament, as feminist-oriented and other mainstream commentaries indicate. Among them are the commentaries by Tammi J. Schneider (2000), Susan Niditch (2008), J. Clinton McCann (2011), and Roger Ryan (2007).[6] None of them worries about the women's fate or

---

6. The commentary by Serge Frolov (2013, 301–29) addresses Judg 19–20 more extensively than Judg 21, although Frolov devotes several paragraphs to what he calls a "sexual liaisons with women without their or their family's consent" (31). He also

their families' loss. Consistently, the commentators ignore the women, refer to the hundreds of rapes as a matter-of-fact, come up with anthropological classifications, or ponder the significance of an absent God in this tale of horror.

A popular commentary by Schneider focuses on the men while also mentioning the rape in a plain way. Schneider organizes her treatment of Judg 21 into three sections, entitled as "Resolving the Situation: Judges 21:1–24" (2000, 277), "Benjamin's Future: Judges 21:1–23" (278), and "The End: Judges 21:24–25" (284). Her interpretation highlights the Benjaminites while the abducted women appear on the margins. Schneider explains, "As a result of that one rape six hundred more women were raped, the difference being that these women were made 'wives' in a fashion that was condoned, in fact recommended, by Israel" (283). Period— no further comment. Here the marriage-after-rape notion emphasizes that the six hundred women had a better fate than the gang-raped concubine of Judg 19 who died in the end. The problem is that Schneider does not further qualify this explanation. Are we supposed to conclude, as other commentators also suggest, that in ancient Israel marriage after rape was an acceptable solution and that, fortunately, we do not live back then?

Interestingly, Schneider classifies the women's abduction unambiguously as "rape/marriage," but again she does not further elaborate on this double terminology even when she comments:

> The book of Judges ends with an episode that could be comical if its results were not horrific. The Israelites fought a civil war because of the rape of one woman, and almost destroyed an entire tribe as a result. That was prevented from happening only by the death of an entire town from which six hundred women were sent to rape/marriage. The Israelites made vows which they only partially kept, and even then kept only in a way that was to their advantage though it led to death and rape/marriage." (285)

In this summarizing statement, rape equals marriage and marriage equals rape. Yet Schneider does not discuss the implications of the terminologi-

---

states clearly that the described event is "in a certain sense … tantamount to an invitation to emulate the gruesome incident in Gibeah" (314). He also classifies the events of Judg 21:19–23 as "the mass rape of Shiloh" (317), although he does not further detail the significance of the "mass rape." Interestingly, he observes that God is among the victims (317–18).

cal equation. Especially in light of the long history of androcentric interpretations, the silence reinforces what other commentators stress, namely,
that the brutal treatment of the attacked people ensures the survival of
the Benjaminites. By not elaborating on the women's violent treatment,
Schneider neither details the women's fate nor considers what the abduction meant for their relatives. In short, Schneider's reading stays within
the storyline although the vocabulary hints at contemporary sensibilities.

Another feminist interpreter, Niditch, goes further in her approach to
Judg 21. She entitles the chapter as "The Reconciliation of Men through
'the Traffic in Women'" (2008, 205). She quotes feminist theorist, Gayle
Rubin, who in 1975 explained that "the relationships between men in a
wide variety of societies are created, maintained, and transformed by the
exchange of females," and this process is called "the traffic of women."
According to Niditch, "Judges 21 describes such a process for the purposes
of reconciliation between warring groups of men." She also observes that
"the androcentric author" tells the story from this vantage point. Yet, sur-
prisingly, this observation does not hinder her from speaking approvingly
of the men. For instance, she explains that the trafficked women domesticate the male warriors who learn to live peacefully in their homes and a
"renewal of order has taken place" (208).

In other words, Niditch grounds her interpretation in a feminist
anthropological explanation, according to which violence and harmony
follow a "natural" cycle with the trafficking of women. Niditch's reading also posits that Judg 21 is "an etiology for customs involving marriage, key passages in the lives of young women." If read accordingly, the
story describes "a yearly 'wife stealing' ritual in which matches are made
between men of Benjamin and daughters of Shiloh," because "such rituals
are common in other cultures" (210). In her reading, then, Judg 21 turns
into a wife-stealing ritual once practiced in ancient Israel and its various
neighbors. This explanation redefines the sexual violence as an ancient
marriage ritual that is also found in other cultures.

For sure, the anthropological comparison helps Niditch to avoid
being outraged about this story. Yet the absence of outrage is not unique to
Niditch. Another commentator, McCann (2011, 138) acknowledges that
"the violence in the book of Judges, especially chapters 17–21, is shocking, but hardly as shocking as the evening news on any given night." To
him, the root cause of the described violence is idolatry, and so he advises
to read the entire book of Judges as "a call to covenant loyalty" toward
"God's incredible perseverance" and "unfailing love" (139). This advice,

when read in the context of mass murder, mass rape, and forced marriage, is dangerous although it is not unique (see, e.g., Butler 2009).

Only one commentator considers the fate of the abducted women with some sympathy, although his interpretation quickly drifts off into concerns about God and idolatry. Ryan (2007, 60) promises to center his reading on the women when he entitles it as "Judges 21: The Survivors of Jabesh-Gilead and the Dancers of Shiloh." He articulates open disapproval with the storyteller when he states about Judg 21:25: "We may consider the storyteller's presentation of a 'happy ending' for this violent horror-fest to be a deeply disturbing conclusion" (164). In contrast to other interpreters, then, Ryan rejects the rationale of the "larger good" to overlook the horrors of the women's abduction. He also bemoans the fate of the other people in Jabesh Gilead, stating: "The inhabitants [of Jabesh Gilead] are ritually annihilated but not before 400 of their children are selected for survival as a living sacrifice of sorts to the cause of Benjaminite survival. The 200 dancing girls who are chosen from the Shiloh vineyards; like the 400, all marry within Israel" (166). Ryan ponders the entire murderous scene, imagining the dancing women and the killing of the villagers when the women are abducted, and he opposes the Benjaminite actions. His protest is rare, as he himself acknowledges. Yet in the end he blames all of it on God and not the rapists when he states:

> It may be argued further that a result of the Mizpah assembly is the restoration of the covenant between Israel and Yahweh by the application of appropriate sacrifices even though the word "covenant" is not mentioned by the storyteller. However, we may protest that the "restoration" is at the high cost of the ruthless taking of so many lives. It is to be noted, therefore, that in these closing chapters it is the character of Yahweh that is most problematic. (166)

Ryan questions the Benjaminite strategy, but then he turns around and explains that the absence of God reflects the storyteller's view of the world in which injustice and unfairness prevails: "Our storyteller writes about what he [sic] observes in the world around him—he tells it as he sees it—which makes the ancient book of Judges essential reading in the modern world" (167). To Ryan, Judg 21 is "ancient protest literature" and, as such, he finds it relevant for today. But he also wonders where God is in all of this violence, asking: "Modern readers may observe much the same in the world around them when they and so many others have cause to rage and demand, 'where is God in all this?'" (168; see also K. Stone 2009, 95). Thus even Ryan, who begins his interpretation with a focus on the women, does not make a special case for them but subsumes them into a general discussion about God's absence in the world.

In short, commentaries do not substantially challenge the idea that "certain women are made for killing" (A. Schmidt 2005, 272) or at least for abduction. Without explicitly admitting to it, US-American interpreters rely on an androcentric perspective that sympathizes with the need for the Israelite tribe to survive. Commentators talk about ancient marriage customs, sometimes even classifying these customs as rape, but none of them articulate substantive positions of solidarity with the abducted and raped women. At best, then, they acquiesce to the violence; at worse, they justify it as the lesser of two evils. Sometimes they also end up questioning God. In sum, all of them contain dangerous teachings that are complicit with violence against women in the text and, by implication, with gender violence in the United States. Most importantly, they claim to read Judg 21 from an apparently neutral space, offering exegetical details, theological judgment, and ethical consideration beyond a partisan approach, while accommodating the sociopolitical status quo of a phallogocentric, kyriarchal society that tolerates misogyny and gender violence. Thus, commentators on Judg 21 do not aspire to resist structures of domination of their time and place, unlike von Rad who conceptualized his work in indirect opposition to the oppressive political-intellectual forces raging in his time and place.

Biblical Interpretation in Neoliberal, Technocratic, and Market-Driven US-American Society: Learning to Resist Violence

Edward W. Said (2004, 135) explained that "the intellectual's role is … to challenge and defeat both an imposed silence and the normalized quiet of unseen power wherever and whenever possible." At their best, Bible scholars are intellectuals who critique religious authority and sociopolitical demands for complicity and silence. In fact, as an academic discipline, the field of biblical studies was born out of challenging the church's insistence that the Bible is the word of God. Bible scholars, employing historical criticism, demonstrated that biblical texts are not God's word but human creations to be critically examined as such. Consequently, biblical scholars brought the question about the Bible's authorship to the forefront of biblical exegesis, and it has occupied generations of Bible readers ever since.

The various answers given over several hundreds of years have successfully torn away the Bible from religious control, so much so that nowadays scriptural authority is usually located in the quest for original meaning and believed to be the central task of reading the Bible. Other events that deeply impacted Old Testament scholarship have further contributed to the importance attributed to the historical-antiquarian approach with its affiliated epistemological assumptions. Nowadays, these developments are still not often seen as coming out of a stance of resistance to political, social, economic, cultural, and religious structures of domination. Thus, much of contemporary biblical exegesis serves the powerful and the few in the United States. Interpretations on Judg 21 illustrate this dynamic, as they do not unambiguously protest the depicted violence; they do not nurture resistance to "unseen power" as it manifests itself in contemporary neoliberal, technocratic, and market-driven US-American society.

It could be argued that such biblical scholarship does not foster democracy and democratic processes. By being complicit with the ethos of empire which requires submission and passivity to violence, the commentaries function in maintaining exploitation, injustice, and violence. They stand in opposition to Schüssler Fiorenza's (2009, 20) proposal that biblical scholars, theologians, preachers, teachers, and communities of faith be educated to participate critically and responsibly in public discourses in which the Bible is used for nondemocratic purposes. Furthermore, commentaries on Judg 21 appear to be oblivious to the pessimism that some theorists articulate regarding neoliberal power. For instance, Teresa J. Hornsby (2011, 137) believes that biblical scholarship has aided Christianity as "an arm of power" in the production of docile, passive, and masochistic bodies and norms in society. Hornsby suggests that the coopting power regime of religion and politics pertains not only to conservative or mainstream conventions of biblical interpretation but also to hermeneutical and methodological innovations in the field of biblical studies. Thus even innovative agendas nurture the powers of the status quo, which makes resistance futile. Hornsby's analytical stance of resignation toward the dominant power structures is depressing, even nihilistic. It suggests that there is no way out of violence. Pamela Milne's (1997, 59) idea of connecting biblical studies to the social, political, legal, and economic goals of politically progressive movements may not solve all forms of domination, but it does not end up in resigned intellectual inaction within a totalitarian-conceptualized neoliberal regime, as identified by Hornsby. Alternative ideas do matter as they help us envision a world that could be more just, more peaceful, and less violent than what people experience today.

In light of these various deliberations about the reading of the Bible in resistance to violence, I want to propose another way of understanding the politics of biblical hermeneutics in the United States. In my view, it is urgent to examine how biblical interpretations participate in structures of domination or, as Davina Lopez and Todd Penner (2011, 166) phrased it so well, we need to investigate "the epistemological effects of scholarly discourses and the ethical implications embedded therein." I suggest developing a sociological framework that fosters analyses of the various interpretation histories of biblical literature to highlight the historical, theological, political, and ideological implications of biblical exegesis in the world. The sociological framework shows that interpreters always participate in debates about violence even when they remain silent on the issue. It exposes interpretations not as "true" or "false," "objective" or "subjective," and "exegetical" or "eisegetical" but as ideological constructs that come from somewhere and are created by readers coming from various contexts. A sociological framework, thus defined, clarifies that interpreters always make culturally, politically, and religiously charged claims about the world when they construct biblical meanings. They articulate positions within the world even when they do not openly disclose assumptions, politics, or convictions. A sociological analysis makes obvious who says what, how they say what they say, what their sayings mean in the context of the interpretative enterprise, and how interpreters see the power dynamics in the world. As such, a sociology of biblical hermeneutics describes, investigates, and evaluates ideologies of power present in exegetical discourse. It contributes to the ongoing democratic discourses in society by critically and responsibly investigating the sociopolitical implications of past and present biblical interpretation. Most importantly, it encourages biblical research to move from a text-centric to a cultural-analytical project, or as Vincent Wimbush (1998, 75) states it so eloquently, it opens up the field to the "complexity of social dynamics as social textu(r)alization."

Furthermore, a sociologically defined biblical hermeneutics resists assimilating the academic study of the Bible into the societal status quo. Following the ideas of Schüssler Fiorenza, it promotes an ethos of radical democracy. It ensures that the nexus between reading and society, reading and culture, and reading and politics is not relegated to an invisible place in the past. It teaches that meaning-making processes and the ensuing exegetical claims are part of the abstract task of contextualizing biblical meanings. It exposes assertions of singular, monolithic, and unilateral biblical meaning as hermeneutical attempts to obfuscate readerly interests in the world. Ultimately, then, a sociology of biblical studies advances an epistemology that challenges claims of objectivity, universality, and value-neutrality, while promoting the hermeneutical appreciation for textual fluidity, multiplicity, and "creolization." A sociology of biblical hermeneutics thus establishes that biblical meanings are created by variously located readers, and that biblical meanings have serious sociocultural, religious-political, and economic-historical consequences throughout history. A sociology of biblical hermeneutics teaches that interpretations of the Bible participate in hermeneutically dynamic as well as politically and religiously charged conversations over sociocultural practices.

In sum, such an approach makes crystal clear that interpretations are always context specific and socially located and never mere descriptions of a long-gone past or expressions of personal piety in a society that is as violent as the United States of America. By exposing readerly assumptions within the violent contexts from which they emerge, a sociology of biblical hermeneutics describes, discusses, and evaluates the politics of biblical studies. It investigates the Bible within its various interpretation histories, and it is neither silent about nor complicit with the various expressions of violence that make people's lives difficult, painful, and limited. Rather, by shedding light on the politics of biblical studies, it aims to contribute to abolishing the pervasive violence experienced by so many people in the United States and around the globe.

Works Cited

Boer, Roland, and Fernando F. Segovia, eds. 2012. *The Future of the Biblical Past: Envisioning Biblical Studies on a Global Key*. SemeiaSt 66. Atlanta: Society of Biblical Literature.

Butler, Trent C. 1978. *Judges*. WBC 8. Nashville: Nelson.

Crenshaw, James L. 1978. *Gerhard von Rad*. Waco, TX: Word.

Dorfman, Jeffrey. 2014. "Middle Class Jobs Are Disappearing and the Fed Is the Culprit." *Forbes*. http://www.forbes.com/sites/jeffreydorfman/2014/06/07/middle-class-jobs-are-disappearing-and-the-fed-is-the-culprit/.

Felder, Cain Hope. 1989. "The Bible, Re-contextualization and the Black Religious Experience." Pages 155–71 in *African-American Religious Studies*. Edited by Gayraud S. Wilmore. Durham, NC: Duke University Press.

Flatow, Nicole. 2014. "The United States Has the Largest Prison Population in the World—And It's Growing." *ThinkProgress.* http://thinkprogress. org/justice/2014/09/17/3568232/the-united-states-had-even-more-prisoners-in-2013/.

Fleenor, Rob, and Mark S. Ziese. 2008. *Judges and Ruth.* The College Press NIV Commentary. Joplin, MO: College Press.

Frolov, Serge. 2013. *Judges.* FOTL. Grand Rapids: Eerdmans.

Gingrich, Newt, and Van Jones. 2014. "Prison System Is Failing America." *CNN.* http://www.cnn.com/2014/05/21/opinion/gingrich-jones-prison-system-fails-america/.

Goldingay, John. 2011. *Joshua, Judges, and Ruth for Everyone: A Theological Commentary on the Bible.* Louisville: Westminster John Knox.

Gongloff, Mark. 2014. "45 Million Americans Still Stuck Below Poverty Line: Census." *Huffington Post.* http://www.huffingtonpost.com/2014/09/16/poverty-household-income_n_5828974.html.

Gunn, David M. 2005. *Judges.* Blackwell Bible Commentaries. Oxford: Blackwell.

Harris, J. Gordon, Cheryl B. Brown, and Michael S. Moore. 2012. *Joshua, Judges, Ruth.* Understanding the Bible Commentary. Grand Rapids: Baker Books.

Heschel, Susannah. 1994. "Theologen für Hitler: Walter Grundmann und das Institut zur Erforschung und Beseitigung des jüdischen Einflusses auf das deutsche kirchliche Leben." Pages 126–70 in *Christlicher Antijudaismus und Antisemitismus: Theologische und kirchliche Programme Deutscher Christen.* Edited by Leonore Siegele-Wenschkewitz. Mainz: von Zabern.

Hornsby, Teresa J. 2011. "Capitalism, Masochism, and Biblical Interpretations." Pages 137–55 in *Bible Trouble: Queer Reading at the Boundaries of Biblical Scholarship.* Edited by Teresa J. Hornsby and Ken Stone. SemeiaSt 67. Atlanta: Society of Biblical Literature.

Hubbard, Robert L., Jr., and Robert K. Johnston. 2012. "Foreword." Pages 13–15 in *Joshua, Judges, Ruth.* Understanding the Bible Commentary Series. Edited by J. Gordon Harris, Cheryl A. Brown, and Michael S. Moore. Grand Rapids: Baker Books.

Ingraham, Christopher. 2014. "Child Poverty in the U.S. among the Worst in the Developed World." *The Washington Post.* http://www.washingtonpost.com/blogs/wonkblog/wp/2014/10/29/child-poverty-in-the-u-s-is-among-the-worst-in-the-developed-world/.

Juzwiak, Rich, and Aleksander Chan. 2014. "Unarmed People of Color Killed by Police, 1999–2014." *Gawker*. http://gawker.com/unarmed-people-of-color-killed-by-police-1999-2014-1666672349.

"Know the Facts about Capital Punishment." n.d. Amnesty International. http://www.amnestyusa.org/our-work/issues/death-penalty/us-death-penalty-facts?gclid=CJuc0sPwy8MCFQtEaQodDVMAlQ.

"Kristallnacht: The November 1938 Pograms." n.d. United States Holocaust Memorial Museum. http://www.ushmm.org/information/exhibitions/online-features/special-focus/kristallnacht.

Lazonick, William. 2013. "The Fragility of the U.S. Economy: The Financialized Corporation and the Disappearing Middle Class." Pages 232–76 in *The Third Globalization: Can Wealthy Nations Stay Rich in the Twenty-First Century?* Edited by Dan Breznitz and John Zysman. Oxford: Oxford University Press.

Lopez, Davina, and Todd Penner. 2011. "Homelessness as a Way Home: A Methodological Reflection and Proposal." Pages 151–76 in *Holy Land as Homeland? Models for Constructing the Historic Landscapes of Jesus*. Edited by Keith W. Whitelam. SWBA 2.7. Sheffield: Sheffield Phoenix.

Matthews, Victor H. 2004. *Judges and Ruth*. New Cambridge Bible Commentary. Cambridge University Press.

McCann, J. Clinton. 2011. *Judges*. IBC. Louisville, KY: Westminster John Knox Press.

Milne, Pamela J. 1997. "Toward Feminist Companionship: The Future of Feminist Biblical Studies and Feminism." Pages 39–60 in *A Feminist Companion to Reading the Bible: Approaches, Methods, and Strategies*. Edited by Athalya Brenner and Carole Fontaine. Sheffield: Sheffield Academic.

Niditch, Susan. 2008. *Judges: A Commentary*. OTL. Louisville: Westminster John Knox.

Osten-Sacken, Peter von der, ed. 2002. *Das mißbrauchte Evangelium: Studien zu Theologie und Praxis der Thüringer Deutschen Christen*. Berlin: Institut Kirche und Judentum.

"Poverty: 2014 Highlights." n.d. United States Census Bureau. https://www.census.gov/hhes/www/poverty/about/overview/.

Rendtorff, Rolf. 1973. "Die alttestamentlichen Überlieferungen als Grundthema der Lebensarbeit Gerhard von Rads." Pages 21–35 in *Gerhard von Rad: Seine Bedeutung für die Theologie*. Edited by Drei Reden von H.W. Wolff, R. Rendtorff, and W. Pannenberg. Munich: Kaiser.

Ryan, Roger. 2007. *Judges*. New Biblical Commentary. Sheffield: Sheffield Phoenix.

Said, Edward W. 2004. *Humanism and Democratic Criticism*. New York: Columbia University Press.

Schmidt, Alicia R. Carmacho. 2005. "Ciudadana X: Gender Violence and the Denationalization of Women's Rights in Ciudad Juárez, Mexico." *The New Centennial Review* 5:255–92.

Schmidt, W. H. 1972. "'Theologie des Alten Testaments' vor und nach Gerhard von Rad." *VF* 17:1–25.

Schneider, Tammi J. 2000. *Judges*. Collegeville, MN: Liturgical Press.

Scholz, Susanne. 2005. "Back Then It Was Legal: The Epistemological Imbalance in Readings of Biblical and Ancient Near Eastern Rape Legislation." *Journal of Religion and Abuse* 7.3:5–35.

———. 2010. "*Lederhosen* Hermeneutics: Toward a Feminist Sociology of German White Male Old Testament Interpretations." Pages 334–54 in *Crossing Textual Boundaries: A Festschrift for Professor Archie Chi Chung Lee in Honor for his Sixtieth Birthday*. Edited by Nancy Nam-Hoon Tan and Zhang Ying. Hong Kong: Divinity School of Chung Chi College.

Schüssler Fiorenza, Elisabeth. 1999. *Rhetoric and Ethic: The Politics of Biblical Studies*. Minneapolis: Fortress.

———. 2007. *The Power of the Word: Scripture and the Rhetoric of Empire*. Minneapolis: Fortress.

———. 2009. *Democratizing Biblical Studies*. Louisville: Westminster John Knox.

Stone, Geoffrey R. 2015. "A Brief History of Academic Freedom." Pages 1–9 in *Who's Afraid of Academic Freedom*. Edited by Akeel Bilgrami and Jonathan R. Cole. New York: Columbia University Press.

Stone, Ken. 2009. "Judges." Pages 87–96 in *Theological Bible Commentary*. Edited by Gail R. O'Day and David L. Petersen. Louisville: Westminster John Knox.

Weaver, Frances. 2014. "The Militarization of America." *The Week*. http://theweek.com/articles/445062/militarization-americas-police

Webb, Barry G. 2012. *The Book of Judges*. Grand Rapids: Eerdmans.

Weber, Cornelia. 2000. *Altes Testament und völkische Frage: Der biblische Volksbegriff in der alttestamentlichen Wissenschaft der nationalsozialistischen Zeit, dargestellt am Beispiel von Johannes Hempel*. Tübingen: Mohr Siebeck.

Wimbush, Vincent L. 1998. "Interrupting the Spin: What Might Happen If African Americans Were to Become the Starting Point for the Academic Study of the Bible." *USQR* 52:61–76.

"They Will Be Yours for Corvée and Serve You": Forced Labor in the Hebrew Bible, Modern America, and Twentieth-Century Communist States

Serge Frolov

Resumen: El presente ensayo estudia la violencia aplicada en los trabajos forzados, tal como muestra el pasaje de Deuteronomio 20:10–14 al ordenar someter a esclavitud a un pueblo conquistado o a asesinar a todos los varones si no se someten de manera voluntaria. El autor analiza esta conducta violenta recorriendo diversos comentarios bíblicos actuales donde identifica cuatro posturas que van desde las que ignoran el pasaje en cuestión hasta las que rechazan su mensaje por injusto y repugnante. Luego narra su propia experiencia de juventud como ciudadano de la Unión Soviética en trabajos forzados y la situación de los pueblos originarios de América al momento de ser conquistados y sometidos a esclavitud o servir como fuerza de trabajo para los amos europeos. Al comparar la práctica de trabajos forzados de la antigüedad bíblica con las prácticas de trabajadores de muy bajo salario aplicadas en nuestro tiempo, señala que hoy se llevan a cabo en general sobre inmigrantes sin papeles o personas pobres que acceden a esos trabajos forzados porque no tienen otra posibilidad y en muchos casos porque resultan trabajos mejores que lo que pueden encontrar en sus país de origen. Finaliza señalando que Dt 20:10–14 tiene la "buena intención" de que se aplica solo a extranjeros pero que a nosotros nos debe servir como advertencia sobre el riesgo de asumir con buenas intenciones actitudes que termina oprimiendo a las personas.

"Horror and fatality have been stalking abroad in all ages." Removed from its context—and thus stripped of the intended Gothic connotations—this maxim of Edgar Allan Poe (1992, 37) succinctly captures by far the broadest common denominator of human social experience. Since at least the advent of the political state—in other words, over the last five thousand years as far as Eurasia and North Africa are concerned—this experience has been most commonly and most predictably that of violence at the hands of fellow humans: war, political oppression, and economic exploitation.[1] The only ones who managed, usually for a very limited time, to avoid finding themselves at the receiving end of violence have almost exclusively been those inflicting war, oppression, and exploitation on others.

Although it does not take more than a rudimentary knowledge of history to notice this pattern, twists and turns of my scholarly career gave me a rare opportunity to observe it on both ends of the chronological continuum and on two different sides of the globe. I started as a student of Latin American history, and although my concentration was on British colonies in the Caribbean (particularly on Jamaica) in the nineteenth century, my studies gave me a clear idea of the extent to which *la violencia* has been pervasive and existentially definitive on the American continent as a whole and especially in its southern and central parts.[2] About two decades ago, I rather abruptly turned to biblical studies—a move that took me thousands of miles and about three thousand years away from postemancipation Jamaica. As with any shift of that magnitude, the landscape that I was looking at drastically changed in almost every respect: new climate, new languages, and, of course, new cultures. The only thing that remained eerily familiar was widespread, persistent violence: faith-

---

1. While oppression and exploitation were most likely unknown until political states began to form towards the end of the Neolithic period, because all three are impossible without food production yielding a substantial surplus, warfare may be much older. Available evidence on the latter issue is inconsistent. On the one hand, Neolithic sites in Eurasia are almost all unfortified and show few traces of large-scale destruction associated with raids or conquests. On the other hand, the actual populations that can be observed today, or could be observed in the past, at the Neolithic or even Paleolithic stage of development for the most part do engage in wars with each other, accompanied by killing of noncombatants, rapes, torture and executions of captives, and cannibalism (see especially Harris 1997, 33–54).

2. The term *La Violencia* ("The Violence") was initially coined in reference to widespread fighting that gripped Colombia in 1948–1958 and resulted in the death of approximately 200,000. It has also been used of the particularly bloody chapter of Guatemalan civil war in the late 1970s and early 1980s. It is, however, applicable to other violent events, including the one that was the subject of my doctoral dissertation in Modern History—the 1865 revolt in Jamaica (Frolov 1986a [Spanish translation: Frolov 1986b]; 1987) as well as to the overall conditions that prevailed for centuries in much of the Americas and still exist in parts of the continent.

fully reflecting the brutal realities of the time and place, it was staring at me from page after page of the biblical text, often denounced by the deity or presented as going against its wishes but just as often endorsed and even demanded by it.

On top of that, unlike the vast majority of those who study both the Bible and the history of the Americas, I have first-hand experience of certain aspects of *la violencia*. I have been fortunate enough never to be directly touched by war, but as a Soviet citizen I have been subjected not only to political oppression (which was especially harsh due to my Jewish origin), but also to the most immediate and naked form of economic exploitation: forced labor. Insofar as the latter has been common in the Americas since at least the arrival of the Europeans in the late fifteenth to early sixteenth centuries and in the biblical world, including ancient Israel, I think that I am uniquely positioned to bring together the two milieus not only in a dispassionate scholarly way, but also from a visceral, experiential standpoint. In particular, it is my belief that my take on a particularly problematic biblical text that appears to endorse forced labor would not be much different from that of its victims in the Americas and that they might be interested in my reflections on the subject.

My discussion proceeds in three parts. In the first part, I introduce the focus text of the present paper, Deut 20:10–14, against its historical background and review the interpretations of this text offered by scholarly studies and popular commentaries of the last few decades. In the second part, I explain what makes these interpretations unacceptable for many readers in the Americas and why I share their standpoint. In the third part, I suggest a reading that makes Deut 20:10–14 meaningful without accepting its problematic content.

Looking the Other Way: Deuteronomy 20:10–14 and Its Recent Interpretations

Forced labor, or corvée, has been common in premodern and early modern societies. In particular, it is amply and broadly attested throughout the ancient Near East, especially in Ugarit and Alalakh (see, e.g., Mendelsohn 1962). In Canaan, the homeland of ancient Israel, a mid-fourteenth century letter of Biridiya, the ruler of Megiddo, mentions corvée workers (Moran 1992, 363), and a late seventh-century Hebrew petition of an involuntary reaper, probably from Judah, found at Metsad Hashavyahu seeks redress against an overseer who falsely accused him of failing to meet a quota and confiscated his garment (Naveh 1960; Mendelsohn 1962).[3] Much more abundant, if arguably less reliable, evidence that ancient Israelites of the preexilic period were closely familiar with forced labor comes from the Hebrew Bible. It uses the term מס, usually translated as "corvée," twenty-three times, claiming that it was practiced both in the premonarchic times (Josh 16–17 and several times in Judg 1) and under the early monarchy. According to 2 Sam 20:24; 1 Kgs 4:6; 12:18, relatively small cabinets of both David and Solomon included officials in charge of מס, and the secession of the northern tribes recounted in 1 Kgs 12 was caused by Rehoboam's refusal to reduce the "hard work"—עבדה קשה—imposed upon them by Solomon. The famous Egyptian bondage of the Israelites as described in Exodus also looks very much like a corvée, complete with a daily quota of bricks (Exod 5), even though in this particular case the text uses the term מס only once, in Exod 1:11. However, the Bible goes far beyond simply documenting the harsh reality of governments and elites imposing forced labor on the dominated populations; it stands alone within the corpus of extant ancient Near Eastern texts in claiming that the practice is divinely sanctioned and even prescribed if those enjoying its fruits belong to the community of the faithful.

In the book of Deuteronomy, the Israelites are stationed on the left bank of the Jordan, poised to enter the land of Canaan that has been promised to their ancestors by the deity as far back as Gen 12. Moses, their leader since the time of exodus from Egypt, lays out the rules of behavior in the promised land and warns the people that only observance of these rules would make it possible for them to take over the land and keep it. Since the deity prohibited Moses to cross the Jordan (Num 20:12; Deut 3:27b; 31:2b; 32:52b; 34:4), the speeches that make up the bulk of the book essentially constitute Moses's last will and testament.

Most of the stipulations spelled out by Moses repeat (sometimes verbatim, sometimes with lesser or greater variations) those voiced by YHWH in Exodus, Leviticus, or Numbers, but some of them do not appear elsewhere in the Pentateuch. One of the latter is found in Deut 20:10–14:

> When you approach a city to fight against it, offer it peace, and if it responds peacefully and opens up to you, then all the people present in it

---

3. Tellingly, the Metsad Hashavyahu plaintiff does not see anything inherently wrong with being drafted into a forced labor detail and punished for real lack of diligence while on it.

will be yours for corvée and serve you. But if it will not make peace with you and will wage war against you, besiege it; and when YHWH your God gives it into your hand, smite all its menfolk with the edge of the sword; only the women, the children, and the cattle, and all that will be in the city take as plunder, and consume the spoils of your enemies that YHWH your God has given you.[4]

As I have put it elsewhere, "The text's addressees are not only permitted, but actually required to kill all adult male inhabitants of a captured city, enslave the women and children, and steal everything of value. Even if the city chooses to surrender (an option that is described, in an almost Orwellian fashion, as *shalom*, or 'peace'), the only major difference is that men are permitted to live; the residents are still essentially enslaved and robbed" (Frolov 2013, 149).

Recent exegetical responses to this passage fall into four categories.[5] The first includes almost all thematic studies of Deuteronomy that carefully avoid covering Deut 20:10–14, as well as those publications, mainly commentaries, that either barely acknowledge the fragment's existence (Mann 1995, 131) or discuss it matter-of-factly, without mentioning any ethical or theological implications (von Rad 1966, 132–33; Craigie 1976, 275–76; Benjamin 1983, 184–98; Tigay 1996, 188–89; Hagedorn 2004, 192–93; Woods 2011, 231).[6] The second group is comprised of writings that see the passage's regulations as either conforming to or, more frequently, improving upon the military practices of the ancient world, especially as exemplified by Assyria or Egypt (Buis and Leclerq 1963, 145; Mayes 1979, 293–95; Preuss 1982, 139–40; Payne 1985, 119; Coffman 1988, 228–29; Miller 1990, 158; Braulik 1991, 69; Cairns 1992, 185–86; Brown 1993, 199–202; Olson 1994, 93–94; Rose 1994, 238–39; Wright 1996, 229–30; Millar 1998, 132–33; Hall 2000, 305, 310–11; Clements 2001, 93; McConville 2002, 320; McIntosh 2002, 243; Rütersworden 2006,

---

4. Unless otherwise stated, all biblical translations are my own.

5. The overview that follows is not meant to be exhaustive. It is, however, based on an extensive survey of books and articles on Deuteronomy, war in ancient Israel, violence in the Bible, etc., published since the early 1960s, mostly since 1980.

6. It is nothing short of amazing that Georg Braulik's article on Deuteronomy and human rights (1988; English translation: Braulik 1994) that begins with a long list of correspondences between the biblical book and the Universal Declaration of Human Rights never mentions Deut 20:10–14.

129; Crouch 2009, 184–86).[7] The next two groups are much smaller. A few authors acknowledge that from today's standpoint the provisions of Deut 20:10–14 are ethically questionable if not downright repugnant (Brueggemann 2001, 207, 210–11; Christensen 2001, 448–50; Nelson 2002, 248–51; Biddle 2003, 316–18; and especially Berrigan 2009, 122–24).[8] Others, by contrast, argue that these provisions are justified, because Israel's security supposedly required such drastic measures (Clifford 1982, 108–10; Merrill 1994, 285–86; Hamlin 1995, 120–21) and because the people's alleged enemies were also enemies of the deity (Munchenberg 1986, 147; Merrill 1994, 285–86; Hamlin 1995, 120).[9]

In sum, apart from a handful of interpreters that unconditionally accept the Deuteronomic endorsement of forced labor, biblical exegesis of the last fifty years has tended to either ignore Deut 20:10–14 or treat it as irrelevant.[10] The latter is particularly true of those who see it as at least preferable to the free-for-all that allegedly characterized ancient warfare—

---

7. A permutation of this strategy is favorable comparison of Deut 20:10–14 to Deut 20:15–18 with its requirement to exterminate the natives of Canaan (e.g., Cairns 1992, 185–86; Niditch 1993, 66–68; Rofé 2002, 156; and, curiously but by no means unexpectedly, Dawkins 2006, 247–48), with the latter mostly seen as an extreme manifestation of Deuteronomic/Deuteronomistic theology and the former as a more "profane" regulation. In fact, as will be shown below, Deut 20:10–14 fits in well with several uniquely Deuteronomic provisions. Moreover, as I have argued elsewhere (Frolov 2013), Deut 20:15–18 may actually be less problematic, indeed not problematic at all, given that it limits the ordained destruction to highly specific groups that not only do not exist today, but also, for all we know, never existed or never lived in Canaan. By contrast, Deut 20:10–14 is explicitly applicable to all cities except those populated by these groups.

8. By no means coincidentally, all books and articles of this category were published in the twenty-first century.

9. Telford Work (2009, 187–88) stands close to the latter group. While admitting that parts of Deut 20 are among "the Bible's most appalling passages" (187), Work claims that they reflect "the ugliness of our afflicted world, and God's horrifying judgment on it" (188), implying thereby that those on the receiving end of the divinely sanctioned violence somehow asked for it. For a deservedly harsh critique of this approach with regard to the genocide of the Canaanites in Joshua, see Seibert 2012, 105–9.

10. Characteristically, although in most cases commentary format makes it impossible to ignore Deut 20:10–18, most authors spend much less time on it than on much more palatable commandments in vv. 1–9, 19–20 of the same chapter. The disproportion is especially striking in Brown (1993, 199–202).

something that today is at most of purely antiquarian interest.[11] But even those who reject the provisions of the piece as "barbaric" (Brueggemann 2001, 207) drive in a similar direction, because almost all of them never try to plumb Deut 20:10–14 for an alternative meaning. This omission is tantamount to saying that the text does not offer anything that might be edifying for a twenty-first century audience.[12] In essence, a vast majority of publications in one way or another invite the readers to avert their eyes from what the authors apparently—and appropriately—view as a discomforting and perhaps even scandalous passage.[13]

That, however, is something I cannot possibly do for the simple reason that over more than a decade forced labor stared me right in the face. Neither, of course, can I approve the Bible's endorsement of the practice, despite considering myself a descendant of ancient Israelites, in other words, of those divinely designated, according to Moses, to benefit from it. In terms of my experience, rather than my identity, I am a resident of the city that Deut 20:10–14 condemns to slaughter and corvée. Although I cannot speak for the residents of the Americas, my educated guess would

---

11. It should also be noted that Deut 20:10–14 arguably goes beyond even the harshest policies documented in the ancient world with regard to the residents of the conquered cities. For example, while several inscriptions of Assyrian kings unflinchingly boast about wholesale slaughter in captured cities (Kern 1999, 68–76), such behavior is not represented—in contrast to Deut 20:13—as mandated by deities. Crouch (2009, 185) argues, moreover, that "the Assyrians usually preferred to specify execution only with respect to the figurehead(s) of the defeated polity."

12. Christensen (2001, 448–50) tries to interpret Deut 20 as a manual of "spiritual warfare," but he does not explain what might qualify as a spiritual counterpart of wholesale slaughter and enslavement.

13. This stance can be irreverently illustrated by a scene from *The Simpsons*. When a naked Homer Simpson, hanging from a helicopter, is dragged across the glass ceiling of a church, the minister, who had just called upon the parishioners to admire this ceiling, newly erected with their donations, shouts: "Now, look at the floor! All look at the floor!" On a more serious note, the "avert your eyes" approach creates more problems than it purports to solve. For example, Davis (2013, 222) wants to consign what she calls "dangerous passages" to "the shelf of cautionary texts, documents, and films … that contaminate our perspectives." Does she intend to put together a new, politically correct Bible? What would she do with the "classical" one? Shred, burn, or bury it in the equivalent of the Soviet "special collections" with goodthinker-only access? Who will decide what is "dangerous"? (Tellingly, Davis's examples include *Mein Kampf*, *Triumph of the Will*, and *Birth of a Nation*, but how about *The Communist Manifesto* or the writings of Chairman Mao?)

be that at least some of them would share this stance. In the next part of this essay, I explain why.

We Are from That City:
Forced Labor in the Soviet Union and the Americas

In the Soviet Union, where I was born, grew up, and spent more than thirty years of my life, corvée was ubiquitous. Except for the party bosses, top administrators, and a handful of distinguished intellectuals, authors, and artists, just about everybody was subject to it. Blue collar and white-collar workers, students and faculty, soldiers and prison inmates could be at any time sent to weed crops, gather the harvest, sort fruits and vegetables at a depot, or work at a construction site. For some of these activities, such as harvesting and construction, a lion's share of workforce was provided by the military and/or the penal system. Fortunately, in the area where I lived, there was little demand for child labor, so in high school I saw only token amounts of corvée, unlike the schoolchildren of Central Asia, who were annually spending up to nine months, that is, the entire summer vacation plus most of the school year, picking cotton. But my second and third years in college both included a September picking potatoes. This kind of obliga-tion was so common and was considered so normal that when somebody was mentioned as being *na kartoshke*, literally "on potatoes," no further explanation was necessary, even though other agricultural staples could be involved. When serving as a lieutenant in the Soviet military, instead of combat training my unit spent days, sometimes weeks at a time loading bales of hay or unloading cement. Again, I was lucky to have never been assigned to participate in wheat or barley harvest, which could amount to months on end away from home with little contact with the family. After discharge, while working at a library I was time and again sent to either a farm or a depot—sometimes for a day, sometimes for weeks.

Admittedly, in terms of hardship and brutality, it was nothing like Egyptian building projects or (looking slightly ahead) the sugar plantations of Jamaica and Barbados. No one was flogged or had their clothes confis-cated for failing to meet the quota, at least not in my time, the late 1970s and 1980s (a few decades earlier, inmates of Stalin's gulag and peasants, newly reduced to serfdom, were worked and starved to death by the hun-dreds of thousands). Those physically unfit because of illness or advanced age were usually excused, and living conditions, although often cramped and devoid of privacy (for example, with dozens of men and women sleeping in one barn, with the sexes separated only by sheets hanging from a rope), were at least bearable most of the time. Indeed, for younger people it often felt like a giant picnic, complete with chatting, singing, making bonfires, boozing, flirting, casual sex, and even some incipient relationships. As a matter of fact, I met my wife when we were both sent to a depot to sort potatoes that had been sitting there for almost a year and therefore mostly resembled compost.[14]

All that said, the experience was neither innocuous nor benign. While probably less taxing physically than many other kinds of forced labor, it was probably just as taxing morally. It is always demeaning to be coerced to do something you have no interest in doing; it is always mortifying to work for a token compensation or no compensation whatsoever; and it is always frustrating not to be able to do anything about it. Moreover, the official propaganda, calling the forced labor a heroic sacrifice alternately for the sake of the motherland or for the (supposedly internationalist) communism project, was making things even worse.

To be sure, one major aspect that is prominent in the Bible is missing in my experience: I was reduced to free labor not as a result of a foreign invasion but rather by the policies of my own government. Deuteronomy 20:10–14 seems to imply that only non-Israelites are subject to forced labor, and the narrator of 1 Kings insists that under Solomon the corvée extended only to "all the peoples remaining ... that are not from the children of Israel" while "the children of Israel Solomon did not turn into slaves" (9:20–22; almost identically 2 Chr 8:7–9). The difference is by no means absolute: giving lie to the narrators' avowals to the contrary, in both 1 Kings (12:4) and 2 Chronicles (10:4), it is the Israelites who transparently allude to the Egyptian bondage in their complaint about Solomon subjecting them to "hard work" (עבדה קשה; compare Exod 1:14; 6:9). Nonetheless, there is no denying that early modern Americas offer a much better parallel to the situation described in Deut 20:10–14. Although written more than two thousand years ago, this passage can be applied with an almost uncanny ease to what happened in the western hemisphere after the arrival of European newcomers in the late fifteenth and early sixteenth centuries.

Even before the first of these newcomers—the Spanish and the Portuguese—realized that the landmass they were exploring was not the eastern

---

14. Our household joke is that our love had heavily fertilized soil on which to flourish.

end of Asia and named it after the Italian merchant Amerigo Vespucci, they were already forcing the indigenous population—whom they continued to call Indians even after discovering that they are not—to work for them. Some had to mine gold and silver, while others were used as dirt-cheap labor in the equally lucrative plantation economy that produced sugar, coffee, cocoa, cotton, tobacco, and other agricultural staples, mainly for European markets (MacLeod 1984, 219–34; Bakewell 1997, 79–80, 82–85, 193–96). In an eerily perfect agreement with the Deuteronomic fragment under discussion, if the natives offered no resistance, the invaders reduced them to forced labor. If they fought, they were slaughtered, and the survivors were still reduced to forced labor. It was by no means a stretch for the conquerors to believe that they were doing everything by the book—the Good Book. After all, since they worshipped the deity of the Bible, it would not be unreasonable to surmise that the aboriginal population was given into their hand by this deity so that they could enjoy the spoils. Just like in the Bible, which never mentions the possibility of conversion, it did not matter much whether those subjected to forced labor joined the religion of their exploiters. Just like in the Bible, where the Israelites are commanded to reduce others to forced labor just a few decades after escaping Egyptian bondage, most of the *conquistadores* were pouring across the ocean—in a replay of the Israelites' crossing of the desert—in search of freedom from the bondage or bondage-like conditions of medieval and early modern Europe.[15]

The similarity began to fade when much of the native American population (including whole ethnolinguistic groups, such as the Arawaks of the Caribbean islands), already decimated by virgin soil epidemics, was thus worked to their slow and painful death (Sánchez-Albornoz 1984, 4–14; Marcílio 1984, 38–45) and when the original colonizers were joined by (in some cases, had to make way for) the British, the French, and the Dutch. Nevertheless, the main feature that made modern Americas look like Deut 20:10–14 come true—prevalence of forced labor—remained in place all the way through the nineteenth and even into the twentieth century. Starting already in the sixteenth century, native Americans who were already reduced to forced labor were joined by almost ten million African slaves (Curtin 1969, 268) and, to a much lesser extent, by inden-

---

15. That, of course, does not obviate the fact that the colonization of America was bankrolled and directed by the European governments and socioeconomic elites that also received the lion's share of the spoils.

tured European workers. Eventually, in Brazil, the Caribbean, and some of the North American British colonies, African slavery became the primary form of the practice (e.g., Marcílio 1984, 52–57; MacLeod 1984, 234–36; Schwartz 1984, 436–42; Bakewell 1997, 164–69, 197, 309–10). In the 1810s and 1820s, newly created independent states of South and Central America technically guaranteed rights and freedoms of all their citizens. In the same century, first slave trade and then slavery were gradually abolished (as late as 1863 in the formerly British United States and 1888 in formerly Portuguese Brazil). Still, forced labor remained in more veiled forms, such as peonage (see, e.g., Daniel 1972; Dore 2006, 110–63) and indentured labor of African, Indian (this time, actually Indian), and Chinese migrants in the Caribbean colonies of Britain (see, e.g., Schuler 1980; Green 1984; Adamson 1984; Ramesar 1984; Lai 2004; Roopnarine 2007).[16] In sum, over hundreds of years that constitute more than four-fifths of the continent's post-Columbian history, the Americas remained by far the world's largest grounds of forced labor, and today descendants of its survivors constitute a large portion of the continent's population, probably a majority in such countries as Brazil, Cuba, and Jamaica. This is why the tacit tendency of modern biblical exegesis to look away from the divine endorsement of corvée in Deut 20:10–14 may be unacceptable not only in my personal situation but also in the much broader American context. In the concluding part of the essay, I suggest an alternative to this tendency.

Meaning Out of Pain: An Alternative Interpretation of Deut 20:10–14

The obvious purpose of Deut 20:10–14 is to prescribe the course of action in a situation where, first, Israel goes to war against a city (20:10a) located "very far" from those "that YHWH gave [it] as a hereditary estate" (20:15–16) and, second, the deity "gives" this city "into [Israel's] hand" (20:13a). Territorial expansion cannot possibly be the purpose of the campaign envisioned by the passage. By trying to establish control far beyond its

---

16. Although African, Indian, and Chinese natives were not forced to sign indenture contracts, for the duration of these contracts, their situation did not differ much from that of slaves. Peonage, practiced not only in Latin America but also in the American South (as well as, under different names, in many other parts of the globe), was, in essence, a type of debt slavery. Its conditions were set up in such a way that paying off the debt was next to impossible or took a very long time. Peons were mostly of indigenous or African stock and their masters mostly of European descent.

"hereditary estate" (נחלה) Israel would, in effect, violate the boundaries
of this estate that the Torah outlines on multiple occasions (Gen 15:18;
Exod 23:31; Num 34:2b–12; Deut 11:24; 34:1b–3). Even assuming that the
people or their leaders might prove greedy or adventurous enough to risk
such a violation, YHWH cannot be expected to reward it by granting a victory over the attacked city. Rather, like any other transgression against the
stipulations of the Torah, the gratuitous war would be likely to result in a
costly and humiliating defeat, if not in loss of independence (as it happens
on multiple occasions in Judges). Neither can Israel's security (cited by Clifford 1982, 108–10; Merrill 1994, 285–86; and Hamlin 1995, 120–21) be
much of a consideration for two reasons. First, a "very distant" city could
not be much of a threat. Second, it is a staple of biblical thought in general and Deuteronomic thought in particular that foreign invasions only
happen when the people are not loyal to their deity (e.g., Lev 26:24–32;
Deut 28:47–57; Judg 2:14–15). If so, why would Israel move against the
"very distant" cities, and why would YHWH support the move?

In trying to answer these questions, it may be worth its while to take
into account that, as mentioned before, the provisions under discussion
occur only in Deuteronomy and that the book contains several other commandments that are unique and patently impracticable as written. To
cite just one example, only Deuteronomy prohibits the addressees both
to deny loans to those who need them and to seek repayment (15:1–11).
In any real economy, it would not only make credit impossible, but also
kill all incentive to work. Everyone would know that there is a guaranteed
loan waiting for them that will never have to be repaid and that if they
earned anything it will have to be given away on demand. By contrast,
Exod 22:24–25 and Lev 25:36–37 only forbid charging interest and taking
the garment of a poor individual as collateral.[17] Likewise, Deuteronomy
not only reiterates the commandment to leave some of the crop for the
poor (24:19–21; see also Lev 19:9–10), but also permits anybody to eat as
much grapes as he or she wants from any vineyard, provided that nothing
is carried away, and to take away as many ears of corn as he or she wants
from any field, provided that no sickle is used (Deut 23:25–26). Again,

---

17. Of course, the prohibition to charge interest is also unrealistic—as evidenced
by the fact that while paying lip service to it neither Jews nor Christians (nor Muslims,
whose scripture follows the Bible in this matter) have ever been able to implement it
literally and in full. Historically, the most common way around the prohibition was
intercommunal lending and borrowing.

these are the kind of regulations that would bring all agricultural activity to a standstill if enforced according to their letter: rapacious crowds would descend on any planted field leaving its owner no choice but to join the crowd until there are only crowds left and no planted fields. Or, more likely, from the moment the stipulation is enacted no one would even try to grow anything, unless coerced to do so.

This, in turn, amply explains why Israel would want to mount military campaigns against "very distant" cities and why YHWH would have no choice but to give these cities into its "hand." If the people observe the Deuteronomic commandments pertaining to credit and agriculture, they will be able to sustain themselves only by forcing others to work for them and plundering their wealth. The endorsement of forced labor in Deut 20:10–14 thus begins to make not only antiquarian but also acutely topical sense: a society in which everybody's property is everybody's for the taking (as it is in Deut 15:1–11; 23:25–26) would inevitably have to rely on the practice.

In this respect, it is hardly surprising that my experience of corvée was routine for a twentieth-century Communist state in which private property was largely or completely abolished. In the Soviet Union, forced labor reigned supreme throughout the seven decades of its history. Peasants, except for a brief respite in 1921–1929, had, under one system or another, to surrender almost all their produce to the government, receiving back what the government deigned to give them (Werth 1999, 146–58). Millions of people were, for all practical purposes, enslaved in the gulag that was, among other things, the source of most of the country's exports (203–6, 213–15). Even unpaid weekend work (*subbotniki* and *voskresniki*), voluntarily initiated by enthusiasts right after the Communist revolution and famously joined by its leaders, including Lenin, very soon became compulsory for all. None of the societies that were organized along similar lines managed to avoid following similar patterns. Suffice it to mention exploitation under the guise of reeducation in China and Vietnam (Margolin 1999b, 499–500; Margolin 1999c, 572–74; on the practice in today's China, see "Prison Slaves" 2012); the Cambodian "agricultural communes," better known as "killing fields" (Margolin 1999a, 619–24); and the disastrous universal drafts for *zafra* (sugarcane harvest) in Cuba (Guillermoprieto 2004, 83–114). Neither were these practices at variance with the writings of Communist theoreticians. The short-term demands laid out by Karl Marx (1988, 75) in the *Communist Manifesto* included "equal liability of all to labor" and "establishment of industrial armies, especially for agriculture," and Josef Popper (Lynkeus) advocated compulsory "labor service" for young men and women (Wachtel 1955, 106). Significantly, both those who envisioned the corvée-based Communist society and those who worked to make it a reality believed, after the manner of the Deuteronomic author(s), that this is necessary for the benefit of the society as a whole (Deut 15:6) and especially for that of the poor (see Deut 15:7–11). Everywhere in the Communist world, official ideology and official propaganda followed the Bible in unflappably claiming that past exploitation was a monstrous crime whose perpetrators richly deserved the ten plagues, up to and including the death of the firstborn sons, while there was absolutely nothing wrong with the forced labor of the present.

Conversely, where private property rights are respected—and to the extent that they are respected—corvée becomes rare and usually disappears altogether. Modern Americas are a case in point. In reducing the continent's natives and then imported Africans and other groups to forced labor, European conquerors were not for the most part motivated by Communist ideals—although similar utopian aspects were visibly present on the fringes of the colonization, for example, in Jesuit reductions in Paraguay (Bakewell 1997, 241–43) or Franciscan missions in Texas.[18] Rather, the newcomers were transplanting the European feudal system, already nearing its demise, across the Atlantic. Nevertheless, given that feudalism, just like communism, has little regard for private property, especially on land, it was entirely logical that the rise of capitalism, a socioeconomic system in which private property reigns supreme, would gradually put an end to this aspect of *la violencia*. Capitalism undermined slavery in the European, especially British, colonies in the Caribbean (Williams 1994), played a pivotal role in its abolition in the United States (which was advocated and then fought for by the industrial North), and eventually rendered peonage and other veiled forms of forced labor obsolete in the republics of Central and South America. By way of a highly ironic contrast, confiscation of land and abolition of other private property by the Castro government in Cuba, ostensibly for the sake of workers and

---

18. Fisher's (1998, 10–11) description of the daily life in San Antonio missions, while brief and on the rosy side, leaves no doubt that their residents were expected to work as much as they were asked to and received housing, clothes, and food rations as determined by the *padres*. That, in turn, explains why the newly converted Native Americans often either resisted work orders or ran away and why their mortality was high, even apart from the virgin soil epidemics.

landless peasants, almost immediately brought corvée—by no means limited to the universal *zafra* draft mentioned above (see Fontaine 1999, 656–61)—back with a vengeance.[19]

Some would rightfully point out that it was precisely the forced labor in the Americas and elsewhere that made capitalism possible by building individual fortunes and that the plight of many nominally free industrial workers—sweatshop employees, both today and in the past, *Gastarbeiter*, or illegal immigrants—is not much better than that of corvée draftees. My response would be, first, that since forced labor has been common throughout human history any present or future society inevitably benefits from it (unless, of course, the humanity renounces everything it has created since the Stone Age).[20] Second, as far as sweatshop workers, *Gastarbeiter*, and illegal immigrants are concerned, being free makes the crucial difference: since they take the jobs that are hard or low-paying voluntarily, it means that they and their families are better off with these jobs than without them.[21]

---

19. An almost identical trajectory can be seen in Russia. Capitalist development led to the abolition of serfdom in 1861 and was slowly but surely eliminating its vestiges in the decades that followed. The anticapitalist Bolshevik takeover in 1917 brought serfdom back in the guise of "collective farms." It should be noted that feudalism and twentieth-century Communism share much more than lack of regard for private property and dependence on forced labor. Other common features include nonmonetary economy based to a large extent on barter, top-down hierarchy held together by personal loyalty, stark contrast between the all-powerful elites and virtually powerless masses, and an official ideology that is not open to criticism and does not tolerate any dissent. From this perspective, it is hardly accidental that the redistributive precepts of Deut 15 are rooted in the idea—occurring elsewhere in the book—that everything the Israelites might own, individually or as a group, is but a conditional grant from the divine suzerain (15:4b–5).

20. That, of course, raises a host of new questions under the rubrics of theodicy and ethics. What kind of deity created the world where humanity's evolvement is inseparable from injustice, suffering, and violent death? For similar concerns with regard to evolution of the natural world, see, e.g., Murray 2008; Southgate 2008; Cowburn 2012, 59–79. What do we do with the undeniable fact that just about everything we enjoy—knowledge, technology, masterpieces of art—rests upon blood, sweat, and tears of countless human beings and that renouncing it would likely make things even worse?

21. Not to mention that currently all these categories of workers come exclusively from the countries where capitalism is either underdeveloped or forcibly suppressed. In another piece of irony, China has become a global sweatshop precisely because it is ruled by Communists. In developed capitalist countries, these workers or their chil-

This does not mean, of course, that the society or the community should not care about the poor, the weak, and the vulnerable. Yet, as the Deuteronomic author(s) emphasize repeatedly, especially in chapter 15, that is precisely what they have in mind—while acknowledging, under their breath, that their stipulations will not be able to eradicate poverty ("for the poor will never be gone from within the land," 15:11). This is what twentieth-century Communism was about: everywhere, from Russia to Cuba, it set out as a bona fide liberation movement, and much of its appeal, especially among the literati, lay in the promise to put an end to all kinds of exploitation of humans by fellow humans, thus establishing a genuinely free society. The result, in both cases, is heavy dependence on forced labor—sometimes of those very people that were supposed to be liberated, sometimes of the unfortunate others. The problem, then, is that of the means. Trying to correct the very real wrongs that exist in the society, be that contemporary West or ancient Israel, by mandating redistribution of property would lead in the wrong direction—back to feudalism, back to Egyptian bondage.

Deuteronomy 20:10–14 can thus be meaningfully confronted head-on by the survivors of forced labor and their descendants if it is read as a warning about the good intentions that can, and will, pave for millions the road to it. By heeding this warning, well-intentioned people the world over, including the Americas, would both pay tribute to the past victims of forced labor and help to prevent it from claiming new victims in the future.[22]

---

dren more often than not eventually join the middle class, with *Gastarbeiter* and illegal immigrants receiving citizenship in the process. It is difficult to deny that capitalism, while by no means perfect, performs far better than any actual (as opposed to imaginary) noncapitalist society of the past or present in just about every respect: from economic growth to human rights (including those of women and racial, ethnic, religious, and sexual minorities) to freedoms (including those of speech and conscience) to protection of natural environment.

22. For this reason, I still cringe every time Western politicians, literati, and glitterati earnestly but thoughtlessly issue irresponsible blanket denunciations of capitalism and "the rich" or, more recently, "the 1 percent." That includes theologians who cite Deuteronomy to justify redistribution of property. They either forget or willfully ignore the fact that the book also includes chapter 20.

Works Cited

Adamson, Alan H. 1984. "The Impact of Indentured Immigration on the Political Economy of British Guiana." Pages 42–56 in *Indentured Labour in the British Empire, 1834–1920*. Edited by Kay Saunders. London: Croom Helm.

Bakewell, Peter. 1997. *A History of Latin America: Empires and Sequels, 1450–1930*. The Blackwell History of the World. Malden, MA: Blackwell.

Benjamin, Don C. 1983. *Deuteronomy and City Life: A Form Criticism of Texts with the Word CITY ('ir) in Deuteronomy 4:41–26:19*. Lanham, MD: University Press of America.

Berrigan, Daniel. 2009. *No Gods but One*. Grand Rapids: Eerdmans.

Biddle, Mark E. 2003. *Deuteronomy*. SHBC. Macon, GA: Smyth & Helwys.

Braulik, Georg. 1988. "Das Deuteronomium und die Menschenrechte. " Pages 301–23 in *Studien zur Theologie des Deuteronomiums*. SBAB 2. Stuttgart: Katholisches Bibelwerk.

———. 1991. *Die deuteronomischen Gesetze und der Dekalog: Studien zum Aufbau von Deuteronomium 12–26*. SBS 145. Stuttgart: Katholisches Bibelwerk.

———. 1994. "Deuteronomy and Human Rights. " Pages 131–50 in *The Theology of Deuteronomy*. BIBAL Collected Essays 2. North Richland Hills, TX: BIBAL.

Brown, Raymond. 1993. *The Message of Deuteronomy: Not by Bread Alone*. The Bible Speaks Today. Downers Grove, IL: InterVarsity Press.

Brueggemann, Walter. 2001. *Deuteronomy*. AOTC. Nashville: Abingdon.

Buis, Pierre, and Jacques Leclerq. 1963. *Le Deutéronome*. SB. Paris: Gabalda.

Cairns, Ian. 1992. *Word and Presence: A Commentary on the Book of Deuteronomy*. ITC. Grand Rapids: Eerdmans.

Christensen, Duane L. 2001. *Deuteronomy 1:1–21:9*. Rev. ed. WBC 6a. Nashville: Thomas Nelson.

Clements, Ronald E. 2001. *The Book of Deuteronomy: A Preacher's Commentary*. Epworth Commentaries. Peterborough: Epworth.

Clifford, Richard. 1982. *Deuteronomy with an Excursus on Covenant and Law*. OTM 4. Wilmington, DE: Michael Glazier.

Coffman, James Burton. 1988. *Commentary on Deuteronomy, the Fifth Book of Moses*. Abilene, TX: ACU Press.

Cowburn, John. 2012. *The Problems of Suffering and Evil*. Milwaukee, WI: Marquette University Press.

Craigie, Peter C. 1976. *The Book of Deuteronomy*. NICOT. Grand Rapids: Eerdmans.

Crouch, Carly L. 2009. *War and Ethics in the Ancient Near East: Military Violence in Light of Cosmology and History*. BZAW 407. Berlin: de Gruyter.

Curtin, Philip D. 1969. *The Atlantic Slave Trade: A Census*. Madison, WI: University of Wisconsin Press.

Daniel, Pete. 1972. *The Shadow of Slavery: Peonage in the South, 1901–1969*. Urbana, IL: University of Illinois Press.

Davis, Patricia H. 2013. "Reflections on 'God Loves Diversity and Justice': A (Modern) Human Rights Perspective." Pages 219–26 in *God Loves Diversity and Justice: Progressive Scholars Speak about Faith, Politics, and the World*. Edited by Susanne Scholz. Lanham, MD: Lexington Books.

Dawkins, Richard. 2006. *The God Delusion*. Boston: Houghton Mifflin.

Dore, Elizabeth. 2006. *Myths of Modernity: Peonage and Patriarchy in Nicaragua*. Durham: Duke University Press.

Fisher, Lewis F. 1998. *The Spanish Missions of San Antonio*. San Antonio, TX: Maverick.

Fontaine, Pascal. 1999. "Communism in Latin America." Pages 647–82 in *The Black Book of Communism: Crimes, Terror, Repression*. Edited by Stéphane Courtois et al. Translated by Jonathan Murphy and Mark Kramer. Cambridge: Harvard University Press.

Frolov, Serge B. 1986a. "The 1865 Revolt in Jamaica." *Latin America* 138:75–91. (Russian)

———. 1986b. "La insurrección de 1865 en Jamaica." *América Latina* 143:46–58.

———. 1987. *The 1865 Revolt in Jamaica*. Ph. D. thesis, Leningrad University. (Russian)

———. 2013. "Diversity, Justice, and the Bible for Grown-Ups: A Jewish Russia-Israeli-American Hebrew Bible Scholar Speaks." Pages 147–60 in *God Loves Diversity and Justice: Progressive Scholars Speak about Faith, Politics, and the World*. Edited by Susanne Scholz. Lanham, MD: Lexington Books.

Green, William A. 1984. "The West Indies and Indentured Labour Migration—The Jamaican Experience." Pages 1–41 in *Indentured Labour in the British Empire, 1834–1920.* Edited by Kay Saunders. London: Croom Helm.

Guillermoprieto, Alma. 2004. *Dancing with Cuba: A Memoir of the Revolution.* New York: Pantheon Books.

Hagedorn, Anselm C. 2004. *Between Moses and Plato: Individual and Society in Deuteronomy and Ancient Greek Law.* FRLANT 204. Göttingen: Vandenhoeck & Ruprecht.

Hall, Garey H. 2000. *Deuteronomy.* The College Press NIV Commentary. Joplin, MO: College Press.

Hamlin, E. John. 1995. *A Guide to Deuteronomy.* SPCK International Study Guide 32. London: SPCK.

Harris, Marvin. 1977. *Cannibals and Kings: The Origins of Cultures.* New York: Random House.

Kern, Paul Bentley. 1999. *Ancient Siege Warfare.* Bloomington: Indiana University Press.

Lai, Walton Look. 2004. "The Chinese Indenture System in the British West Indies and Its Aftermath." Pages 3–24 in *The Chinese in the Caribbean.* Edited by Andrew R. Wilson. Princeton: Markus Wiener.

MacLeod, Murdo J. 1984. "Aspects of the Internal Economy of Colonial Spanish America: Labour; Taxation; Distribution and Exchange." Pages 219–64 in vol. 2 of *The Cambridge History of Latin America.* Edited by Leslie Bethell. Cambridge: Cambridge University Press.

Mann, Thomas W. 1995. *Deuteronomy.* Westminster Bible Companion. Louisville: Westminster John Knox.

Marcílio, Maria Luiza. 1984. "The Population of Colonial Brazil." Pages 37–63 in vol. 2 of *The Cambridge History of Latin America.* Edited by Leslie Bethell. Cambridge: Cambridge University Press.

Margolin, Jean-Louis. 1999a. "Cambodia: The Country of Disconcerting Crimes." Pages 577–635 in *The Black Book of Communism: Crimes, Terror, Repression.* Edited by Stéphane Courtois. Translated by Jonathan Murphy and Mark Kramer. Cambridge: Harvard University Press.

———. 1999b. "China: A Long March into Night." Pages 463–546 in *The Black Book of Communism: Crimes, Terror, Repression.* Edited by Stéphane Courtois. Translated by Jonathan Murphy and Mark Kramer. Cambridge: Harvard University Press.

———. 1999c. "Vietnam and Laos: The Impasse of War Communism." Pages 565–76 in *The Black Book of Communism: Crimes, Terror, Repres-*

sion. Edited by Stéphane Courtois. Translated by Jonathan Murphy and Mark Kramer. Cambridge: Harvard University Press.

Marx, Karl. 1988. *The Communist Manifesto*. Edited by Frederic L. Bender. New York: Norton.

Mayes, A. D. H. 1979. *Deuteronomy*. New Century Bible Commentary. Grand Rapids: Eerdmans.

McConville, J. G. 2002. *Deuteronomy*. ApOTC 5. Downers Grove, IL: InterVarsity Press.

McIntosh, Doug. 2002. *Deuteronomy*. Holman Old Testament Commentary. Nashville: Broadman & Holman.

Mendelsohn, Isaac. 1962. "On *Corvée* Labor in Ancient Canaan and Israel." *BASOR* 167:31–35.

Merrill, Eugene H. 1994. *Deuteronomy*. NAC 4. Nashville: Broadman & Holman.

Millar, J. Gary. 1998. *Now Choose Life: Theology and Ethics in Deuteronomy*. New Studies in Biblical Theology. Grand Rapids: Eerdmans.

Miller, Patrick D. 1990. *Deuteronomy*. IBC. Louisville: Westminster John Knox.

Moran, William L., ed. and trans. 1992. *The Amarna Letters*. Baltimore: Johns Hopkins University Press.

Munchenberg, Roger H. 1986. *Deuteronomy*. Chi Ro Commentary. Adelaide: Lutheran Publishing House.

Murray, Michael J. 2008. *Nature Red in Tooth and Claw: Theism and the Problem of Animal Suffering*. Oxford: Oxford University Press.

Naveh, Joseph. 1960. "A Hebrew Letter from the Seventh Century B.C." *IEJ* 10:129–39.

Nelson, Richard D. 2002. *Deuteronomy: A Commentary*. OTL. Louisville: Westminster John Knox.

Niditch, Susan. 1993. *War in the Hebrew Bible: A Study in the Ethics of Violence*. New York: Oxford University Press.

Olson, Dennis T. 1994. *Deuteronomy and the Death of Moses: A Theological Reading*. OBT. Minneapolis: Fortress.

Payne, David F. 1985. *Deuteronomy*. The Daily Study Bible (Old Testament). Philadelphia: Westminster.

Poe, Edgar Allan. 1992. *The Complete Stories*. Everyman's Library. New York: Knopf.

Preuss, Horst Dietrich. 1982. *Deuteronomium*. ErFor 164. Darmstadt: Wissenschaftliche Buchgesellschaft.

"Prison Slaves: China Is the World's Factory, but Does a Dark Secret Lurk behind This Apparent Success Story?" 2012. Al Jazeera. http://www.aljazeera.com/programmes/slaverya21stcenturyevil/2011/10/2011101091153782814.html.

Rad, Gerhard von. 1966. *Deuteronomy: A Commentary*. OTL. Philadelphia: Westminster.

Ramesar, Marianne D. 1984. "Indentured Labour in Trinidad, 1880–1917." Pages 57–77 in *Indentured Labour in the British Empire, 1834–1920*. Edited by Kay Saunders. London: Croom Helm.

Rofé, Alexander. 2002. *Deuteronomy: Issues and Interpretation*. London: T&T Clark.

Roopnarine, Lomarsh. 2007. *Indo-Caribbean Indenture: Resistance and Accommodation, 1838–1920*. Kingston, Jamaica: University of the West Indies Press.

Rose, Martin. 1994. *5. Mose*. Vol. 1: *Mose 12–25. Einführung und Gesetze*. ZBK 5. Zürich: TVZ.

Rütersworden, Udo. 2006. *Das Buch Deuteronomium*. NSKAT 4. Stuttgart: Katholisches Bibelwerk.

Sánchez-Albornos, Nicolás. 1984. "The Population of Colonial Spanish America." Pages 3–35 in vol. 2 of *The Cambridge History of Latin America*. Edited by Leslie Bethell. Cambridge: Cambridge University Press.

Schuler, Monica. 1980. *"Alas, Alas, Kongo": A Social History of Indentured African Immigration into Jamaica, 1841–1865*. Baltimore: Johns Hopkins University Press.

Schwartz, Stuart B. 1984. "Colonial Brazil, c. 1580–c. 1750: Plantations and Peripheries." Pages 423–99 in vol. 2 of *The Cambridge History of Latin America*. Edited by Leslie Bethell. Cambridge: Cambridge University Press.

Seibert, Eric A. 2012. *The Violence of Scripture: Overcoming the Old Testament's Troubling Legacy*. Minneapolis: Fortress.

Southgate, Christopher. 2008. *The Groaning of Creation: God, Evolution, and the Problem of Evil*. Louisville: Westminster John Knox.

Tigay, Jeffrey H. 1996. *Deuteronomy*. The JPS Torah Commentary. Philadelphia: Jewish Publication Society.

Wachtel, Henry I., ed. 1955. *Security for All and Free Enterprise: A Summary of the Social Philosophy of Josef Popper-Lynkeus*. New York: Philosophical Library.

Werth, Nicolas. 1999. "A State against Its People: Violence, Repression, and Terror in the Soviet Union." Pages 33–268 in *The Black Book of Communism: Crimes, Terror, Repression.* Edited by Stéphane Courtois. Translated by Jonathan Murphy and Mark Kramer. Cambridge: Harvard University Press.

Williams, Eric. 1994. *Capitalism and Slavery.* Chapel Hill: University of North Carolina Press.

Woods, Edward J. 2011. *Deuteronomy: An Introduction and Commentary.* TOTC 5. Downers Grove, IL: InterVarsity Press.

Work, Telford. 2009. *Deuteronomy.* Brazos Theological Commentary on the Bible. Grand Rapids: Brazos.

Wright, Christopher J. H. 1996. *Deuteronomy.* NIV Biblical Commentary. Peabody, MA: Hendrickson.

Trauma All Around: Pedagogical Reflections on Victimization and Privilege in Theological Responses to Biblical Violence

Julia M. O'Brien

Resumen: La autora encara el problema de aproximarse a los textos de violencia en la Biblia dentro de las aulas de educación teológica. Presenta su experiencia de muchos años conduciendo cursos donde los estudiantes son confrontados con la realidad de textos bíblicos que muestran violencia extrema y que en muchas ocasiones son avalados por la misma voluntad divina. A su vez, la lectura crítica se revela débil la afirmación de que el Dios del Antiguo Testamento es violento mientras que el mostrado en el Nuevo es amoroso y pacífico. Los estudiantes suelen sufrir en el aula el golpe de descubrir que hay violencia en la Biblia y que muchas cosas que hoy rechazamos son corrientes en las narrativas bíblicas: esclavitud, abuso sexual, mentiras, asesinatos, traiciones, infidelidad. Se estudia la opresión de género como la forma más común de violencia bíblica, la que por extensión es asumida como normal en la vida de muchos estudiantes. También se analiza la realidad de vivir en los Estados Unidos dentro de una sociedad privilegiada en comparación con la realidad de otras naciones muchas veces avasalladas por su política exterior. El artículo concluye que es necesario que en la clase se expliciten las diversas formas de violencia que los participantes han sufrido o sufren a fin de poder desentrañar el sentido de la violencia en los textos bíblicos. De este modo se revisará el concepto de autoridad de la Biblia, de su modo de ser "Palabra de Dios," de la imagen de Dios que los textos nos ofrecen.

In the past three decades, an increasing amount of biblical scholarship has explicitly addressed the ethical dimensions of the biblical violence. Methodologies and perspectives have ranged widely, including feminist (Scholz 2010; Kirk-Duggan 2003), historical (Collins 2004; Rowlett

1996), literary (Lapsley 2005), psychological (Daschlke and Kille 2010), Girardian (Williams 1992), aesthetic (O'Brien and Franke 2010), comparative (Ellens 2004; Nelson-Pallmeyer 2003), and confessional (Seibert 2012). Anthologies and bibliographies offer diverse readings of texts and perspectives (Murphy 2011; Bernat and Klawans 2007; Matthews and Gibson 2005). Many of the essays in this volume bring a cultural studies perspective to bear, tracing the resonances between ancient and modern expressions of violence.

These approaches, as well as others, have profoundly influenced my own work and teaching. I attest to the power of diverse perspectives to transform both the theory and the practice of humane biblical interpretation. Increasingly, however, I have come to recognize and struggle with another factor in readers' responses to biblical violence. From my experiences with seminary students inside and outside of the classroom, I have learned the key and often neglected role that lived experiences of trauma play in the way that readers transact[1] with the Bible. Indeed, personal abuse histories are far more determinative for some students' understanding of the Bible's relation to violence than any critical analytical tools they may learn to use. While the personal is profoundly political, my reflections begin with what has happened in the classroom before I will contextualize my discussions.

The essay thus provides possible answers to the problem of what constitutes a responsible pedagogy in core areas in our students' lives. It includes the issue of sexual violence and God-talk. A first section reports on my multiyear teaching experiences in which I have helped students to engage with the ethical issues contained in many biblical texts, especially as they relate to violence. A second section reflects on these teaching experiences in terms of chosen pedagogy, assigned readings and assignments, the significance of biblical scholarship, and the issue of classroom dynamics. A third section investigates how gender scripts, national privilege, and patterns of racial oppression reinforce students' perceptions that violence is primarily a personal matter and how to deal with these stereotyping issues in the teaching environment. In my conclusion, I wrestle with the lessons learned from and for classroom settings in which biblical texts on

---

1. In referring to this process as a transaction, I am employing Louise Rosenblatt's language for the interactions between texts and readers (Rosenblatt 1978). Similarly, Norman Holland describes the psychological "work" that reading entails (Holland 1975).

violence are central. I suggest that students must name and process their own experiences with violence before they can successfully expand their views about violence in the Bible.

The Learning and Teaching Experiences

Throughout my fifteen years of teaching in the seminary context[2] and, to a lesser degree, during my previous ten years of undergraduate teaching, I have consistently pushed students to grapple with the ethical dimensions of biblical texts. In a two-semester sequence of Introduction to the Hebrew Bible/Old Testament, we not only explore the historical and literary dimensions of ancient texts, but also the ethics of their composition and reception. We struggle with the ancient and modern significance of the Sarah/Hagar conflict; the Akedah; Joshua's *herem;* Judges' accounts of Jephthah's daughter and the Levite's concubine; Hosea's marriage analogy; and God's wrath. We share our reactions to these stories and also reflect on the writings of biblical scholars attempting to craft ethical responses to these and other "texts of terror,"[3] including Renita Weems (1988), Cheryl Exum (1995), Carol Delaney (1998), Robert Warrior (2005), and various authors in the *Theological Bible Commentary* (O'Day and Petersen 2009) and the *Global Bible Commentary* (Patte 2004), as well as my own *Challenging Prophetic Metaphor* (O'Brien 2008). Students reflect in small groups and written papers on questions, such as "Does knowing when Joshua was written affect your reactions to its violence?" or "Does reading the story of the Levite's concubine in the context of the book of Judges as a whole make it sound any less violent?" They reflect not only on the real-life consequences of specific biblical texts, but also on the way they use the Bible: "Does the way you talk about the Bible accurately reflect all that it contains and the way you really use it?" I raise such questions in all of the electives I

---

2. Lancaster Theological Seminary was founded within the German Reformed tradition, which in 1959 became part of the United Church of Christ. The student body of 130 includes more than twenty Protestant denominations, including United Methodist, Presbyterian USA, African Methodist Episcopal, Mennonite, Pentecostal, and Unitarian Universalist. A faculty of nine full-time professors and a wide array of adjuncts administer three degree programs and provide additional educational programs that attract 3,000 clergy, lay leaders, and youth each year. It is located in Lancaster, Pennsylvania. More information can be found at www.lancasterseminary.edu.

3. The language, of course, derives from Trible's influential book (1984).

teach, including "Women and the Bible," "Ruth and Esther," "Psalms," and "Prophets of Divine Wrath" (Nahum, Obadiah, and Malachi).

One elective course that I taught in 2010 and 2012 placed these questions at the center of our learning. The course on "Violence and the Bible" was designed as an opportunity for students to engage with violent texts of the Protestant canon from exegetical and theological perspectives. In 2012, the course asked students to name their assumptions about the Bible, violence, and God's nature. We then worked through Eryl Davies's *The Immoral Bible* (2010) to develop a common vocabulary for approaches to biblical ethics. The bulk of the semester was devoted to close exegetical and experiential encounters with biblical texts, facilitated by our conversation with each other and with authors such as Kathleen O'Connor (2011), Jacqueline Lapsley (2005), Erich Zenger (1996), Donald Capps (1995), and Richard Horsley (2005). At the end of the semester, we devoted two full three-hour sessions to processing our learning and "applying" it to commonly held assumptions about the Bible's relation to violence.

In all of my courses, I seek ways for students to "feel" the violence of the Bible in addition to talking about it. We journal our reactions to Caravaggio's horrific depiction of the Akedah and, following the lead of O'Connor (2011), we have imagined the human realities of the Babylonian destruction of Jerusalem in 587 BCE through role-play. Consistently, I push students to take seriously the significance of biblical texts for human living and to consider the strengths and weaknesses of various interpretative strategies. While my own specialty is Hebrew Bible, the "Violence and the Bible" course addresses the entire Protestant canon to avoid the easy assumption that violence is "an Old Testament problem."[4]

Overall, student feedback from these courses has been predominantly positive. On course evaluations and final papers, participants report learning much about the ancient world, gaining new appreciation for the biblical text, and having their horizons widened. Students rarely mention, however, how they have come to interpret the violence in the Bible or the ways in which the Bible should and should not be used to promote violence.

My own observation is that the inability to process the violence of the Bible is the biggest gap in student learning. While I have seen students grow in their awareness of what is in the Bible and why it is complex, I

---

4. This is why I do not assign readings from Seibert (2012), whose work does not take seriously New Testament violence, the significance of ideological and/or structural violence, or the anti-Semitic implications of his own hermeneutics.

have been disturbed by the apparent disconnect between what they claim to have learned and the way they continue to respond to violent biblical texts. In various introductory classes, at midterm students write insightful papers reflecting on various dimensions of biblical accounts of God's anger, but by the end of the semester they primarily remember that the biblical God gets angry a lot. In the "Violence and the Bible" course, the same students who in one class session articulately describe the historical context in which Joshua was written and the literary patterning of violence in the book of Judges nonetheless struggle at semester's end to incorporate historical, literary, sociological, or ideological perspectives into their responses to statements, such as "The Old Testament God is violent, but the New Testament God is loving" or "Using the Bible to promote violence is obviously a misreading of the text." Students can list (ad nausem, it seems) the biblical texts that disturb them and answer basic questions about methodological approaches, and they remember the conclusions drawn in their own exegetical projects. But they struggle with two key learning goals of the class: "to articulate one's own understanding of the Bible and its role in religious and political life" and "to formulate one's own use of the Bible in regard to violence." In all courses, the degree of disconnect between theory and praxis in regards to biblical violence has differed among students, but it has not neatly correlated with the effort they have invested in the class or with their general academic success. Something else, something specific about the relation between violence and the Bible, seems to be at work.

Reflection on Learning and Teaching Experiences

Witnessing students' struggles to connect biblical scholarship with the ethics of violence has led to me reconsider various aspects of my courses, such as pedagogy, assigned readings and assignments, the relative importance of critical biblical scholarship, and classroom dynamics. I regularly modify courses in light of what I have discovered.

One insight, however, stands out among others, and it is changing the way I think about teaching in the area of the Bible and violence. I now believe that students are much less disturbed by the critical methodology used to *study* violent biblical texts than with the *content* of the biblical canon itself. Many students are so shocked and disoriented by learning just how much violence is *in* the Bible that they find it extremely difficult to take the next step and to analyze the Bible's violent content from multiple perspectives. At the end of their study, they are able to talk about various approaches to biblical violence, but their enduring, existentially significant learning—the real "take-away"—is that the Bible is not the "Good Book" in the simple ways they once assumed.

For some students, this disillusionment is a variation on the "normal" process witnessed by most of us who teach introductory biblical studies courses. In introductory courses, learning that Moses might not have written the Pentateuch, that Abraham passed off his wife as his sister, that Leviticus condemns more than same-sex relations, or that the book of Exodus accepts slavery shakes students' conviction that they know the content of the Bible and that the Bible is God's word. Encountering biblical violence, however, intensifies their reaction, making them question not only the Bible's historicity but also its morality. Students coming to seminary with a high degree of biblical literacy are especially disturbed by this "content shock": self-professed "scholars of the Bible" are embarrassed by the difference between what they have taught others about Leviticus, Judges, and Hosea and the violence that they now see within these books. Biblically illiterate students are disturbed in a different way: because they had assumed that academic Bible study would be uplifting and spiritually enriching, they now feel naïve in their prior assumptions and thinking about the Bible.

For another set of students, however, disillusionment with the Bible's purity cuts even deeper to the bone. Increasingly, I recognize that those who have suffered violence in any form, but especially those with experiences of systematic abuse by parents, caregivers, and/or intimate partners, encounter the violence in the Bible in ways that are profoundly painful and often paralyzing. I usually have learned students' abuse histories in the course of private conversations in my office, when in moments of intense pain and vulnerability they trust me with their stories. The details of those office conversations are not mine to share, but I can report that many have been truly horrific. The suffering that human beings inflict on one another, especially on those closest to them, is heart breaking.

Strikingly, students themselves rarely recognize the correlation between their experiences of abuse and their intense reaction to the violence in the Bible. Many believe firmly that their abuse is behind them or at least adequately addressed elsewhere. I am the one who recognizes the connections: students who feel paralyzed by encountering violence in the Bible are often the ones with the most intense histories of abuse.

After the disclosures in my office, I have a deeper insight into how and why some students react as they do. Most if not all abused students experience my demand to consider multiple perspectives for processing and responding to the violence in the Bible not only as just unhelpful but also often as retraumatizing. Unable to hide from problematic texts, they linger over descriptions of human pain that are all too familiar: rape by intimate partners, blows by enraged parents, sexualized verbal abuse, abandonment, or gang rape. Even to those who have undertaken years of therapy, the reading of biblical texts in light of human experience reactivates past sensations of emotional and physical pain.

The issues go even deeper. When students recognize the violence of the Bible, they do not only re-live past trauma but actually experience new pain caused by losing faith in the very means of their own survival. Abused students repeatedly recount how the Bible saved them from their former lives. In times of trauma, a key biblical verse, perhaps about love, about being chosen, about God's care, or about the wisdom of God's plan for their lives, had become their mantra and their strength. To use the language of Alice Miller, the Bible had been their "enlightened witness,"[5] the lone voice countering the narrative of their abusers. They had read—and still read—the Bible as if it were a note slipped by God/Jesus under the locked door of their captivity. To them, the Bible confirms that someone on the outside knows their predicament and is sending help.

The reality and prevalence of abuse in students' lives is not new to me. Sadly, I long have known that many of my students are victims and survivors of abuse, and I have long been attentive to the cognitive and emotional dimensions of discussing violent biblical texts in my classrooms. My new insight instead relates to the role that students' relationship with the Bible has played in their recovery and healing process and how devastating it is to lose faith in one's rescuer.

My pedagogy has been based on the assumption that by giving abused persons permission and tools to resist the violence of the Bible and to talk back I would help them continue on their path to wholeness. Seeing now how many of the formerly abused students depend on the Bible for their ego strength, I recognize why an entire semester devoted to exploring one violent text after another has left them feeling battered. My firm insistence on considering the historical, literary, and ideological dimensions of texts and on *understanding* and *explaining* them in an academic setting may

---

5. This is the language of Alice Miller, as employed by D. Capps (1995).

be the equivalent of asking the abused to empathize with their rescuer-turned-abuser.

I see, too, the vocational challenges of rethinking the Bible's goodness. Perhaps even more than our general seminary student population,[6] students with severe abuse histories define their ministries as "helping," by which they usually mean helping others heal from the very abuse they once experienced. Before taking biblical studies classes, they had assumed that the Bible would be a key resource for "help." They had assumed that the "Good Book" would be as liberating for others as it was for them. When they are asked to rethink their own relationship with the Bible, they have to reevaluate what good news they have to offer others. Thus they wonder what to do if Bible study cannot help other abused women as it once helped them.

Reflecting on student reactions to violent biblical texts has deepened my understanding of how personal histories of abuse affect the way many learners process what they encounter in the classroom. For abused students, beliefs about God, the Bible, and faith derive far less from the theological formulations of their religious traditions than from their own survival strategies. They do not primarily interact with the Bible as Lutherans or Presbyterians or Pentecostals but as hurting people. The violence done to them, largely unaddressed, is a hidden lens through which they read the Bible.

Reflecting on the Larger Dynamics of the Learning and Teaching Experiences

While the experience of abuse varies from individual to individual, broader ideologies undergird classroom encounters with the Bible's violence. Gender scripts, national privilege, and patterns of racial oppression conspire to reinforce students' perceptions that violence is primarily

---

6. In addition to training students to serve as pastors, Lancaster Theological Seminary offers training for specialized ministries. In partnership with Lancaster General Hospital, we offer an accelerated degree in chaplaincy, allowing students to complete a Masters of Divinity and four units of clinical pastoral education in three years. Our joint program with the Shalem Institute of Washington, DC, offers students the ability to complete a certificate in Spiritual Direction while completing the M.Div. Students in the M.Div. and Master of Arts (Religion) degrees also can pursue specializations in youth and young adult ministry.

a personal matter and the unique result of a single dysfunctional family or a matter of private shame. Various ideologies thus shape not only the stories students tell themselves and others, but also my own assumptions about the purpose of studying violent biblical texts.

Ideologies of Gender

Gender-based oppression and socialization is perhaps the most obvious ideology informing these dynamics. In over twenty-five years of teaching, every student who has disclosed to me a history of abuse has been female. In my current institution in which sixty percent of the students are female, I hear (through personal disclosure or appropriate institutional channels) at least ten new stories every year. Many more students are willing to acknowledge having been affected by domestic violence when they are invited to offer a show of hands in a classroom exercise. In the past five years, I have seen this number rise either due to a greater prevalence, students' increased comfort with disclosure, or deeper awareness on my part. In some of my small classes, I estimate that at least half of the students are victims-survivors of childhood sexual abuse, domestic violence, and/ or sexual assault during adolescence or adulthood.

Such numbers are consistent with national trends. Various agencies estimate that one in four women have been physically assaulted by an intimate partner. Furthermore, women from all ethnicities, races, educational backgrounds, and social classes are targets, although the incidence rate does vary between ethnic groups ("Domestic Violence Statistics" n.d.). As stressed in Michael Kimmel's study, ninety percent of domestic violence victims are women:

> According to the U.S. Department of Justice, of the one million cases of "intimate partner violence" reported each year, female victims outnumber male victims by more than five to one. (2001, 5)

Despite the ubiquity of gender-based violence and despite over three decades of public domestic violence education, most women continue to consider their abuse as unique and private. Those who have undertaken therapy talk about family dynamics in psychological terms, and those with education in domestic violence talk about the warning signs of abuse and exit strategies. But most separate their "family matters" from broader social dynamics. For instance, "my father's rage" is rarely linked with the logic of the patriarchal household. "My childhood sexual abuse" is rarely linked with the sexualization of children and rape as power. "My dependency on my husband" is rarely linked with gender socialization and the gendered distribution of economic resources.

Students' tendency to interpret abuse through the lenses of family dynamics and personal psychological processes not only encourages them to keep their "private" stories out of the classroom, but also reinforces the invisible but real power of gender ideologies. In courses such as "Women and the Bible," most female students easily grasp the realities reflected in the tropes of gendered violence in the prophetic books. They sympathize with Hosea's wife and are appalled by Ezekiel's depiction of Jerusalem and Samaria. Yet the same students resist viewing their own interactions with the divine as shaped by the very gender paradigms inherent in abuse. They want to be able to say that "I need God to be the father I never had" or "I need God to be a comforting Mother" without being reminded that such statements reflect not only their families of origin, but also deeply internalized patriarchal constructs of gender roles and the privilege of the nuclear family.[7] Many of them want to save other women but are not willing to interrogate the gender scripts that inform their own experiences of reality. They want to address their situations as women without making men uncomfortable and without changing their own patterns of dependency.

Many female students downplay the role of gender ideology in domestic violence, insisting that "men are victims of domestic violence, too." Kimmel's study thoroughly challenges such assertions. Integrating data from crime statistics and family conflict studies, he concludes that men actually overestimate their own victimization by women while underestimating the frequency and severity of their own acts of violence:

> Initiating violence is never legitimate according to the norms of traditional masculinity in America; retaliating against a perceived injustice with violence is always legitimate. As a result, men will tend to overestimate their victimization and women will tend to underestimate theirs … men who are assaulted by intimate partners are actually more likely to call the police, more likely to press charges, and less likely to drop them. (2002, 1345)

---

7. I explore the ideological dynamics of God the Father in O'Brien 2008.

While female-on-male domestic violence does occur, it differs in severity and motivation from male-on-female violence: "women use violence as a tactic in family conflict while … men tend to use violence more instrumentally to control women's lives…. These two types of aggression are embedded within the larger framework of gender inequality" (1355–56). While Kimmel counsels compassion for all victims of violence, he insists that public policy makers and family counselors must remain aware that the perpetrators of violence "both in public and in private, at home or on the street, and whether the victim is male or female, are overwhelmingly men" (1358).

Confronting North American Privilege

The privilege of living in North America also shapes classroom responses to biblical violence. Only on rare occasions have male or female students drawn significant correlations between biblical violence and today's corporate violence unless specifically asked to do so. Each year, several students compare the Canaanites in the book of Joshua to Native Americans in the United States, but their analysis remains fairly superficial and reflects a vague guilt informed by middle school American history textbooks rather than a deep recognition that their communities continue to benefit from the colonization of this land and that their theological discourse is complicit in that colonization.

Consistently, students struggle to identify any example of violence beyond the individual. When asked to empathize with the trauma of the destruction of Jerusalem, many students imagine the fates of individuals in military zones, but they find it difficult to envision how the Babylonian defeat shaped Judean theological reasoning. Most explain in detail what is "wrong" with the story of the Levite's concubine but stare blankly when asked how the bombings in the United States on September 11, 2001, affect them and their churches. Even those recently returning from our seminary's cross-cultural trips, newly sensitized to the situation of India's Dalit communities or the Palestinians in the West Bank and Gaza or impoverished Haitians, still respond much more quickly to the victimization of individuals in the Bible than to the inherent violence in a statement such as "God destroyed Judah, because the people were sinful." Even African American students who powerfully articulate daily insults of racism, gang violence, and racial profiling in their communities struggle to see the systemic dimensions of violence in biblical texts. Most students recoil from the horrific brutalization depicted in the story of the Levite's concubine but never consider why biblical writers (and modern film makers) find graphic accounts of women's victimization so useful for instruction and entertainment. Most embrace the language of love in the Gospel of John on a personal level but struggle to notice the gospel's pervasive anti-Judaism—even after reading the work of Adele Reinhartz (2005).

Their difficulties in recognizing structurally experienced violence and terror reflect the privilege of living in a country in which the military fights its wars elsewhere and in which acts of terrorism are not experienced daily but as horrific "events." Many believe that "the U.S.A. is the strongest nation in the world," that "people only hate us because they are jealous of our success," and that "our military keeps the world safe." Even when tempered by revelations about Guantanamo, Benghazi, and covert operations, these convictions are still alive and well in most students' thinking. Some students in my North American classroom speak the language of Liberation Theology, but even those most burdened by liberal guilt struggle to empathize with Judah's national failure and understand how such failure might have shaped Judah's testimonies to divine sovereignty and deserved punishment

Student responses reflect other forms of privilege as well, such as white privilege, political privilege, and religious privilege, all of which render the oppression of others invisible and account for one's own oppression in individual rather than structural terms. Privilege thus makes it possible for my students to overlook that the Gospel of John characterizes Jews as "children of the devil" and uses darkness as the symbol of evil. Because of their privilege, my students fail to recognize that Hagar is not Sarah's romantic rival but a slave forced into surrogacy. Privilege leads them to accept at face value the Deuteronomists' claim that King David bore no responsibility for the disappearances of his rivals. Recognizing these and other effects of privilege on one's own interpretation is difficult for all students, but it is especially difficult for those whose abuse histories lead them identify themselves as champions of the oppressed.

Challenging Class Privilege

Witnessing student interactions with biblical violence has not only spurred my reflections on the ideologies that shape their responses. Perhaps even more, it has deepened my recognition of the ideologies that shape my own thinking and pedagogy. As I explain more fully in *Challenging Prophetic*

Metaphor (O'Brien 2008), I claim that violence in the Bible is only a problem when readers make particular assumptions about the canon. Those who eschew violence are troubled by violence in the Bible only when they engage the Bible within the conceptual framework of "authority" and believe that the Bible is a set of guidelines to be followed, "life's instruction book," or "the only rule of faith and practice."

This dilemma can be mapped as in the diagram below. In this scheme, the observation to be processed is that "the Bible shows God acting violently." As long as this observation is undisputed, at least one of the assumptions numbered in my graphic must be challenged: if violence is always bad and God is always good, then God cannot be violent. Readers working within the "authority frame" go to great lengths to avoid rethinking assumption number 3 ("The Bible reflects God perfectly"). Their first response to the dilemma is to attempt to discredit the presenting problem ("The Bible shows God acting violently"). They reinterpret passages that "seem" to depict God in violent acts and latch on to critical scholarship that could "fix" the problems of

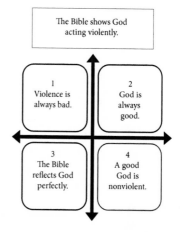

Figure 1. Considering the "Problem" of Biblical Violence

the Bible: alternate translations, symbolic rather than literal meanings, and historical explanations of "how things were back then." Perhaps, they believe, "If historical criticism can prove that the events of the book of Joshua were the wishful thinking of exiles, then I don't have to worry that God really condones genocide." When such fixes fail and they must rethink their assumptions, they are more likely to question assumption number 1 ("Violence is always bad") rather than to challenge the more key assumptions number 3 ("The Bible reflects God perfectly") or number 4 ("God is always good").

Decades ago, my encounter with feminist readings of the Bible convinced me that no interpretation truly "fixes" the violence of the Bible. Indeed, violence is far more prevalent in the Bible than most readers recognize. It is built into the Bible's very structure. In the language of Toni Morrison (1992, 46), ideologies such as patriarchy and racism are the "fish bowl" of biblical rhetoric, invisibly giving shape to and providing the boundaries for biblical language and characters.

Given my own convictions, the most logical response has been to rethink assumption number 3 ("The Bible reflects God perfectly"). Instead of a rule book, I see the Bible as a privileged anthology of testimonies from people shaped by the ideologies of their own world. I believe the Bible is worth reading, not because it tells us how to live, but because it shows how people have thought about God and spurs us to do the same. Rather than challenge assumption number 1 ("Violence is always bad"), number 2 ("God is always good"), or number 4 ("A good God is nonviolent"), my response to those who see the violence of the Bible as a problem is this: Change your relationship with the Bible. Change your expectations of it. Quit thinking about it as a set of rules to be obeyed. Think about it instead as expressions of faith to listen to, learn from, and if necessary, respectfully challenge.

Why has this solution that is so unsatisfying and sometimes even traumatic for students been so life-enriching for me? In my view, one factor relates to my socialization within the "educational class." I was raised by parents who were not wealthy but well-educated. My father, a United Church of Christ pastor, completed college and seminary degrees, and my mother completed college and worked as a public high school teacher. At home, I was rewarded for being smart, for reading, and for thinking on my own as long as I was respectful. In church, I heard my father preach that science and logic deepen one's experience of faith as long as they were not taken to absurd extremes. At home and in class, I watched my mother (who was also my tenth grade English teacher) insist on well-structured argumentation and reward creative thesis statements.

My family's socialization in the ethos of mid-twentieth century North American education prepared me well for small-town public school college-preparatory classes, for the private college I attended, and the masters and doctoral programs I completed. Throughout my education, I was consistently rewarded for defending novel theses, for interpreting existing material through new lenses, and for renegotiating power relationships through rethinking and reframing. Intellectual autonomy was lifted up as a value. Even when it was not honored in practice, even when professors or parents dismissed claims that contradicted their own convictions, the *rhetoric* of academic freedom remained uncontested.

As an academic, I now belong to a guild informed by many of these same values. Of course, my current political and social views are not identical with those of my parents, teachers, or colleagues, and differentiating myself from key figures in my education has not come without emotional and professional cost. Nonetheless, in little of my experience has obeying authority for its own sake been valued, imposed, or financially-incentivized. It has never been forced upon me with physical violence.

My story differs markedly from the stories of those abused by parents and/or partners. While I have been rewarded for intellectual autonomy, they have been battered for any attempt at the same. As Donald Capps (1995, 60–64) argues, childhood abuse systematically denies a child intellectual autonomy to the decree that "a key factor in breaking the vicious cycle of child abuse" is intellectual autonomy for children. The denial of autonomy of any kind also shapes the abuse of women, as Kimmel's study stresses. While women do strike men in situations of family conflict, "violence that is instrumental in the maintenance of *control*—the more systematic, persistent, and injurious type of violence—is overwhelmingly perpetuated by men, with rates captured best by crime victimization studies. More than 90% of this violence is perpetrated by men [against women]" (2002, 1358).

The "solution" that I offer students by asking them to rethink their relationship to authority and to honor the Bible without obeying it may resonate with those in a social location similar to mine, but not with those students who live with current or remembered experiences of abuse. In their experience, challenging or leaving one's abuser increases the likelihood of fatality.[8] For those with the life experience of abuse, the uncontested power of God and God's Bible to outrank and outflank any human threat is far more appealing than any pep talk on intellectual autonomy I can give. Yet, as a theological educator, my goal is to help students develop ethically-responsible modes of biblical interpretation, to help students recognize the ways in which their views of the Bible, God, and sin can perpetuate the logic of abuse for those who hear their sermons, learn from their teaching, and receive their pastoral care. Therein lies the dilemma. How does an educator shed light on the abusive potential of the survival strategies to which the fragile cling?

---

8. According the website of the Domestic Abuse Shelter of the Florida Keys, "Approximately 75% of women who are killed by their batterers are murdered when they attempt to leave or after they have left an abusive relationship" ("Information on Domestic Violence" n.d.).

Lessons from and for the Classroom: Toward Concluding Comments

My experience suggests that it is difficult, if not impossible, for learners to change their understandings of violent texts without having named and processed in some way their own experiences with violence. As long as a particular relationship with the Bible is fundamental to a student's survival strategies, she will experience any threat to that relationship as further trauma or, at the very least, an academic exercise irrelevant to her own life.

This observation poses the pressing question of what constitutes responsible pedagogy in areas so core to students' sense of life. The question is not whether education *should* contain a psychological component, since it always does. As Norman Holland (1975, 14) argues, all reading is a "transaction" with one's own core identity issues: "Meaning, that is, the act of making sense of a text, works as a defense against some source of anxiety. Each reader, therefore, will seek out a unifying idea that matches his particular needs for sense and logic." The question, instead, concerns how to *address* the therapeutic dimensions of the educational process, especially in cases in which unacknowledged trauma impedes learning goals.

Obviously (at least to me), while the educational process may have therapeutic outcomes, its primary goal is not therapy. Moreover, neither professors nor fellow students can or should serve as the student's primary therapeutic community. The professor responsible for assessing a student's academic progress (and, in my case, assessing her "fitness for ministry") should never underestimate the real power she holds over students, and while some students may find another's public disclosure of an abuse history liberating, classroom dynamics can be derailed when self-defined "helpers" begin to assume responsibility for the wounded person's pain.

Professors and administrators obviously need wide and deep networks for referrals, but the classroom cannot and should not avoid the realities of people's lives. Issues of abuse and lived violence cannot be isolated from student learning. When I next teach the "Violence and the Bible" course, I will likely assign a "violence journal," in which students record their reactions to biblical passages, assigned readings, and violence in the news. I hope that my occasional, nongraded reflections on their entries give me a better sense of what students are actually experiencing, as opposed to what I am inferring from their behavior in class. Their reflections may allow me to make earlier referrals, if necessary.

Such insight also may enable me to modify class plans in response to what I glean. For example, the class role-play based on O'Connor's *Jeremiah: Pain and Promise* (2011) was designed to help students empathize with the pain of exile so that they grasp how Jeremiah's theology is a response to trauma. Because I incorrectly assumed that students would have difficulties in identifying with the pain of dislocation, I devoted more class time to creating empathy rather than to helping students appreciate O'Connor's claim about Jeremiah's theology. Had I understood the high rate of trauma histories among my students, I would have reversed the priorities of the session and crafted an exercise to help students more deeply consider O'Connor's claim that Jeremiah's theology should be read empathetically but provisionally: a theology forged in the context of trauma may not be adequate for one's whole life. A well-crafted journal question following our classroom exercise may spur student reflections on the contexts in which their own theologies have been forged and how well that theology is—and is not—serving them today. Journaling may help students (and me) come to a deeper understanding of how what we define as "good news" and "bad news" is profoundly contextual and provisional.

I do not know if my experience is representative of other educational contexts, but domestic violence statistics suggest that every female student in every classroom has a 25 percent chance of having been sexually or otherwise assaulted. In mainline Protestant theological institutions where women constitute 60 percent of the student body, the number of abused women might be higher, given the frequency with which the wounded seek to heal others. In addition, every male student in every classroom has a high likelihood of being affected in some way by violence, such as in the domestic setting as a child, by being an observer, an adult victim, a perpetrator, or in the context of military service.[9] The likelihood that students have some history with violence should inform all class sessions and all interactions with students.

This awareness should also inform congregational life and denominational structures. As the increasing number of female students complete theological education and enter ministry professions, the number of traumatized clergy will continue to rise. Surely sermons preached, pastoral

---

9. Army chaplain Rev. Mel Baars reflects how violent texts such as Nahum help the healing of those suffering from combat-induced PTSD in Baars 2008. Her blog is available at http://www.melbaars.blogspot.com.

care offered, and education provided will be affected. Bishops, conference ministers, and those in similar leadership positions would do well to factor these realities into clergy placement, care of clergy, and the mediation of conflicts between clergy and parishioners.

What I have learned about myself in this process has pushed me to a deeper recognition of the dynamics of power in my classroom. In retrospect, I see how the design of my courses privileges those who share my willingness to challenge traditional views of biblical authority. In my "Violence and the Bible" course, the Davies (2010) volume chosen as our scaffolding for ethical discourse *seemed* to invite diverse views, as it discussed the strengths and weaknesses of various approaches to biblical ethics. Yet its final chapter presented the resisting reader most sympathetically. Explicitly and implicitly, I do the same in my teaching. By pushing students to accept that there is no simple fix to the "problem" of violence in the Bible, I prod students to deal honestly with the texts in front of them and come to their own conclusions. Yet in failing to present viable alternatives to my "solution" of rethinking biblical authority, I do not offer students the same intellectual autonomy that I claim to value. While I have not based students' grade on their conclusions about violence and the Bible, I also have not helped them to construct an approach to the Bible and violence that works for them at this stage in their lives.

These and other questions face me as a plan for upcoming teaching. As I develop a new course on homosexuality and the Bible, prepare to teach the "Violence and the Bible" course again, and redesign the introduction course to the Hebrew Bible/Old Testament for a hybrid classroom/online format, I continue to question how intellectual autonomy really works in the classroom. What forms of student resistance to content and concepts should be challenged? What forms should be honored—temporarily and long-term? How do I recognize my own privilege more quickly and respond more appropriately?

James Joyce (1938, 210) claims that "we walk through ourselves meeting robbers, ghosts, giants, old men, young men, wives, widows, brothers-in-love. But always meeting ourselves." I hope that the next time students and I gather in the classroom I will remember that none of us has finished meeting ourselves. I also hope that we will find ways to meet each other as biblical interpreters and as human beings while we are processing our own life experiences.

Works Cited

Baars, Mel. 2008. "Confession and Lament in Nahum 3: Journeys of Healing after War." Gender Certificate Project. Durham: Duke University.

Bernat, David A., and Jonathan Klawans. 2007. *Religion and Violence: The Biblical Heritage*. Sheffield: Sheffield Phoenix.

Capps, Donald. 1995. *The Child's Song: The Religious Abuse of Children*. Louisville: Westminster John Knox.

Collins, John J. 2004. *Does the Bible Justify Violence?* Philadelphia: Fortress.

Daschlke, Dereck, and D. Andrew Kille, eds. 2010. *A Cry Instead of Justice: The Bible and Cultures of Violence in Psychological Perspective*. New York: T&T Clark.

Davies, Eryl. 2010. *The Immoral Bible: Approaches to Biblical Ethics*. New York: T&T Clark.

Delaney, Carol. 1998. *Abraham on Trial: The Social Legacy of Biblical Myth*. Princeton: Princeton University Press.

"Domestic Violence Statistics." n.d. American Bar Association. http://www.americanbar.org/groups/domestic_violence/resources/statistics.html.

Ellens, J. Harold, ed. 2004. *The Destructive Power of Religion: Violence in Judaism, Christianity, and Islam*. Westcort, CT: Praeger.

Exum, Cheryl. 1995. "The Ethics of Biblical Violence against Women." Pages 252–71 in *The Bible in Ethics: The Second Sheffield Colloquium*. Edited by John Rogerson, Margaret Davies, and M. Daniel Carroll R. Sheffield: Sheffield Academic Press.

Holland, Norman N. 1975. *5 Readers Reading*. New Haven: Yale University Press.

Horsley, Richard. 2005. "'By the Finger of God': Jesus and Imperial Violence." Pages 51–80 in *Violence in the New Testament*. Edited by Shelly Matthews and E. Leigh Gibson. New York: T&T Clark.

"Information on Domestic Violence." n.d. Domestic Abuse Shelter of the Florida Keys. http://www.domesticabuseshelter.org/InfoDomesticViolence.htm.

Joyce, James. 1938. *Ulysses*. New York: Random House.

Kimmel, Michael S. 2001. "Male Victims of Domestic Violence: A Substantive and Methodological Research Review; A Report to the Equality Committee of the Department of Education and Science." National Online Resource Center on Violence against Women. http://vawnet.org/Assoc_Files_VAWnet/GenderSymmetry.pdf.

————. 2002. "Gender Symmetry in Domestic Violence: A Substantive and Methodological Research Review." *Violence against Women* 8 (11): 1332–63.

Kirk-Duggan, Cheryl, ed. 2003. *Pregnant Passion: Gender, Sex, and Violence in the Bible.* Atlanta: Society of Biblical Literature.

Lapsley, Jacqueline. 2005. *Whispering the Word: Hearing Women's Stories in the Old Testament.* Louisville: Westminster John Knox.

Matthews, Shelly, and E. Leigh Gibson, eds. 2005. *Violence in the New Testament.* New York: T&T Clark.

Morrison, Toni. 1992. *Playing in the Dark.* Cambridge: Cambridge University Press.

Murphy, Andrew R., ed. 2011. *The Blackwell Companion to Religion and Violence.* Malden, MA: Wiley-Blackwell.

Nelson-Pallmeyer, Jack. 2003. *Is Religion Killing Us: Violence in the Bible and the Quran.* Harrisburg, PA: Trinity Press International.

O'Brien, Julia M. 2008. *Challenging Prophetic Metaphor: Theology and Ideology in the Prophets.* Louisville: Westminster John Knox.

O'Brien, Julia M., and Chris Franke, eds. 2010. *Aesthetics of Violence in the Prophets.* New York: T&T Clark.

O'Connor, Kathleen. 2011. *Jeremiah: Pain and Promise.* Philadelphia: Fortress.

O'Day, Gail R., and David L. Petersen, eds. 2009. *Theological Bible Commentary.* Louisville: Westminster John Knox.

Patte, Daniel, ed. 2004. *Global Bible Commentary.* Nashville: Abingdon.

Reinhartz, Adele. 2005. "Love, Hate, and Violence in the Gospel of John." Pages 109–23 in *Violence in the New Testament.* Edited by Shelly Matthews and E. Leigh Gibson. New York: T&T Clark.

Rosenblatt, Louise M. 1978. *The Reader, the Text, the Poem: The Transactional Theory of the Literary Work.* London: Southern Illinois University Press.

Rowlett, Lori. 1996. *Joshua and the Rhetoric of Violence: A New Historicist Analysis.* Sheffield: Sheffield Academic.

Scholz, Susanne. 2010. *Sacred Witness: Rape in the Hebrew Bible.* Philadelphia: Fortress.

Seibert, Eric A. 2012. *The Violence of Scripture: Overcoming the Old Testament's Troubling Legacy.* Philadelphia: Fortress.

Trible, Phyllis. 1984. *Texts of Terror: Literary-Feminist Readings of Biblical Narratives.* Philadelphia: Fortress.

Warrior, Robert. 2005. "Canaanites, Cowboys, and Indians." *USQR* 59: 1–8.

Weems, Renita. 1988. *Just a Sister Away: Understanding the Timeless Connection between Women of Today and Women in the Bible*. San Diego, CA: LuraMedia.

Williams, James G. 1992. *The Bible, Violence, and the Sacred: Liberation from the Myth of Sanctioned Violence*. San Francisco: Harper San Francisco.

Zenger, Erich. 1996. *A God of Vengeance? Understanding the Psalms of Divine Wrath*. Louisville: Westminster John Knox.

PART 3
RESPONSES

"The Earth Was Filled With Violence": Reading the Hebrew Bible against *La Violencia*

Nancy Bedford

One of the most problematic misconceptions that circulate in our societies is the idea that incidents of violence are surprising, unexpected, and rather like an act of nature that could not have been foreseen. On the contrary, violence in its various forms is knit into the very structure of our globalized economy and into the dominant "common sense" norms of our cultures. By focusing on the notion of *la violencia* as a hermeneutical key in reading the Hebrew Bible, the essays in this book help us perceive how the institutional and systemic components of violence permeate society, traversing cultural, political, economic, and religious institutions.

Slavoj Žižek (2008) suggests that, in order to understand violence, we should look at it "sideways" or "awry." When we observe violence, there tends to be more to what is going on than is visible at first. According to Žižek, there are, in fact, multiple dimensions involved. At the most obvious level, we perceive or experience *subjective* violence clearly in the foreground, performed by an "identifiable agent." However, if we respond only to that dimension, we miss the backdrop of the violence we have perceived, which is instrumental in generating it. Žižek calls that background the *objective* side of violence. This objective dimension can be further divided into *symbolic* violence (at work at and embodied in our languages and in our universes of meaning) and *systemic* violence, resulting from the way our economic and political systems work (1–2).

Žižek's taxonomy is helpful, because it allows for a deeper and wider context by which to understand violence when it flares up. Violence does not emerge out of nowhere against a normal background of peace and absence of violence. Rather, the norm is already violent both symbolically and systemically (Žižek 2008, 1–2). When we become caught up in the narrative about one crisis of violence after the other in the world, our response to that violence will be inadequate if we only take into account the subjective effect and forget the objective (systemic and symbolic) depths whence violence arises. At most, they will treat the symptoms without really getting a handle on the disease itself. It is therefore vital not only to "do" or "act" viscerally in response to violence, but also to take the time to analyze and to use the instruments of theory to understand it, which is also a form of praxis. In other words, we should not fall prey to what Žižek calls the "anti-theoretical edge" of the urgent injunctions to action that emerge every time we feel outraged by violence (Žižek 2008, 6). Rather, understanding and discernment are called for.

This is where the essays in this book can lend us a hand. By focusing on *la violencia* in its various historical and contextual manifestations, they help us in discerning and understanding how the Hebrew Scriptures, whose stories and cadences are so formative for many of us, can be complicit in the manufacture of violence as well as provide inspiration in resisting and interrupting violence.

Several distinct themes emerge in the essays and serve to connect them to each other. One discovers throughout the book a threefold dynamic that appears to some extent in most of the essays. First, they analyze how biblical interpretation can condone and contribute to violence, with reference to concrete texts and contextualized examples. The awareness on the part of the authors about the realities of empire, of its subaltern subjects, and its colonized territories, both in biblical times and in the history of the American continent since the European invasion that began in 1492, shines a spotlight on the complexity and urgency of the task of biblical interpretation. Second, they recognize the need for biblical interpreters to be vigilant against any sort of hermeneutic that condones violence and injustice. A hermeneutic can become violent by remaining silent and not recognizing its own complicity with violence. Some forms of interpretation even actively promote violence. Third, they offer concrete examples of how to interpret Scripture in a way that pushes back against violence and resists symbolic and systemic violence, particularly manifestations that have to do with the political, cultural, and economic oppression of the most vulnerable in a given society.

As the essays make clear, in order for us to be able to resist the violent use and abuse of biblical texts, it is not enough to react instinctively to the violence we perceive in Scripture or to believe it is justified ideologically by Scripture. It is also not enough to think about the problem (Žižek's discernment and understanding), even though such theoretical ground-work is indispensable and provided in various ways in each of the essays. The process of constructing a contextually appropriate, nonviolent inter-pretation in a given time and place requires us also to come to terms with our own stories, trajectories, privileges, and indeed with trauma at personal and collective levels. Our social location and history inevitably color our readings in ways that are sometimes helpful and sometimes less so. To the extent that we are unable to recognize our complicities with a given injustice, it is also difficult to recognize the complicities of given biblical texts or interpretations with the violence that upholds that injustice.

A liberating, decolonial, nonviolent hermeneutic requires humility, honesty, self-awareness, and an openness to continual conversion, growth, and transformation. Expressed theologically, what is required is the prac-tice of personal and communal discernment and persistent openness to the transformative work of the Spirit. In what follows, I would like to engage in some musings about what most struck me about each of the essays. I do so not as a biblical scholar, but as a Christian theologian who loves Scripture and engages with it regularly in writing, teaching, and preaching in Span-ish and in English, both in Latin America and in the United States, where I now live.

I confess that in reading the Hebrew Bible since childhood I have most often skipped over the oracles, wanting to get to the promises or eschato-logical visions that tend to appear near the end of prophetic books. I had rarely stopped to ask myself what the ideological function of the oracles might be. Steed Vernal Davidson's explanation that they are literary-colo-nial devices emanating from a colonized elite that ends up supporting the ideology of the Persian Empire gave me a way into those texts that is illu-minating to me as a theologian, particularly for the task of spiritual dis-cernment. After all, I belong to a fairly large cadre of Latin American born theologians living and working in the United States. I have to ask myself to what extent my own theological production is co-opted by living and working in this present day Babylon (or Persia or Rome), so that simi-larly to the redactors of those texts, I consciously or unconsciously am entrapped by an ideology of empire that warrants violence. In other words, I am reminded by this interpretation of the oracles to check to what extent I am colonized or co-opted by the symbolic violence of this empire.

I think we probably all sometimes fall into this sort of violence in our theologies, regardless of our intentions and loyalties. For example, how much of my teachings should be dedicated to informing students about realities such as United States military and economic interventions in Latin America with which many of my class participants are usually unacquainted? Does a tactical decision to devote more time to addressing other burning questions of the day end up skewing my theological pedagogy in the direction of imperial interests? The biblical oracles as presented by Davidson serve as reminders as to how empire colonizes our imagination, our desires, and our theological production. They challenge me to continue to struggle pedagogically and in my writing against the normalization of imperial violence and the myth of redemptive violence that permeate life, including the life of many churches, in the United States.

That the United States-Mexico border is a site of racial and imperial violence is clear to anyone who has paid attention to the history of the borderlands. Gregory Lee Cuéllar's essay links some of that violence to specific Protestant readings of Scripture that legitimize it, including the particular form of physical and symbolic violence exercised by the Texas Rangers or *Rinches*. This brings the matter very close to home to me as a reader, not only because I am a Protestant, but because according to family lore my father's side includes a number of men (mostly Baptists) who in the nineteenth century belonged to the Rangers, including my great-grandfather. These men were "Anglos" in the sense that they spoke English and had English surnames (one of which I bear). Several of them had Native American mothers or wives, but that did not stop them from identifying with the Anglo-Protestant project, that is, with US-American expansionism and "Manifest Destiny" interpreted as the result of divine providence. Their stories illustrate how the forces of white racism, patriarchy, colonialism, and biblical hermeneutics came together for my white ancestors as an aspirational project even if they were barely surviving as sharecroppers and subsistence farmers. It would be a mistake to presume that the hermeneutical underpinnings of this project have fully dissipated from the white Protestant tradition and the white evangelical tradition in particular, which is why understanding the history of the borderlands continues to be crucial for a liberating theology.

Indeed, it would be difficult to understand white racist resistance to Mexican and Central American immigration specifically, as well as the opposition to the legalization of undocumented Latin Americans in the United States more broadly, without understanding the religious and indeed scriptural undertones of the discussion. Though securing or maintaining an economic advantage is certainly part of the dynamic, purely

economic explanations of the rationale for the persecution of undocumented immigrants today, carried out by paramilitary groups (such as the
"Minutemen") at the border, fall short. Such groups are also bolstered by
their appropriation of a "divine right" to the land their white forefathers
wrested away by force from people with brown skin. Majority white Evangelical and Protestant denominations and organizations in the United
States have put out statements decrying violence toward immigrants,
quoting the Hebrew Bible's injunctions to respect and protect the stranger,
the widow, and the orphan and calling for comprehensive immigration
reform.[1] Such initiatives will likely be insufficient to sway their base to
change its attitudes if the basic sin of white racism and the myths that
underlie white privilege are not dealt with head on, including both family
and national lore about the "glorious" deeds of the past and the religious
justification for US-American expansionism, militarism, and imperialism.

The analysis of gang violence in Honduras and other Central American countries, offered by Renata Furst, unpacks the logic of violence from
the perspective of its victims. She does not forget the connection between
personal experiences of violence and the wider web of symbolic and systemic violence that helps generate them. By hewing to the perspective of
the victims and not of the victimizers in her reading of Habbakuk, Furst
reads the text against the grain and to subvert the interpretive habit of
reading from the perspective of the powerful. It is not easy to do so, as she
points out. It takes an act of deconstruction.

As a theologian what comes to my mind in reading her essay is how
dangerous it is to try to resolve the theodicy question theoretically in a
way that distances God from the suffering of the world. If the cost of
defending God's "justice" is to obscure the experience of the vulnerable,
then that cost is too high. Paradoxically, the insistence on keeping the
experience of the victims of violence in the foreground (Žižek's "subjective" dimension), as Furst does, makes the connections to systemic and
symbolic violence (Žižek's "objective" dimension) clearer, rather than
obscuring them.[2] Her approach allows for a narrative that cannot resolve
the trauma of suffering such violence, but it *can* be part of a response to

---

1. See, e.g., the "Evangelical Statement of Principles for Immigration Reform"
(n.d.) of the Evangelical Immigration Table endorsed by many evangelical leaders;
available online at http://evangelicalimmigrationtable.com/.

2. Unlike Furst, Žižek does not privilege the perspective of the most vulnerable
and tends to speak of the experience of violence as mediated to relatively privileged

it. Theologically speaking, her work challenges me to articulate hope in God not as one who works "through" violence, but rather works "against" it, empowering us to resist its appeal and its mystique as the best way to resolve problems.

It is admittedly very difficult to articulate hope in God as one who resists violence rather than justifying it (i.e., a liberating eschatology), if we live in a state of fear. Through his reading of Judith and Tobit, José Enrique Ramírez-Kidd illustrates how an imperial politics of domination instills fear and leads us (as subjects of empire) to internalize it, to express that fear as submission, and in turn to become complicit with imperial violence. The essay serves as a reminder that not all violence is physical, taking us once again into the terrain of symbolic and systemic violence. It describes the psychological suffering entailed in the "normalization" of violence as a way of life along with the colonization of our imaginations, so that we have a hard time visualizing options and possibilities outside of what has become the norm. Theologically, it leads me to wonder what concrete ways there might be to resist this "pedagogy of fear" and to imagine alternatives. After all, we are "subjects" of empire both in the sense of being subjected to it and in that of having a subjectivity that resists being entirely colonized. Pablo R. Andiñach's reading of a biblical narrative as a protest against imperial violence seems to open some space for such resistance by rereading the mythical text about Babel found in the Hebrew Bible in light of reigning myths in our own time.

If one of the characteristics of an imperial politics of domination and violence is to impose its own logic as the only "door to the divine" and therefore to divine favor (however it might be defined), Andiñach presents us with a key to resisting such domination. We must refuse to believe, that is, internalize, the dominant conception of the divine. In other words, the "subjects" of a given imperial system exercise their subjectivity by refusing to recognize the divinity that has become an instrument of oppression. As Andiñach suggests, we can fashion counter-narratives that demythologize imperial "doors to God" in part by retrieving or improvising language that allows us to do so creatively. Perhaps one concrete way for us to denormalize a regime of fear and violence is to explore the possibilities of "poetic reason" found in novels, poetry, songs, dance, movies, and many other

---

subjects through images and reporting: as information *about* violence, not as violence felt in our own bodies or in the bodies of those we love.

forms of cultural production. Such poetic reason invites the construction of knowledge that is the outcome of both the intellect and poetic sensibility, guided and directed by the latter.[3] It seems to me that a biblical hermeneutics sensitive to poetic reason can be a powerful instrument of hope and love. It is a practice of "casting out fear."

By tackling Gen 19 and Judg 19, Cheryl B. Anderson provides a concrete example of the power of biblical hermeneutics for good and ill, as seen in the outworking of the HIV/AIDS crisis in the African American community in the United States. She specifically challenges us to consider how our reading of Scripture contributes (or not) to the maintenance of a "mythical norm" that privileges those who are male, heterosexual, light-skinned, and privileged. What I find especially helpful about Anderson's work is that she models how to evaluate our habits of interpretation by looking at them from the perspective of a very concrete reality, in this case the transmission and perception of HIV/AIDS in a given population. She uncovers how a form of implicit violence, that is, the apparently "innocent" and "objective" exegesis of certain texts in the Hebrew Bible, leads to explicit violence experienced in bodies that do not conform in whole or in part to the mythical norm. There are many other concrete realities that affect the most vulnerable in a given society and could be used in a similar way: feminicide, police and military violence against people of color, the systematic despoiling of land belonging to native communities, environmental racism, erosion of civil and political rights of citizens alongside the expansion of the rights of corporations, clergy sexual abuse, hate crimes against persons identifying as LGBTQ, mistreatment of undocumented migrants, and many other such situations. As Anderson shows, it is not a matter of saying simply that it is the Bible's "fault" that such things happen, but rather of learning ways to identify interpretations that legitimize violence and conversely of developing a hermeneutics of retrieval that is life-giving.

Susanne Scholz provides just such an exercise in her essay. She shows how dominant modes of biblical hermeneutics in the United States contribute to a culture of internal violence both by omission (silence) and by commission (specific interpretations that condone violence). From a Latin American perspective, we sometimes think primarily about the violence

---

3. The expression *razón poética* was coined by Spanish philosopher María Zambrano (1904–1991) (see Zambrano 1939).

exercised by the United States as going outwards. However, the United States also polices its subaltern subjects internally with particular vehemence. It also allows the myth of redemptive violence to permeate the very fabric of its national project, as the rhetoric of its political leaders illustrates.[4] In light of this dynamic, it is vital to pay attention to the ways in which biblical scholarship contributes directly or indirectly to structures of domination. Scholz proposes a sociological framework in order to do so. Her analysis of three approaches to the interpretation of Judg 21 is a helpful exercise, because it illustrates how scholars are already always embedded in violent structures. The sociological framework allows her to uncover the politics of such exegetical argumentation. It is up to us as readers and interpreters, then, to learn to be transparent about our own complicities with the dominant logic of violence and domination, and to propose interpretations that contest systemic and symbolic violence.

Our hermeneutical contestations of violence will always be tentative, partial, and fraught with ambiguity. We can never fully escape our complicities with violence, and expressed theologically, we cannot achieve "perfection." The ambiguity even of what we think of as our best work becomes particularly evident in Serge Frolov's treatment of the problem of forced labor in Deut 20. He connects this biblical passage to concrete historical examples of forced labor practices in the former Soviet Union and on the American continent. He underlines how very unhelpful blanket denunciations of a given system, such as capitalism, and glib readings of Scripture are. They are too simplistic and do not take into account the unintended consequences even of well-intentioned policies and decisions. I have to ask myself as a theologian how often I fall into the ease of blanket denunciations rather than careful nuanced analysis. One of the challenges of a critical theology is to be clear about the censure of injustice and violence while also being aware of the intricacy and at times the

---

4. US-American political leaders ritually ask "God" (which god?) to "bless the United States of America" (in what way?). They also ritually thank the police and the military for their service in making "us" (whom?) "safer" (from whom or what?). Any variation from these ritual assertions or any association with those who question them can endanger the viability of a political candidate, as the case of Barack Obama's relationship with his former pastor Jeremiah Wright illustrates. Obama distanced himself from Wright in part as a result of Wright's sermon on "Confusing God and Government" (delivered on April 13, 2003 at Trinity UCC in Chicago), which critiqued US-American civil religion, militarism, and colonialism and questioned the myth of redemptive violence (for a transcript, see FreakyBoy 2008).

opacity of reality. It probably impossible to achieve both at once, which is one reason a multiplicity of voices and interlocutors, such as those in this book, is vital.

The essays indeed point to the complexity and ambiguity of our hermeneutical task. Admitting such complexity does not belie our responsibility to tackle interpretive practices that condone violence. It also has distinct consequences specifically for pedagogy. It is no coincidence that all of the authors are engaged in teaching and in learning, and I suspect the same will hold for most of this volume's readers. Julia M. O'Brien engages the contours of a pedagogy in her essay that addresses the ethical dimensions of biblical violence, taking us straight back to direct experiences of violence and to its resulting trauma. It is Žižek's "subjective" dimension. O'Brien thus takes us to the heart of the matter when people confront both the violence contained in the biblical text itself and in the various ways it has been interpreted throughout time. They wonder if the "good book" is really such a good book after all.

O'Brien centers on the problem of the double trauma when those who have survived profoundly abusive and violent situations and relationships have to read about biblical violence. In studying violent texts and by attempting to interrupt violent habits of interpretation with others, O'Brien worries that this very practice retraumatizes them. What I find helpful about her concern is that she engages in a hermeneutical spiral that returns her back to her assumptions and explicit or implicit presuppositions about how to engage Scripture. She realizes so clearly that different students are affected differently by her practices of interpretation. In other words, she knows that what is liberating for her work on biblical violence may not be as effective or as liberating to other people. This is a vital acknowledgment about the limits of any one person's pedagogical efforts.

Rather than disheartening, I find O'Brien's recognition about our intrinsic limitations as interpreters very encouraging. We need each other as companions on the hermeneutical journey. We need each other's correction and mutual encouragement. We need each other for dispute and for dialogue, for insight and for challenge, and for continued instruction on how la violencia manifests itself. As a theologian, I add that we also need God's Spirit to prod us toward discernment, engagement of difficult topics, the recognition of our own complicity with violence, so that we feel encouraged along the way. As in the Genesis story of the deluge, from God's perspective and from ours, the earth is still full of violence (Gen 6:11) on the experiential, systemic, and symbolic levels. Yet the earth is also filled with signs of nonviolent resistance and hope for shalom that we can help each other discover.

Works Cited

"Evangelical Statement of Principles for Immigration Reform." n.d. Evangelical Immigration Table. http://evangelicalimmigrationtable.com/.

FreakyBoy. 2008. "God Damn America." The Sluggite Zone. http://www.sluggy.net/forum/viewtopic.php?p=315691&sid=4b3e97ace4ee8cee02bd6850e52f50b7.

Zambrano, María. 1939. *Filosofía y poesía*. Morelia: Publicaciones de la Universidad Michoacana.

Žižek, Slavoj. 2008. *Violence: Six Sideways Reflections*. New York: Picador.

La Violencia and the Return of the Monstrous: A Response

Todd Penner

> And the lord [Marduk] stood upon Tiamat's hinder parts,
> And with his merciless club he smashed her skull.
> He cut through the channels of her blood,
> And he made the North wind bear it away into secret places.
> His fathers beheld, and they rejoiced and were glad;
> Presents and gifts they brought unto him.
> Then the lord rested, gazing upon her dead body.
>
> Enuma Elish (King 1902)

> Then a mighty angel picked up a boulder the size of a large millstone and threw it into the sea, and said: "with such violence the great city of Babylon will be thrown down, never to be found again."
> After this I heard what sounded like the roar of a great multitude in heaven shouting: "Hallelujah! Salvation and glory and power belong to our God, for true and just are his judgments. He has condemned the great prostitute who corrupted the earth by her adulteries. He has avenged on her the blood of his servants."
>
> Rev 18:21; 19:1–2 (NIV)

The authors in this volume have provided us with a rich and varied discussion of *la violencia* as it is manifested both globally and locally through acts of violence, discursive ideological formations that bolster systemic violence, and the repercussions of the oppressive socioeconomic conditions that result from the interrelationship of acts and discourses, deeds and words.[1] The authors further link their varying discus-

---

1. I am grateful to the editors of this volume for the invitation to offer a response. I am particularly appreciative of Susanne Scholz for her editorial efforts and encour-

sions to the Hebrew Bible in multiple ways, exploring the deployment of biblical discourses in recent history towards violent ends, the violence inherent in the biblical text itself, and the possible resistant models that biblical discourses might offer to sustained violence. Additionally, many of the authors wrestle with the failure of biblical scholarship to address head-on some of the difficulties that the Hebrew Bible poses ethically with respect to its sustained investment in violence. As well, many engage the general tensions that exist in the text between a hope for a world without violence and the violent means by which such hope is frequently imagined to materialize. The authors are keen to draw, when they can, on their own experiences of violence and certainly on their assessments of the urgent contemporary questions and issues that confront our local and global communities—and these are legion! Overall, taken as a whole, this volume offers a testament to the ongoing struggles by scholars to bring the ancient texts to bear on our world, making the Bible speak to us anew, even as we also ask it to account for itself, perhaps at times even putting God on trial in a court of our own design. In the midst of what is clearly an interpretive struggle, one that involves a force and fierceness of its own, the scholars in this volume work doubly hard not to leave us in a hopeless and helpless state, in the darkness of a deep, unsettling malaise.

In its original usage, *la violencia* refers to a particular period in Colombian history (1948–1958) that was marked by an epidemic of ferocious violence that killed nearly 200,000 people (Roldán 2002). More generally, it has been applied to other periods of violence in Colombia as well as in neighboring countries such as Guatemala (where it is used to identify the civil strife of 1978–1984). In its original usage, the "violence" designated by *la violencia* focuses on the tragedy and horror of civil war and not the structural matters involved in state violence. "The violence" is a period or

agements, as well as her incisive feedback on the essay. I owe Davina Lopez a great debt for her substantive feedback on this piece and for the enriching and sustained exchanges on the subjects contained herein. Thanks also to Doug McMahon for the many conversations over the past year that have helped rekindle the spirit and nurture thinking about difficult and complicated matters—his friendship has been life-giving. This essay is dedicated to Janette, an eight-year old whirling dervish of a girl, who lives in Mott Haven, Bronx, New York. She tutored a professor on many subjects, including the ways that trauma and joy, terror and delight, neglect and curiosity, violence and caring could co-mingle in the same moment—perhaps even consubstantiate. Life goes on, wherever it goes on.

an epoch of violence, and certainly the Hebrew Bible resonates here, as one might well frame the majority of the narrated history of Israel as one long period involving internal and external violent entanglements, often in the extreme.

As it is used throughout this volume, *la violencia* signifies "structural violence" in its discursive and physically manifested forms. When one refers to structural violence and the discursive and physical apparatuses of oppression, one moves into the territory of constructing those who dominate and those who are subdued. To be sure, the Hebrew Bible fuels such conceptions with its portraits of wicked tyrants who rise up to punish the people of Israel. Granted, in the biblical tradition there is the ever present thread of "but the people asked for it," not unlike the caricature of the domestic abuser who says: "Well, if she wouldn't lip off, I wouldn't have to hit her." In the biblical tradition, this notion is framed by "covenant faithfulness," with the people being punished for failing to live up to their covenantal obligations. Whatever the specifics of the biblical logic are, it is evident that this volume highlights the nature of biblical discourse as problematic while at the same time reinscribing some of the larger structural problematics in the very act of critiquing them. In other words, within the framework of biblical referents, it is almost impossible to escape the "us" versus "them," "good" versus "evil," construct. The Bible does not just invite adopting such an optic, it more or less demands it. Indeed, the deity of the Bible demands "justice," and it is a demand that divides those who will be justified and those who will be judged most harshly. When someone like Job builds up the confidence to inquire so as to make sense of this framework, particularly in situations where it does not make sense or seem to reflect reality, God responds by making clear that it is always a zero sum game: "Would you discredit my justice? Would you condemn me to justify yourself?" (Job 40:8; NIV).

In some sense it is very difficult for any interpreter of the Bible to escape that framework. How could we? One might well argue that it matters little whether one views the Hebrew Bible as an authoritative text or sees it as something to resist—either way someone is on top (and justified) and someone is at the bottom (and receives the swift hand of judgment). The only difference is who occupies those positions. Some twenty-five years ago in his *Myth of Innocence*, New Testament scholar Burton Mack (1988) addressed this point clearly as it related to the development of the Christian tradition, particularly the Gospel of Mark (see also Lopez and Penner 2015). He argued that the portrayal of Jesus as the innocent victim was constructed in such a way so as to justify the actions of Christians against Jews and others at later points in time. The narrative thus provides a discursive framework in which there are the "innocents" and the "perpetrators," and the latter deserve whatever violence may be enacted against them in the future. Mack goes on to argue that this gospel logic is embedded in American discourses of exceptionalism. Moreover, scholars who study the gospel texts are similarly influenced by this biblical rhetoric, which itself was designed to justify later actions rather than reflect historical realities per se. As a result, and pertinent to the discussion of *la violencia* here, is the idea that the biblical texts, even in their most seemingly innocent moments, may in fact be operating at much more suspect levels. Now, perhaps this should not surprise us. The Bible is, after all, a most human book. As such, it is comprised of the same contradictions and complications and confoundings that mark human activity through time.

In the end, however, we arrive back at the burning question of this volume: What does the Hebrew Bible have to offer to us in our time of violence? Is the Bible just part of the problem? Can it be a component of the solution? But then, what exactly do we want to solve? Do we want the world to be less violent? Do we just want to point out the horrific travesties and transgressions that mark the global scene? Do we want to feel virtuous about ourselves for asking these questions, for being the kind of people who think deeply and profoundly about issues related to violence and suffering? What are we willing to give up so that this world would be better? And, of course, better in what way and for whom? Who gets to determine which violence is bad and which is not, which is liberative and which is destructive? Whose ideology should be operative here? Moreover, if ideologies are as powerful as we continually suggest they are, then to what extent might our own justifications for justice in fact be products of discursive formations that have shaped us in directions that support violence in the very act of our decrying it? As I read through the essays in this volume, these are the kinds of questions that haunt me. To engage human violence at all, on any level, is a work of mourning. Perhaps in this the Hebrew Bible does offer us a site for reflection and lament, a place from which to meditate upon the larger structures of those structures of violence we are wont to envision. Perhaps this is a good place to start: what do we make of and do with a world in which violence must always be with us, and in which every attempt to address violence of necessity brings more violence into being?

In the Beginning Was Violence

The creation stories of the ancient Near East are rife with violence. The Enuma Elish provides something of a paradigm in this respect, wherein we find monstrous creatures rising up to wreak havoc, only to find themselves torn asunder in turn. Heads roll. Blood flows. The heavens and the earth are formed from the broken body of Tiamat. Life comes into being through death. And not just any kind of death—one that is ferociously violent. The story of the ascension of Marduk to the status of chief deity of the pantheon brings with it the necessary suffering and destruction of hideous monsters. Indeed, in these so-called *Chaoskampf* narratives chaos, represented in the form of a monster, not infrequently a sea serpent functioning as a representation of the sea as a primordial force of disruption and disorder, finds itself in a cosmic struggle with the principle of order, usually represented by one of the chief gods of the pantheon (e.g., Marduk, Baal, Seth, Yahweh). When ancient Near Eastern peoples came to imagine the creation of their worlds, they did so in language and conceptions that seemed most familiar to them, that is, in terms related to conquest, domination, and violence. Making sense of the worlds they inhabited, violence was not merely an aberration, it was the structural principle of the world itself. No doubt the fierce destruction of a Tiamat was understandable and justifiable. After all, she represented the monsters that come in the night, those demons that terrorize and threaten the ordering principle that keeps the world in balance. Of course, that very ordering principle is itself a force of reckoning, holding out the threat of force to anything that opposes the imperium. Violence is not the purview of either chaos or order; it is, rather, what keeps the world in balance. That is a sobering thought. Rather than being a "necessary evil," violence seemingly exists as a natural force: it is the way the world is. After all, it is how the world was brought into being, forming the birth canal for the origin of life.

The biblical narratives that relate to creation are often taken to be radically different than those of the surrounding cultures, something set apart, offering a challenge to the polytheistic models that were prevalent. To be sure, within the Hebrew Bible there are traces of creation traditions that echo the kinds of chaos models we find elsewhere (Batto 1992). Passages such as Job 9:13 and 26:12–13, Isa 27:1 and 51:9, Ps 89:9 and especially 74:12–17 provide ample attestation that some ancient biblical traditions cohered more closely with the accounts such as the Enuma Elish. The *Chaoskampf* motif, as it relates to the sea and its monstrous inhabitants, also quite possibly underlies the narrative of Exod 15, wherein the "Song of the Sea" presents the birth narrative of the people of Israel, similarly connected to God subduing the sea and destroying enemies (Batto 1992, 102–27). Throughout the Hebrew Bible, we also see references to tyrants and foreign kings constructed in semi-mythological categories as the monstrous, relating back to the theme of Yahweh's triumph over the forces of chaos at creation (Grottanelli 1999, 47–72).

These motifs, however, seem remote from the dominant account in Gen 1–2.[2] Yet I ask whether the Genesis creation account is all that different from the chaos narratives that it is assumed to categorically reject. In my view, this argument is important for our understanding of violence, because the biblical text, as it now stands, creates something of the "myth of innocence" mentioned above. The key element is the rhetorical force of the text, or, more precisely, the force of the rhetoric of God. In point of fact, despite all of the apparent eschewing of the so-called "mythological" trappings of other ancient Near Eastern creation stories, the Genesis text maintains one fundamental connection: the investment of the cosmos arising in the midst of order being sustained over against chaos. At the root of the creation narrative in Genesis lies an effort by the deity to provide a bulwark against disorder, to tame chaos, and, indeed, to conquer it. Perhaps we lack the specific personifications or names of deities in the text, but the principle is the same: order conquers chaos. The biblical account is even more obsessive about the ordering process. The commands and prohibitions—the law—that come into play in Eden among the first humans in effect are the obvious outcomes of the ordering process that brings creation into being. That action is swift when there is a violation—and the consequences are severe: pain, suffering, and death—makes clear that order is paramount.

---

2. As is well known, the creation narrative in the book of Genesis is comprised of two accounts, one (Gen 1:1-2:4a) traditionally attributed to the Priestly (P) source and the other (Gen 2:4b-25) to the Yahwist (J) source. For the purposes of my discussion I refer to them as a collective whole (Gen 1:1-2:25). My understanding is that both narratives reflect a similar rhetorical and logical structure in their original literary traditions with respect to their focus on order. Moreover, the two narratives are the "introduction" to the Hebrew Bible canon as it has been put together in the early CE centuries, and before that they introduced the Torah proper, and thus ideologically they cohere within the same rhetorical structure. Hence, even if there were a difference in the conception of order in J over P at one time, the rhetoric of the final redactor structures the entire account of Gen 1–2.

Do we really find a gentler, kinder deity in Genesis in comparison with Marduk in the Enuma Elish? In Genesis, we certainly find a more palatable god from the standpoint of modern sensibilities. This deity speaks from the heavens, forcing the process by words rather than through the bludgeoning of a rival. Dare we say we have a more "civilized" version, perhaps something to be contrasted with the "barbarism" of the Canaanites or the Babylonians—something more "rational," "logical," or "moral"? After all, do not our myths say something about who we aspire to be as a community? Jon Levenson (1988) holds up the creation story in Genesis as a model for how we should think about evil in the world: just as God sought to control evil and chaos in the beginning, so we should continue that same battle. Here the civilizing, ordering creation narrative provides an ample model for ethics, addressing how we should think about violence in the world—from the perspective of modeling the created order. There is something reassuring about this vision about the order of things. It is certainly comforting and comfortable, as it takes care of the "monsters under the bed." Where are they? God shines the light on them, and they disappear. We too can continue this struggle against the monstrous by similarly shining the light.

At the same time, the phenomenon is disquieting and should give us pause. The Hebrew Bible traditions are rife with justified violence, actions taken against monstrous evil-doers. The biblical traditions affirm that the obedient, those who "walk in the ways of God," will be protected, although there are biblical traditions that raise the question as to why the righteous suffer. As it turns out, not everyone who is obedient manages to avoid suffering. Even if we put to one side that conundrum, there is still the question regarding the nature of the required obedience. Obedient to what, to whom, and for what reason? The fact is that the content of the obedience—that which frames those who are "righteous"—is still regulated by law-givers. True, there is a deeply rooted system of social justice in the Bible. Yet that is not all there is. What if, at the end of the day, one does not want to serve Yahweh. Then what? What if one does not fall within the categories of biblical obedience? What happens then?

The justification for violence enacted by the deity—based on the rationale that the creator God has the divine right—is well attested in the Hebrew Bible. Indeed, God frequently acts violently to save God's people, as is the case with Egypt in the book of Exodus. The Jewish philosopher Emil Fackenheim (1972) draws on this dynamic in his book *God's Presence in History*. There, in wrestling with one of the most difficult questions of modern theology and ethics, Fackenheim seeks to understand the events of the Holocaust in view of the key question: where is God? Fackenheim does not offer a simple answer, if he really offers one at all. He notes the rather lopsided nature of God's actions in history. When God comes to deliver the people, in order to save them God destroys the "Egyptians." In other words, God's presence in history is not one that sidesteps violence. God's action in history often demands violence, and sometimes, especially in the face of some of the most horrific monsters of our time, it is required of God's people to deploy violence similarly, even if we are uncomfortable with it or unable to rationalize it.

It is striking that no matter where the Bible takes us, violence persists in the end. While we may take some comfort in the contrast between "good" and evil" that the Bible offers, it is another matter altogether how this works out in the real world. It is not by accident that the great theo-ethical mind of Reinhold Niebuhr detailed real-world responses through a form of Christian realism rather than a straightforward rendering and application of biblical ethics. Making world-defining decisions requires more than simply asking: what would the Bible have us do? However, we rarely engage the world in nuanced or complex ways. All too often we construct the "Other" in terms of the monstrous, readily replicating simplistic configurations of the moral compass. It becomes much easier to act with a biblical conviction when we know that the enemy we strike out against is one like Tiamat, Rahab, or Babylon. Not unlike what Mack suggests with respect to the portrayal of the innocent death in the Gospel of Mark (as a basis for the justification of all kinds of violence against those who were made complicit in the death of the innocent *in the narrative*), our conceptions of "good" versus "evil" rely heavily on caricatures and black-and-white modes of perception and evaluation. Only when we dehumanize individuals, communities, whole cultures, or races can we fully envision the righteous acts of violence against them. *They have to deserve it.* Every tyrant in the Bible and every monster outside of it *deserves* the fate that awaits them. While we often focus on the humanizing function of Scripture, the Bible frequently demands the opposite: the dehumanizing of the object of our fears. When the human is taken out of the equation, one acts with clarity and conviction.

Babylon in the book of Revelation provides an illustration. It is a bad day for Babylon when God decides to visit vengeance on her for her many sins and atrocities. As the text from Revelation cited above outlines, Babylon is treated almost identically by God as Tiamat is by Marduk. It is not surprising to see the end of world repeat in significant ways the moments of its beginning. Indeed, Revelation is saturated with the combat myth theme (Collins 1976). Here we see God, again, in a struggle with the forces of chaos, this time locked in a final battle, with monsters and beasts from both land and sea. This decreative moment involves speaking, and it certainly is accompanied by many declarations. However, in the final analysis it entails most fully the violence we associate with the ancient Near Eastern creation myths: God gets down and dirty through fierce intermediaries and warriors.

Yet the troubling question is what exactly Babylon did to deserve this type of treatment. Even if she deserves the punishment for committing violence against the weak and oppressed, does being monstrous represent the totality of who she is? Did she laugh and play with her children? Did she ever enjoy a good meal just for the meal's sake? Did she lend a helping hand to a family member? Did she not perhaps say a kind word of gratitude to a stranger? Did she ever stop to reflect on the poetry of Sappho or contemplate the philosophy of Plato's *Republic*? Did she ever look up at the stars and wonder what was beyond her, perhaps even marveling at her own finitude, if but for a fleeting moment? Must the monstrous be so conceptually hideous that nothing but the most gruesome death is deserved? Most importantly for my purposes here, which is the greater violence: the violent acts of Babylon against the "innocent," the violent acts of God against Babylon, or the violently dehumanizing conceptual and rhetorical categories that frame the entire interaction?

Locking Down *La Violencia*

In his book on the subject of "Lockdown America," Mark Lewis Taylor (2015) presents a compelling case for redeploying the early Christian resistance against imperial Roman rule within a context of a new imperialism in the United States. In the second edition of this book, Taylor expands his argument further, demonstrating the substantively oppressive nature of America's fixation on mass incarceration and the death penalty. Taylor argues that there exists a close relationship between the United States war on terror abroad and the attempt to lockdown America domestically. It is not uncommon in times of imperial expansion to see corollary efforts to domesticate the home front. Such efforts of domestication come at a price. For instance, everyone knows about the killing of young men of color, predominantly African American men, by the police. The death of Michael Brown in Ferguson, Missouri, provided a flashpoint for this concern in summer 2014, galvanizing local and national communities and even the federal government and producing substantive criticism of the use of brutal/brutalizing police force. Similarly, the recent suicide of Kalief Browder, who was held for three years at Rikers Island as a teenager whilst he awaited trial on the charge of stealing a backpack, demonstrates not just the brokenness of the judicial system and the alarming absence of accountability, but also the overarching societal indifference to the plight of young men of color. Clearly the conversations about Lockdown America are much needed.

At the same time, we must ask how we, in society, maintain the balance between order and chaos or between one kind of order and another form of order we consider "deviant." Do we want safe streets? At what cost? Do we want to be safe in the world? At what cost? Lockdown America is an excessive regime of violence, indiscriminate and indifferent—and to be sure, racist, sexist, and fully tainted by economic and class biases—but is it not necessary too? Do we really want a "kinder, gentler" police force or military? Here the classic, culturally resonant, court scene played out between Tom Cruise and Jack Nicholson in *A Few Good Men* comes to mind, the one in which Jack Nicholson's character, Colonel Nathan Jessep, offers up his "You Can't Handle the Truth" speech, which is apropos to the discussion at hand:

> Son, we live in a world that has walls, and those walls have to be guarded by men with guns.... My existence, while grotesque and incomprehensible to you, saves lives. You don't want the truth, because deep down in places you don't talk about at parties, you want me on that wall—you *need* me on that wall. We use words like "honor," "code," "loyalty." We use these words as the backbone of a life spent defending something. You use them as a punch line. I have neither the time nor the inclination to explain myself to a man who rises and sleeps under the blanket of the very freedom that I provide and then questions the manner in which I provide it. I would rather that you just said "thank you" and went on your way. (Reiner 1992)

Colonel Jessep has a point. The balance between differing regimes of order and ordering is delicate. It is easy to be idealistic about how things ought to be over against the realities of how they actually are. While I do not make an argument here condoning military or police brutality, we do need to realize that when the military and police act they often must do so in violent ways—this is a tension. And this tension should push us to reflect more broadly on the nature of violence, what we mean by it, what we want from it, what we want it to do for us, and our overall relationship to it.

We all benefit from the enforcement of Lockdown America. No one wants to live in a world that permits the "orders of horror" to be unleashed, what we might perceive as "chaos." We desire "taming." It is "deep in our bones," "in our DNA," a key component to evolutionary survival. This desire/need has enabled us, ironically, to pursue an unencumbered analysis and critique of "taming" and "ordering," as I do here. Yet, I am deeply uncomfortable with that relationship and balance, as it brings us back to the discussion of the biblical creation account. I find myself embracing a model in which violence that is used to my benefit (and, of course, to the benefit of the greater social good, as defined by my segment of society and my "better self") is "good" violence, even as I maintain that we need to be more humane, more understanding, and less aggressive in our enforcements, including our understanding of how one regime of violence such as racism, which we categorically reject, infiltrates and shapes another regime of violence, such as policing, which we may endorse on some level. Admittedly, this is a luxury position. Someone in the Armed Forces or one charged with policing gang-infested streets would probably not find this social logic comforting, as their lives are on the line. How we relate to violence, what we think about it, what we consider just and fair, *is very much a matter of our social location.* I do not say that people cannot respond to violence differently as history has shown that many people do. However, for most of us, we are socially located with respect to violence in ways that shape what we see as legitimate and what we perceive as nonlegitimate. Largely, we do not give much thought to the violence—physical, social, or economic—that sustains our ways of life. We take this violence for granted. It is part of the "background noise." Rather than being an act of thoughtlessness, such taking for granted functions well for us: it is not to our advantage to examine these issues too closely, as matters become less clear and more unsettling when we do. While the unexamined life might not be worth living, the examined one can be difficult to bear.

If violence and our relationship to it is a matter of social location, then our social location relates to *la violencia* in various ways. The observation about the effect of our relationship to violence on our perceptions of violence, including legitimate and illegitimate uses, extends far beyond our local contexts. When the famed drug lord Joaquín Guzmán Loera, known by his nickname "El Chapo," escaped from a Mexican high security prison through a mile long tunnel dug into his cell in July 2015, the Mexican authorities allegedly conducted a massive manhunt. The United States authorities were dismayed and perplexed at the lapse in security, given that this particular individual was responsible for violence on a massive scale. However, in his hometown of Culiacán, Mexico, many people participated in a parade celebrating his escape. As it turns out, people in his home region viewed him as a mythic local hero, something of a Robin Hood figure, who opposes the corrupt Mexican government and stands up to the United States, seen by some as an oppressive force. This example is a reminder that even the most tyrannical monsters of our time, responsible for unimaginable acts of violence, are appreciated and valued by others, even if not by us. One's response to the violence of others depends on one's relationship to these various entities and who is seen to benefit. Our constructs of violence are not universal, and this is a most perplexing conundrum.

Bloody gang violence, drug trafficking viciousness, the tactics of terrorists, the brutality of human trafficking, and the ruthless regimes that make international news headlines are everywhere. We could go far afield and still always find our way back home, not far from the "killing fields of Wall Street." There is an intimate connection between the centers of power and the manner in which violence plays out elsewhere, on the seeming margins. We are closer to these places of horror than we or they realize. Most unsettling is that in all of this violence spread worldwide, manifesting itself in ever more diverse and hideously innovative forms, how we think about it is intimately connected to our social and economic class and our position in particularly privileged countries, those at the so-called "center." Perhaps not unlike our understanding of the creation accounts of the ancient Near East when compared to the biblical narrative, we similarly find our own assessments and deployments of violence—our mechanisms for ordering, for taming chaos—more civilized than the barbarism we are wont to find elsewhere.

It is almost impossible for us to think about violence except outside of our *habitus*, which includes our social class and value system. Yet, for all of our talk about reading the Bible "from this place" and for all of our efforts to do so, we have given rather feeble attention to examining "this place" in all of its complexities and contradictions and contestations. Perhaps the most disturbing thought is this: what if "this place" exists as it does only because "that place" exists as it does? What if violence elsewhere is necessary for us to have our lives as we want them here, including more sustainable and justice oriented forms of life? What if God can only save people by destroy-ing the Egyptians? Is our plentiful talk about violence and our passionate attempts to bring the Bible to bear on the critical questions of our own day an effort to assuage our guilt?

I do not find any easy answers to these questions. I certainly do not suggest we wash our hands of the matter and step away. However, I do think that we have only scratched the surface of the immense problem of violence in our world, and we do not yet seem to have categories in which to think about violence beyond the rhetoric we have found throughout time: that of the monstrous, the horrifying spectacle, the dehumanized subject. We live in the time of violence. We always have. We always will. Among the many questions that one could pursue here, I choose to end on this one: Who will we choose to be and become in and through our rhetorics and logics of violence?

Monsters Are Us: The Violent Return of the Repressed

In his general lectures on psychoanalysis, Sigmund Freud (1953, 26–27) summarizes succinctly his theory of the repression of sexual impulses and their consequent "return." For Freud, civilization arises precisely in diametric relationship to increased impulse renunciation, the deferral of personal gratification for the sake of the larger communal good. He notes: "The sexual are amongst the most important of the instinctive forces thus utilized: they are in this way sublimated, that is to say, their energy is turned aside from its sexual goal and diverted towards other ends, no longer sexual and socially more valuable" (27). For Freud, sexual impulse is both the source of great cultural and social achievement as well as the root of mental and emotional rupture. Speaking with the voice of a prophet, Freud notes that this great civilization that we have built up is "insecure, for the sexual impulses are with difficulty controlled; in each individual who takes up his part in the work of civilization there is a danger that a rebellion of the sexual impulses may occur" (27). Sexual impulses, as part of the untamable part of human biology, lurk just beneath the surface. Avoiding the engagement and denying the reality of this impulse serves to make life more precarious; it puts civilization and society at greater risk. As some impulses are pushed down forcefully, they can return in other, more ominous, forms. Moving beyond the pure psychology of it and rather seeing Freud as something of social theorist and critic, I think we have laid out here a valuable lens through which to understand something about the problem of violence in our world. I do not suggest that violence is tied to the repression of sexual impulses, although there probably is some connection to be made. For my purposes, I am interested in the idea that repression leads to distortion and to the denial of the self. That is to say, the more we push the monsters under the bed, pretending they are not there, the more likely they are to appear in all the more hideous formations. In light of Freud's suggestions, it is now quite clear why it is that Babylon must be treated like Tiamat at the end of time: repressing violent desire leads to its expressed overdetermination when it eventually is unleashed.

We live in a time period and culture (here in the United States) that is fixated on discourses of blame and shame. For all of our talk of tolerance, we are increasingly becoming more intolerant. Greg Lukianoff (2014) has provided excellent documentation that even in the last great bastions of free liberal thought in this country—institutions of higher education—there too we find increasingly a lockdown on open discourse and a move to public shaming. For a long while Wendy Brown (2008) has detailed how neoliberalism regulates "aversion" and uses "tolerance" as a means to limit discourses and frank exchange. In this respect, the discourses of radicalism and identity-based resistance frequently serve to tame the wilder human impulses while being thought to do the opposite (Penner and Lopez 2015, 169–213). To this end, Mack's analysis of the early Christian "myth of innocence" and its afterlives and after-effects is ever more relevant today. We experience daily a world wherein innocence is the operative discursive framework in which we embody current "technologies of the self," to borrow a concept from Michel Foucault. We continually domesticate our bodies and regulate our interactions as if people *were* innocent. And such social logics have had long-ranging impact on political, legal, and economic regulation.

More to the point of this response and the larger concerns of this collection of essays, our conceptions of violence are inevitably bound up with these current discursive and embodied trends. It seems to be the case that, as we conceptualize the world in terms of blame and shame discourse and as we configure and imbibe the "myth of innocence" ethos, we cannot help but theorize structures of oppression and violence in fairly one-sided, dehumanizing, and monstrous terms. But is this the best way to labor in this world? Is this the most life-giving expression of our imagination? More importantly, if in this one-sided process we fail to acknowledge our own monstrousness, our own lack of innocence, what are the consequences of this kind of repression? In other words, and taking Freud as a guide here, discourses of monstrosity inevitably repress our own, often very natural, impulses—those we consider monstrous, fierce, and brutal—and this denial can have devastatingly personal, communal, and societal ramifications. It is one thing to act out (even in justifiable ways) against violence (even perhaps using violent physical or rhetorical tools to do so). It is quite another to conceptualize the object of such action in monstrous terms. In the latter instance, the personal and communal rhetorics deployed in configuring monstrosity inevitably repress our own personal and communal "demons," and it is we who are dehumanized through our own dehumanizing rhetoric. The worst scenario is that in these acts of conjuring up monsters, real and imagined, we often feel justified and even smug in doing so. In moments where we both have massive repression combined with considerable self-assurance in the rightness of our actions, we are at great risk of the monstrous being unleashed in our midst.

Constructing otherness on the basis of a myth of innocence lends itself to sustaining a world in which we must create monsters in order to act out in our best interests and to seek justice and even liberation for our communities. After all, we can only envision bringing about a "New Heaven and Earth," a "New Jerusalem," through the monstrous characterization of Babylon as the obstacle that stands in the way. By operating within the signifying field of "innocence," we will inevitably utilize discourses of purity to define our motivations, to contextualize our moment, and to construct our self-identities. As Edward Ingebretsen (2001) pointedly argues, the monsters we envision *are us*. Indeed, our dehumanizing characterizations of others ultimately represent our own repressed impulses, our failure to confront our other selves, which, in point of fact, only become monstrous through being repressed.

In the final analysis, then, when we talk about *la violencia* and discuss its relationship to the biblical tradition, we should do so with a view to our own complicity in such networks of violence. I do not intend a move towards sanctimonious naming practices, nor do I imagine the onset of paralysis. Rather, how we speak about violence, how we articulate the categories and structures of *la violencia*, speaks volumes to who we are as individuals and as communities of scholars, people of faith, and Bible readers. Failing to observe the complexities and conundrums and contradictions in our articulations of violence and the violent, including in how we view the Bible in relationship to violence, only serves to repress essential aspects of who we are as human beings. In the end, the monsters we envision in and through our discourses, those beastly creatures we bring to life, are hidden parts of ourselves and our lived realities in and for others. This dynamic does not mean that we refrain from speaking about and to violence. It means, however, that we do so mindful that every monster we describe is also an essential part of us. No evil is so great that it exists outside of who we are personally and communally. Such a recognition should give us pause in our conversations about violence. It should also encourage a deep and abiding humility. At the same time, such recognition also empowers us, as the impetus for change in this world lies less in our high-minded ideals and more in precisely those forces we often fear, those parts of us tucked away under the bed.

Works Cited

Batto, Bernard Frank. 1992. *Slaying the Dragon: Mythmaking in the Biblical Tradition.* Louisville: Westminster John Knox.

Brown, Wendy. 2008. *Regulating Aversion: Tolerance in the Age of Identity and Empire.* Princeton: Princeton University Press.

Fackenheim, Emil L. 1972. *God's Presence in History: Jewish Affirmations and Philosophical Reflections.* San Francisco: HarperCollins.

Freud, Sigmund. 1953. *A General Introduction to Psychoanalysis.* Translated by Joan Riviere. New York: Permabook.

Grottanelli, Christiano. 2001. *Kings and Prophets: Monarchic Power, Inspired Leadership, and Sacred Text in Biblical Narrative.* New York: Oxford University Press, 1999.

Ingebretsen, Edward J. 2001. *At Stake: Monsters and the Rhetoric of Fear in Public Culture.* Chicago: University of Chicago Press.

King, L. W., ed. and trans. 1902. *The Seven Tablets of Creation [Enuma Elish.* London: Luzac.

Levenson, Jon D. 1988. *Creation and the Persistence of Evil: The Jewish Drama of Divine Omnipotence.* Princeton: Princeton University Press.

Lopez, Davina C., and Todd Penner. 2015. "Burton Mack and the Loss of Our Innocence." *JAAR* 83:827–37.

Lukianoff, Greg. 2014. *Freedom from Speech.* New York: Encounter Books.

Mack, Burton L. 1988. *A Myth of Innocence: Mark and Christian Origins.* Minneapolis: Fortress Press.

Penner, Todd, and Davina C. Lopez. 2015. *De-introducing the New Testament: Texts, Worlds, Methods, Stories.* New York: Wiley-Blackwell.

Reiner, Rob, dir. 1992. *A Few Good Men.* Columbia Pictures.

Roldán, Mary. 2002. *Blood and Fire:* La Violencia *in Antioquia, Columbia, 1946–1953.* Latin America Otherwise. Durham, NC: Duke University Press.

Taylor, Mark Lewis. 2015. *The Executed God: The Way of the Cross in Lockdown America.* 2nd ed. Minneapolis: Fortress.

Yarbro Collins, Adela. 1976. *The Combat Myth in the Book of Revelation.* HDR 9. Missoula, MT: Scholars Press.

THE INTERCONNECTEDNESS OF *LA VIOLENCIA*: A RESPONSE FROM BRAZIL (IN PORTUGUESE)

Ivoni Richter Reimer

Abstract: Reading the contributions of this book from her Brazilian perspective, Reimer agrees that violence against people takes place all over the world and biblical scholars need to address this problem. In her country, too, there was a time when a military regime controlled people on all levels of society, killing thousands of people and torturing and exiling many. Yet even in today's democracy, violence is still present even though it appears in different forms and shapes. Nowadays, Brazilian society is ruled by laws, some of them recently established, but the existence of a law does not necessarily ensure the fulfillment of a person's right. According to Reimer, violence is an expression of power and dominion over territories and bodies. Its goal is to seize society and to make people submissive and silent, mainly by instilling fear and terror. At the same time, violence also occurs in our daily lives and personal relationships. For instance, Reimer suggests that we include studying how we live out our gender relationships and concepts of masculinity. She thus acknowledges in her response that the contemporary world faces many challenges in light of ongoing violence in people's lives. Foremost among those challenges is the urgent need to make visible the victims of violence. Often, they remain victims, because they are controlled by fear. They need to get the necessary support and strength from their cultural, religious, and political systems to overcome their fear so that they, too, can contribute to building societies with less violence and more justice.

Leio os nove ensaios de SEMEIA num contexto bastante específico, mas não restrito a situações do meu país, Brasil.

Ontem, 26 junho 2015, no mesmo dia em que, no Vaticano, o Papa Francisco sinalizou o reconhecimento do Estado da Palestina e no mesmo dia em que se iniciaram as festas de romaria do Divino Pai Eterno (Trindade/Goiás) e dentro do mês de uma das centrais festas religiosas islâmicas, o Ramadã, o mundo inteiro presenciou mais três ações terroristas de matiz religioso-política em três continentes (França, Tunísia e Kuwait), sendo que, até o momento, os ataques numa praia em Susa/Tunísia e numa mesquita em Kuwait foram assumidos pelo grupo Estado Islâmico. Esta expressão de violência ocorre, mais uma vez, dentro do Ramadã, mês do jejum ritual muçulmano e, num dos casos, tratou-se de um ataque contra um lugar sagrado islâmico, no qual uma comunidade de fiéis estava celebrando sua fé.

No Brasil, pela primeira vez na história, realizam-se investigações, prisões e punições em casos de escândalos de corrupção e de tráfico de influência político-econômica não só na Petrobrás, fator este que se torna um dos pivôs da crise política do atual governo. Os muitos bilhões desviados criminalmente por pessoas de diversos partidos políticos e empresas manifestam-se como ações violentas contra o povo e a nação brasileiras, porque este dinheiro é público, estava destinado e deveria ser usado em instituições de serviço público (saúde, educação, infraestrutura) para o benefício da população. É crime que atenta contra os direitos básicos da população, sendo que os criminosos, após acurada investigação, devem ser punidos e o dinheiro, restituído aos cofres públicos e monitorado também pelos(as) cidadãos e organizações populares por meio de 'portais da transparência' online. A indignação é imprescindível, mas não basta. Levantar vozes moralizantes e proféticas pode ajudar a amenizar a raiva de quem foi lesado, mas somente uma profunda conscientização e posturas proativas poderão ajudar a construir uma cultura de desconstrução do 'jeitinho brasileiro' e da cultura da impunidade que vigora em todos os níveis da sociedade.

Simultaneamente continua a violência no campo, na disputa de terras entre grupos indígenas, pequenos camponeses, trabalhadores sem-terra e latifundiários. Nas cidades, principalmente mas não só nos grandes centros urbanos ou metrópoles, a violência se expressa brutalmente na conquista e manutenção de poder em favelas-comunidades por parte de gangues que exercem seu poder em disputa com o poder institucional, representado pela polícia ou exército. Nestas relações de força, que podemos nomear de 'intencional, categóricas e calculáveis,' uma parte das vítimas da violência são membros desses dois grupos, mas, para além deles, trata-se principalmente de milhares de pessoas que se tornam alvos aleatórios desta ação violenta de ambos os grupos.

Além desses 'tipos clássicos' de violência, existem inúmeros outros que, para além de questões estruturais em nível socioeconômico, que abarcam também as neocapitalistas formas de trabalho escravo, acontece diariamente uma infinidade de violências nas relações de gênero, bem como em relação à etnia, à idade, ao ambiente.... A violência contra as pessoas idosas, contra as crianças e adolescentes e a violência doméstica tem sido realidade durante décadas discutida e tratada em movimentos sociais e eclesiais, e resultaram em debates em nível nacional e político-jurídico, resultando em leis protetivas e punitivas. Trata-se do Estatuto da Criança e do Adolescente (1990), do Estatuto dos Idosos (2003), e da Lei Maria da Penha (2006).[1] Observe-se que uma das mais antigas leis é o Estatuto do Índio (1973) e a lei da Política Nacional do Meio Ambiente (1981), e entre as mais recentes consta o Estatuto da Igualdade Racial (2010).

É óbvio que estas, como as demais leis, não fazem o direito e a justiça se realizarem automaticamente, mas elas contribuem substancialmente de duas maneiras fundamentais para o acesso e a garantia de direitos das pessoas e dos grupos envolvidos: (1) para o conhecimento da história e dos direitos, o que também pode contribuir, em médio e longo prazo, com a construção de uma mentalidade e cultura nacionais de respeito, responsabilidade e solidariedade; (2) para o conhecimento de procedimentos a serem adotados para a realização e a proteção desses direitos. Por outro lado, os Estatutos também podem ocasionar o acirramento de posturas em relação ao tema e objeto em questão, o que faz parte da dinâmica da interação de poderes e organizações, o que renovadamente precisará de ações e medidas educativas, também legais.

Os nove ensaios de SEMEIA trouxeram à memória milênios de história de violências sofridas por 'povos bíblicos' e por povos nos continentes americanos, mas também de caminhos trilhados em busca de transformação, superação e muitas vezes de acomodação. Teço, a seguir, algumas considerações acerca de algumas questões evocadas.

Algumas percepções e reflexões a partir dos ensaios

No Brasil-república, *la violencia* foi conhecida massivamente durante o período da ditadura militar, com todos seus procedimentos e implicações

---

1. Trata-se das leis 8.069, 10.741 e 11.340, respectivamente, sancionadas pela Presidência da Republica. Observe-se que todas as leis aqui referidas são encontradas em: http://www.planalto.gov.br/ccivil_ 03/leis, motivo pelo qual não serão arroladas individualmente na Bibliografia.

(controle, perseguição, tortura, morte, desaparecimentos, atos institucionais, exílio), incluindo os traumas que marcaram a vida de sobreviventes e seus familiares através do medo e das ações sofridas. Passado o regime ditatorial, contudo, não cessou a violência. Ela continua se manifestando, de forma muito incisiva principalmente em lugares nos quais o poder constituído é questionado, desobedecido e transgredido por parte de forças paramilitares e por forças policiais e militares que enfrentam forte e organizada oposição, como em comunidades-favelas em grandes metrópoles brasileiras. A violência, porém, não é uma forma de expressão apenas desses poderes e organizações e não resulta apenas por meio de suas ações. Ela se expressa em igual intensidade em outras relações de poder, em que atuam os mesmos mecanismos de controle e dominação, em nível privado, doméstico e íntimo, enfim, em espaços que deveriam ser de total confiança, aconchego e proteção.[2]

Em qualquer nível de relações, a violência pode se tornar instrumento sempre quando alguma forma de poder é questionada e desobedecida, e um dos mecanismos para manter o controle e o próprio poder sobre alguém é a tessitura do medo, instrumento subjetivo com bases vivenciais, cujo objetivo é alcançar e preservar a submissão de outrém. Este medo se constrói a partir de experiências 'exemplares' e por meio do imaginário e da memória sempre reconstituídos. Para vencer o medo é preciso coragem, perspicácia, união, criatividade, organização, perseverança, apoio e solidariedade ... renovadamente! Este 'vencer o medo' igualmente se constrói por meio do acesso a memórias e imaginários ancestrais que registraram experiências de resistência às violências de então, gerando transformação e esperança! É preciso, sim, mas não basta apenas olhar para as tradições bíblicas de terror e violência; faz-se cada vez mais urgente superar estas tradições recorrendo a outras, presentes também no mesmo corpo de literatura sagrada, que ajudam a construir novos olhares, perspectivas e relações de vida, incluindo toda a criação! Neste sentido, é preciso continuar analisando e questionando os imperialismos em nível macro, mas sem deixar de observar simultaneamente as relações 'imperiais' que se reproduzem em níveis de relação micro, doméstico e privado.

Considero que todos os ensaios constam de uma riquíssima abordagem exegético-hermenêutica e histórico-cultural, também porque estão

---

2. Ver as formas de violência doméstica, em Singh 2005.

permeados pelas próprias vivências de seus autores e autoras, com seus pertencimentos étnicos, confessionais, de gênero e sociais distintos. Registro, aqui, minha alegria de ler um volume em que a autoria dos ensaios é quase equitativa entre homens (5) e mulheres (4). Cada ensaio apresenta fragmentos de uma perspectiva. É assim que posso compreender a análise realizada por Cuéllar que, como pastor e cientista, relê criticamente o processo de anexação do norte do México aos EUA no contexto das lutas entre protestantes de origem anglo-saxã e católicos de origem espanhola e o faz com base na releitura crítica da concepção de 'povo escolhido' de Israel, que fora transferido para os referidos protestantes; isto, contudo, não impede uma leitura igualmente crítica das políticas de colonização e dominação espanhola católica ou portuguesa católica, como no Brasil.... Esta riqueza de perspectivas também palpita no texto de Furst, de origem hondurenha, que relê parte da história de violência de gangues urbanas em Honduras em busca das verdadeiras vítimas, com a inquietante pergunta de Habacuque: por que e até quando vítimas inocentes haverão de suportar tudo isto?

É o conjunto destes ensaios que talvez permita constituir um mosaico que represente mais proximamente realidades específicas da violência, e mesmo assim ainda parcial, porque sempre multifacetária e complexa. O mesmo acontece com os referenciais teóricos para sua abordagem e compreensão. Gostei de perceber que, no conjunto, o objetivo é olhar analiticamente para a realidade atual marcada pela violência em todos os contextos e para textos bíblicos, buscando compreender parte da posição desta tradição religiosa, e mais especificamente deste Deus, frente às realidades da violência. Nem sempre, porém, como mostra a análise de Furst, o texto bíblico responde 'satisfatoriamente' às demandas atuais. Mesmo assim, no conjunto dos ensaios, percebe-se uma 'colisão' de interesses e interpretações da Bíblia hebraica no contexto das relações geopolíticas, culturais e religiosas no continente americano. Isto evidencia que não só a violência, mas também as interpretações bíblicas da violência são contextuais, por um lado, mas dizem respeito ao conjunto das tradições religiosas do cristianismo, como herança a ser trabalhada, por outro lado. Estes aportes exegético-hermenêuticos sul-centro-norte americanos certamente encorajam e inspiram para exercícios semelhantes, também acerca de outras temáticas.

Os textos bíblicos selecionados e analisados neste volume de SEMEIA são parte central da linguagem religiosa judaico-cristã e em parte também islâmica. Como tal, eles configuram eixos construtores de identidade e identificações, de coesão grupal e de valores constitutivos daquelas culturas, fazendo parte de um complexo sistema simbólico, de crenças, doutrinas, representações e imaginários que contribuem para estabelecer, consolidar, legitimar, manter, questionar e transformar relações entre pessoas, povos e seu ambiente. No caso específico, foram selecionados textos que narram acerca de experiências de violências, suas abordagens e inserções no conjunto do fenômeno religioso judaico antigo, seu processo interpretativo e suas relações com dinâmicas e experiências de violência, hoje, no continente americano.

Assim, percebo que os textos de Davidson, Andiñach e Cuéllar se ocupam em perceber e relacionar o fenômeno da violência em sua expressão imperialista no mundo bíblico com seus efeitos interpretativos na política exterior dos EUA no Caribe, nas políticas de consolidação de uma só língua hegemônico-dominante no mundo imperialista globalizado, e na anexação do norte do México aos EUA. As relações político-ideológicas, presentificadas por meio de forças militares e econômico-sociais, estão presentes no passado e na nossa história recente, sustentadas por um discurso de segurança e paz imperiais, por meio das tradições bíblicas dos 'oráculos contra as nações', do 'povo escolhido e bom' e do mito de uma língua hegemônica (Gn 11) que é questionada. Há que se refletir, aqui, que, em comparação com 'aqueles tempos', alguns mecanismos e instrumentos da violência até podem ter sido tecnologicamente desenvolvidos, mas seus efeitos continuam agredindo na mesma intensa profundidade a dignidade do ser humano, como em tempos (i)memoráveis. É o que também evidencia o estudo realizado por Frolov, que tematiza o trabalho escravo no mundo bíblico a partir das realidades que ele próprio vivenciou e que os povos originários das Américas enfrentaram por ocasião das conquistas com subsequente colonização. Esta é uma faceta da violência que sempre fez e ainda faz parte de sistemas imperiais de dominação, adentrando nossos tempos sob novas formas, como trabalho mal remunerado e semelhante ao trabalho escravo, também presentes no Brasil. Textos bíblicos e suas interpretações, como Dt 20,10–14, não mais deveriam servir de base e legitimação para tais expressões de violência, não só por causa dos avanços jurídico-legais, tecnológicos e das ciências humanas, mas por serem discriminatórios em si mesmos. Por isto, concordo que os tomemos criticamente como advertência e alerta para não cair na armadilha de 'boas intenções' que acabam cometendo injustiça por discriminação, que já é, ela mesma, expressão de violência. Nesta parte e motivando um diálogo com autores brasileiros, indico para as análises de textos proféticos, realizados, p.ex., por Milton Schwantes, Haroldo Reimer e Tânia Mara V. Sampaio.[3]

Além das expressões de violência até aqui tratadas, José Enrique Ramírez-Kidd chama a atenção para o fato de que as várias formas de violência acabam criando condições culturais que promovem obediência e submissão. O fenômeno da violência internalizada com base na pedagogia da violência, do terror e do medo é por ele tratado com base nos livros de Judite e Tobias, bem como seus efeitos em sistemas de dominação no antigo Oriente e na história da América Latina.[4] Esta pedagogia fez com que a violência física e a violência psicológica penetrassem a consciência do povo exilado, e ajudou a produzir formas de acomodação e indiferença ao sistema injusto e ao sofrimento por ele causado, e repercute até hoje na história ocidental. A afirmação básica é que a cultura do medo e a violência internalizada são fruto e fonte de várias outras formas de violência.

É neste ponto que agradeço as contribuições de Cheryl B. Anderson, Susanne Scholz e Julia M. O'Brien. Analisar as complexidades e ambigüidades das relações de poder a partir da intimidade e da sexualidade, do público e do privado tem sido desafio e compromisso importante de hermenêuticas feministas de libertação. Assim também se fez aqui, infelizmente realizado novamente só por mulheres.... O'Brien chega a afirmar que a violência de gênero é a forma mais comum de violência bíblica e que, por extensão, é assumida como 'normal' na sociedade estadunidense. Furst constatou o silêncio acerca das mulheres na narrativa de opressão e sofrimento em Habacuque, e questionou que é preciso trabalhar concretamente pela sua visibilização, quando se pergunta pelas vítimas das dominações imperialistas. Junto com a necessidade de se revisitar o conceito da autoridade bíblica (O'Brien), há também, de acordo com Scholz, a urgência de considerar hermeneuticamente as questões do político nos EUA, o que inclui realidades de violência nos âmbitos que envolvem a pobreza, a pena de morte, a violência policial e a violência sexual, como bem demonstrado na interpretação de Jz 21.

Para mim foi muito interessante e proveitoso observar como algumas realidades e percepções coincidem naquilo que li e 'presenciei' por meio dos ensaios e aquilo que se vive e elabora hermenêutica e teologicamente

---

3. São muitos os textos produzidos por estes e outros autores brasileiros. Aqui, no caso, remeto a Schwantes (2000, 2004), Reimer (1992, 2000), Sampaio (1999).

4. Preciosas contribuições exegéticas e hermenêuticas foram realizadas, no Brasil, por Sandro Gallazzi e Ana Maria Rizzante (2001).

no Brasil. Teço aqui algumas considerações em busca de diálogos que possam fortalecer mutuamente.

Em termos de fenômeno religioso, não só de matriz cristã, é perceptível o crescimento de tendências fundamentalistas, principalmente no meio (neo)pentecostal e carismático, para as quais não interessa evidenciar e questionar a realidade da violência nos textos bíblicos, principalmente em se tratando de violência de gênero. Quando muito, a violência é tratada em perspectiva da vontade disciplinar de Deus e para testar a fé. Obediência e submissão a outrém é visto como parte desta vontade de Deus, para manutenção da boa ordem divina no mundo. Neste sentido e neste contexto, a experiência feita pela professora O'Brien com suas alunas também é realizada em vários centros de formação teológica de todas as denominações cristãs no Brasil. Contudo, em centros de formação teológica que se orientam mais pela exegese histórico-crítica e sociocultural, estas realidades multifacetárias de violência tem sido trabalhadas em sala de aula, em eventos científicos e resultaram em produções relevantes.[5] Também em centros de formação teológica popular e ecumênica, como o Centro de Estudos Bíblicos (CEBI), há décadas que se exercita a análise de textos bíblicos em perspectivas socioculturais, ambientais e de gênero, para o que muito contribuíram Milton Schwantes, Carlos Mesters, Nancy Cardoso Pereira, Haroldo Reimer, Elaine Neuenfeldt, Sandro Gallazzi e Ana Maria Rizzante, entre muit@s outr@s.[6]

Teorias interacionistas e fenomenológicas da violência[7] aplicadas aos (con)textos do mundo bíblico podem ajudar a perceber e articular que as estruturas imperialistas com seus instrumentos de ocupação e manutenção de territórios ocupam simultanea e similarmente os territórios corporais, expressando violência em todos os âmbitos da vida. Neste quesito, aponto para duas realidades do contexto do Novo Testamento:

A violência da cruz como representação de um sistema e estratégia de dominação imperial por meio do medo e controle de movimentos e corpos de homens, mulheres e crianças. Esta violência se fez presente no processo de colonização portuguesa no Brasil, quando 'cruz e espada' eram instrumentos de missão, ocupação de territórios e controle; ela esteve pre-

---

5. Veja-se, p.ex., os livros organizados por Neuenfeldt, Bergesch, e Parlow (2008) e Richter Reimer e Matos (2011), produzidos a partir de disciplinas e congressos acadêmicos.

6. Ver, p.ex., o *link* Publicações em: www.cebi.org.br/#.

7. Texto elucidativo de Monsma (2007).

sente durante a ditadura militar por meio das múltiplas formas de tortura e morte; ela ainda se faz presente, nas inúmeras formas violentas de ocupação de terras e nas pedagogias de medo por meio de ações 'exemplares.' Ressignificar a violência multifacetária da cruz em símbolo de vida nova, ressurreição, esperança e ânimo para as lutas de resistência pacífica faz parte de uma estratégia contracultural que desaloja poderes imperialistas patriquiriarcais de todos os tempos e em todos os lugares.

A violência da guerra imperialista romana como avassaladora de lugares e de relações transparece em textos apocalípticos, como Mc 13,17 par., quando lidos junto com a narrativa de Josefo (GJ 4,106ss), que reporta a situação do caos e das fugas geradas por aquelas guerras. A fuga do comandante judeu, João, com a população da cidade de Gischala, evidencia a dupla crueldade, da guerra e do abandono, que é vivenciada em situações de extrema aflição: num certo momento, ele ordenou que se deixasse para trás as mulheres e as crianças que já não conseguiam acompanhar o ritmo dos homens: "Digna de piedade era a perdição das mulheres e crianças que, colocando as mãos no peito, clamavam a seus maridos e parentes, entre soluções e clamores, para que esperassem por elas" (GJ 4,110). Esta ocupação e aniquilação de territórios geopolíticos e corporais fazia parte de um sistema patriquiriarcal de dominação, elaborado por filósofos/ideólogos e implementados por regimes político-ideológicos greco-romanos,[8] aos quais a proposta de Reino de Deus se contrapõe, fornecendo elementos conceituais e pragmáticos como partilha, comunhão, solidariedade, paz, justiça e integridade da criação. Esta proposta pode sustentar ainda hoje anseios e vivências heterotópicos em todos os contextos não só do continente americano.

Se entendemos violência como expressão arbitrária de poder e domínio imposto sobre territórios geopolíticos e corporais, que se manifesta como instrumento principalmente em situações de crise e como estratégia de ocupação e manutenção do poder, então é preciso urgentemente

---

8. A este respeito ver Richter Reimer (2006), que apresenta distintos níveis de dominação que interagem no cotidiano da vida das pessoas e dos povos, desde a situação das guerras de ocupação, o estabelecimento do controle, seus mecanismos e infraestrutura, como exército, pedágios e alfândegas, praças e templos, estradas e sistema penal. Neste estudo, ela referencia Luise Schottroff, Klaus Wengst, Néstor O.Míguez, Moses I.Finley, Bruce J. Malina, Carolyn Osiek, Uwe Wegner, e Kuno Füssel.

também rever nossas relações de gênero e concepções de masculinidades.[9] Como parte das construções e dinâmicas culturais, elas interagem cotidiana e diretamente na experiência, reprodução ou superação de violências domésticas e político-sociais, também expressas por meio de todas as formas de *bullying*.

Se textos e tradições bíblicas ainda continuam sendo relevantes na (re)construção de identidade religiosa, então o seu conjunto deve ser urgentemente elucidado e trabalhado, em nível de trabalho pastoral, de estudos e de formação teológicas em todos os níveis. Assim, os textos que narram violências e também os textos que se opõem a ela, apresentando outras possibilidades de construção de relações humanas, devem ser colocados lado a lado e analisados conjuntamente, porque são oriundos da mesma mat(r)iz cultural, a fim de melhor conhecer nossas tradições que, desde suas origens, não são unívocas, mas polifônicas, complexas, ambíguas e até contraditórias.

Como tal e como já se vem fazendo em todos os continentes, é preciso continuar trabalhando no sentido de reconhecer que, em interação dialógica entre passado e presente, em vistas de um futuro mais justo, é preciso visibilizar e reconstruir renovadamente a história de personagens bíblicos, desses sujeitos históricos que foram silenciados durante milênios em suas experiências de opressão, mas também de resistência, protagonismo, libertação e transformação em suas relações culturais, ideológicas, sociopolíticas e econômicas! Neste sentido, não se pode negar ou esconder a experiência de várias formas de violência também nos textos sagrados do cristianismo, nem tampouco as formas inventadas para resistir e se opor aos vários tipos de violência. Ao contrário, é preciso conhecer sua arqueologia e sua engenharia, a fim de poder proativamente tecer um presente-futuro qualitativamente diferente, de respeito e realização da vida plena, justa e prazerosa de todos os seres!

Especificamente, a opressão das mulheres foi e continua sendo construída historicamente, com ajuda poderosa de bens religiosos e da história interpretativa e efeitual de textos sagrados. Esta opressão, caracterizada por dominação, subordinação, submissão, discriminação e toda sorte de violência não mais precisa ser explicada como fatalidade, vontade de Deus ou destino. Os avanços também nas ciências bíblicas podem contribuir no

---

9. Ver, p.ex., o livro organizado por Musskopf e Ströher (2005) a partir do I Congresso Latino-Americano de Gênero e Religião, em São Leopoldo.

sentido de redobrar e renovar esforços para, em todos os níveis de formação e educação, evidenciar estratégias e dinâmicas, mecanismos e sistemas com os quais esta opressão foi construída, consolidada, justificada e legitimada e como estes textos bíblicos podem ser reinterpretados juntamente com outros textos que testemunham que viver sem violência é possível e urgente. E que neste trabalho, o conhecimento dos homens se juntem aos conhecimentos das mulheres.

Alguns desafios permanecem atuais, entre os quais estão a necessidade ética de visibilizar as vítimas, todas elas, no texto e na vida e, em solidariedade, prestar apoio e acolhida e vencer o medo, sempre de novo!

Bibliografia

Gallazzi, Sandro, e Ana Maria Rizzante. 2001. "*Judite:* A mão da mulher na história do Povo." Petrópolis: Vozes; Série Comentários Bíblicos: AT.

Monsma, Karl M. 2007. "Teorias interacionistas e fenomenológicas da violência com aplicações à pesquisa histórica." *MÉTIS* 6.11:23–37. http://www.ucs.br/etc/revistas/index.php/metis/article/viewFile/ 822/579.

Musskopf, André, e Marga J. Ströher, eds. 2005. *Corporeidade, etnia e masculinidade: Reflexões do I Congresso Latino-Americano de Gênero e Religião.* São Leopoldo: Sinodal.

Neuenfeldt, Elaine, Karen Bergesch, e Mara Parlow, eds. 2008. *Epistemologia, violência, sexualidade: Olhares do II Congresso Latino-Americano de Gênero e Religião.* São Leopoldo: Sinodal.

Richter Reimer, Ivoni. 2006. "Patriarcado e economia política: O jeito romano de organizar a casa." Pages 72–97 in *Economia no mundo bíblico: Enfoques sociais, históricos e teológicos.* Edited by Ivoni Reimer Richter. São Leopoldo: Sinodal; CEBI.

Richter Reimer, Ivoni, e Keila Matos. 2011. "Silencioso desespero: Violência e silêncio contra a mulher em casa e na Bíblia." Pages 73–90 in *Direitos Humanos: Enfoques bíblicos, teológicos e filosóficos.* Edited by Ivoni Richter Reimer. Goiânia: Ed. da PUC Goiás; São Leopoldo: Oikos.

Sampaio, Tânia Mara Vieira. 1999. *Movimentos do corpo prostituído da mulher.* São Paulo: Edições Loyola.

Singh, Priscilla, ed. 2002; 2005. *As igrejas dizem "NÃO" à violência contra a mulher: Plano de ação para as igrejas.* Genebra: Federação Luterana Mundial; São Leopoldo: Sinodal.

Contributors

Cheryl B. Anderson, Ph.D., is Professor of Old Testament at Garrett-Evangelical Theological Seminary in Evanston, Illinois, and she is an ordained elder in The United Methodist Church (Baltimore-Washington Conference). Her current research interests involve contextual and liberationist readings of Scripture in the age of HIV and AIDS. Her publications include *Women, Ideology, and Violence: Critical Theory and the Construction of Gender in the Book of the Covenant and the Deuteronomic Law* (2004), and *Ancient Laws and Contemporary Controversies: The Need for Inclusive Biblical Interpretation* (2009).

Pablo R. Andiñach, Dr. Theol., is Professor of Old Testament and Ancient History at the Pontificia Universidad Católica Argentina in Buenos Aires, Argentina. His main fields of interest and research are biblical hermeneutics, Latin American theology of liberation, and Hebrew Bible theology. Among his many publications are *Cantar de los Cantares: El fuego y la ternura* (1997); *El libro del Éxodo* (2006); *Ser Iglesia* (2007); *Éxodo, comentario para su traducción* (2009); *Introducción hermenéutica al Antiguo Testamento* (2012); *El Dios que está. Teología del Antiguo Testamento* (2014). With Alejandro Botta, he co-edited *The Bible and the Hermeneutics of Liberation* (2009).

Nancy Bedford, Dr. Theol., is Georgia Harkness Professor of Applied Theology at Garrett-Evangelical Theological Seminary. Her areas of research include global feminist theories and theologies, Latin American theologies, Latino/Latina theologies in North America, theologies in migration, and theological hermeneutics. Her latest book is *Galatians: A Theological Commentary* (2016).

Gregory Lee Cuéllar, Ph.D., is Assistant Professor of Old Testament at Austin Presbyterian Theological Seminary. His major research interests include postcolonial theory and borderlands hermeneutics. His research also seeks to integrate archival theory and museum studies with the study of modern biblical interpretation. His is author of *Voices of Marginality: Exile and Return in Second Isaiah 40–55 and the Mexican Immigrant Experience* (2008).

Steed Vernyl Davidson, Ph.D., is Associate Professor of Old Testament at McCormick Theological Seminary in Chicago. His research centers on postcolonial studies and the Bible. He is the author of *Empire and Exile: Postcolonial Readings of the Book of Jeremiah* (2013).

Serge Frolov, Ph.D., is Professor of Religious Studies and the Nate and Ann Levine Endowed Chair in Jewish Studies at Southern Methodist University. His areas of research include biblical hermeneutics and theology, history and religions of the ancient Near East, and Jewish history and thought. He is the author of *The Turn of the Cycle: 1 Samuel 1–8 in Synchronic and Diachronic Perspectives* (2004), *Judges* (2013), and about 250 articles.

Renata Furst, PhD., is Assistant Professor of Scripture and Spirituality, at the Oblate School of Theology in San Antonio, Texas. Her research interests are in prophetic literature, narratology, the Hispanic interpretation of Scripture, and the relationship between Scripture and spirituality. She published *De Josué a crónicas: From Joshua to Chronicles* (2007) and *Rut, Esdras, Nehemias y Ester* (2009).

Julia M. O'Brien, Ph.D., is Paul H. and Grace L. Stern Professor of Hebrew Bible/Old Testament at Lancaster Theological Seminary. Her research interests include prophetic literature and the intersections of gender studies and the Bible. Among her publications are *Micah* (Wisdom Commentary Series; 2015); editor-in-chief, *Oxford Encyclopedia of Bible and Gender Studies* (2014); co-editor, *The Aesthetics of Violence in the Prophets* (2010); *Challenging Prophetic Metaphor: Theology and Ideology in the Prophets* (2008); *Nahum, Habakkuk, Zephaniah, Haggai, Zechariah, Malachi* (2004); and *Nahum* (2002; 2009).

Todd Penner, Ph.D., specializes in ancient Jewish and Christian religious and cultural traditions and has broad interests in modern interpretations of the Bible, method and theory in the study of religion, and cultural study of religion in the modern world. Among his books are *In Praise of Christian Origins: Stephen and the Hellenists in Lukan Apologetic Historiography* (2004); *Contextualizing Gender in Early Christian Discourse: Thinking beyond Thecla* (with Caroline Vander Stichele; 2009); and *De-introducing the New Testament: Texts, Worlds, Methods, Stories* (with Davina C. Lopez; 2015). He was a senior editor of *The Oxford Encyclopedia of the Bible and Gender Studies* (Julia O'Brien, ed.; 2014).

José Enrique Ramírez-Kidd, Dr. Theol., is Director of the Escuela de Ciencias Bíblicas at the Universidad Bíblica Latinoamericana in Costa Rica. His research involves the relationship between the ancient Near East and the Hebrew Bible, narrative literature, and Bible and literature. Among his recent publications are *Para comprender el Antiguo Testamento* (2009) and *El libro de Ruth: Ternura de Dios frente al dolor humano* (2010).

Ivoni Richter Reimer, Dr. Theol., is Professor of Bible, Hermeneutics, and History at Pontifícia Universidade Católica de Goiás (PUC Goiás) in Goiânia, Brazil. She holds a doctorate in theology/philosophy from the University in Kassel, Germany (1990) and in Social Science from the Universidade Federal de Santa Catarina/Brasil. Among her publications are *Women in the Acts of Apostles: A Feminist Liberation Perspective* (1995); *O Belo, as Feras e o Novo Tempo* (2000); *Vida de las mujeres en la sociedad y la iglesia: Una exégesis feminista de los Hechos de los Apóstoles* (2003); *Gravame como selo sobre teu coração: Teologia bíblica feminista* (2005); *Economia no mundo bíblico: Enfoques sociais, históricos e teológicos* (2006); *Milagre das Mãos: Curas e exorcismos de Jesus em seu contexto histórico-cultural* (2008); *Terra e água na espiritualidade do movimento de Jesus: Contribuições para um mundo globalizado* (2010); *Ananias e Safira nas origens do cristianismo e suas interpretações: Reler e reconstruir Atos 5:1–11* (2011); *Compaixão, cruz e esperança: Teologia de Marcos* (2012); and *Maria, Jesus e Paulo com as mulheres: Textos, interpretações e história* (2013).

Susanne Scholz, Ph.D., is Professor of Old Testament at Perkins School of Theology at Southern Methodist University in Dallas, Texas, USA. Her research focuses on feminist biblical hermeneutics, epistemologies and sociologies of biblical interpretation, and cultural and literary methodologies. Among her publications are *Feminist Interpretation of the Hebrew Bible in Retrospect* (Vol. 1: Biblical Books; Vol. 2: Social Location) (ed., 2013; 2014); *Hidden Truths from Eden: Esoteric Readings of Genesis 1–3* (co-ed.; 2014); *God Loves Diversity and Justice: Progressive Scholars Speak about Faith, Politics, and the World* (ed., 2013); *Sacred Witness: Rape in the Hebrew Bible* (2010); *Introducing the Women's Hebrew Bible* (2007); *Biblical Studies Alternatively: An Introductory Reader* (ed., 2003); *Zwischenräume: Deutsche feministische Theologinnen im Ausland* (co-ed., 2000); and *Rape Plots: A Feminist Cultural Study of Genesis 34* (2000).

Index of Ancient Sources

Index of Modern Authors

CPSIA information can be obtained
at www.ICGtesting.com
Printed in the USA
LVOW08s1705251116

514358LV00001B/18/P